HUMAN,

ALL TOO HUMAN

D0144957

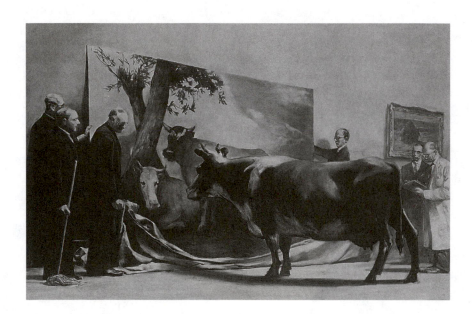

Mark Tansey, *Innocent Eye Test*, 1981.

ROUTLEDGE

NEW YORK

LONDON

HUMAN,

ALL TOO HUMAN

Edited with an Introduction by

DIANA FUSS

1-97

Published in 1996 by

Routledge
29 West 35th Street
New York, NY 10001

Published in Great Britain in 1996 by

Routledge
11 New Fetter Lane
London EC4P 4EE

Library of Congress Cataloging-in-
Publication Data

    Human, all too human / Diana Fuss,
    editor.

        p.   cm. — (Essays from the
        English Institute)
    Includes bibliographical references.
    ISBN 0-415-91499-X (hb).   ISBN 0-
    415-91500-7 (pb.)
      1. Man I. Fuss, Diana. 1960–. II.
    Series.
    BD450.H854 1995   95-14690

CONTENTS

ESSAYS FROM
THE ENGLISH INSTITUTE

Since 1944, the English Institute has presented work by distinguished scholars in English
and American literatures, foreign literatures,
and related fields. A volume of papers selected for the meeting is published annually.

Also available in the series from Routledge:

Comparative American Identities:
Race, Sex and Nationality
in the Modern Text
Edited with an Introduction by
Hortense J. Spillers

English Inside and Out:
The Places of Literary Criticism
Edited with an Introduction by
Susan Gubar and
Jonathan Kamholtz

Borders, Boundaries and Frames:
Essays on Cultural Criticism
and Cultural Theory
Edited with an Introduction by
Mae Henderson

Performativity and Performance
Edited with an Introduction by
Andrew Parker and
Eve Kosofsky Sedgwick

ACKNOWLEDGMENTS

Human, All Too Human brings together some of the most important work on the problem of the human in a posthuman era. For making such an ambitious enterprise possible, first thanks must go to the supervisors and trustees of the 1994 English Institute at Harvard University (where these papers were first imagined, solicited, and finally presented) and to the volume's contributors for seeing the exact contours of the project even more clearly than its planners. Thanks also to the many individuals who helped to launch *Human, All Too Human*: Anthony Appiah for chairing the conference and for suggesting our title; Marjorie Garber for selecting the cover art; the entire staff at the Harvard Center for Literary and Cultural Studies for sharing their ideas and resources; Rey Chow, Nancy Vickers, and Richard Yarborough for their coordinating genius; and Jeff Masten and Suzanne Marcus for magnificently pulling off the whole show. This book owes its genesis to the many colleges and universities around the country that together comprise the English Institute.

HUMAN,

ALL TOO HUMAN

DIANA FUSS

"**W**HAT SHALL WE call human in humans?" Jean-François Lyotard asks in a collection of essays entitled, knowingly, *The Inhuman*.[2] The political stakes of this preeminently philosophical question today pose themselves with special urgency, as debates over the significance of genetic surgery, virtual reality, reproductive technology, artificial intelligence, and other forms of "posthuman" reconstruction dramatically disorganize traditional Enlightenment conceptions of the human. The question of what it means to be human has never before been more difficult—and more contested. In the wake of humanism's recession, what has become of the human? Our task here is to rethink the category of the human, opening a door to an encounter with what one of our most fearless poets of humanity calls the "human after human."[3]

INTRODUCTION

HUMAN,

ALL TOO HUMAN

One thing is necessary above all if one is to practice reading as an *art* ... something for which one has to be a cow and in any case not a "modern man": *rumination*.

—Friedrich Nietzsche,
On the Genealogy of Morals[1]

Before the human was the *humanus*: of or belonging to man, a derivative of the same root as *homo, hominem*. Not until the early eighteenth century does the human finally stray from its earlier etymological incarnations—humayn, humain, humane—gradually taking on the function of a metaphysical predicate to "man." A sign whose history has rarely been examined, the human is a linguistic, cultural, and sociopolitical construct of comparatively recent date. That the human has a history comes as no surprise to those subjects so routinely and so violently excluded from its ideological terrain. In the past, the human has functioned as a powerful juridical trope to disenfranchise slaves, immigrants, women, children, and the poor. Some of the most ferocious and unthinkable events of our century—mass extermination in Europe, genocide in Armenia, apartheid in South Africa, repression in Latin America, ethnic cleansing in Bosnia—have all been waged passionately in the name of *humanitas*. In America, the human continues to be deployed as a weapon of potent ideological force, its unstable boundaries perpetually challenged and redrawn to exclude entire groups of socially disempowered subjects: the homeless, mothers on welfare, blacks in prison, people with HIV/AIDS, illegal "aliens." The human is not, and has never been, an all inclusive category.

Simply to rechart the topography of the human risks leaving in place the colonizing designs of that very mapping. Our purpose in this volume is not to broaden the category of the human to include previously abjected and excluded others, but to engage in a more radical interrogation of *the process by which the human comes to mean* in the production of cultural difference. The human has always been a politically charged referent with a complicated and difficult social history. Just who counts as human, and why, underwrites a long saga of contentious debate within humanist discourse, a discourse mired from the start in the amalgamated histories of imperial expansion, scientific experimentation, and industrial revolution. The human may, in fact, be one of our most elastic fictions. As the dividing lines between humans and "nonhumans" have been historically redrafted to accommodate new systems of classification and new discourses of knowledge, the human has proceeded to mutate many times over.

In its most canonical metaphysical guise, the human as thinking animal claims a privileged position of cognitive authority within the Enlightenment's great chain of being. But what happens when the investigating agent becomes its own problem, or when the knower becomes the known? The essays in this volume invite us to place the traditional subject of knowledge in the unsettling position of object, calling into question the very boundary that would render the human transparent while subjecting its imaginary others to relentless scrutiny and obsessive reclassification. Suspending the humanistic claim to authoritative knowledge, these essays interrupt and interfere with traditional cultural taxonomies that exempt the category of the human from the rigorous ideological critique it so urgently requires. More than ever before, the human—part social fiction, part political fantasy—demands careful, discerning, and exacting analysis.

The terrain is arduous: What is being done, or undone, when the human ceases to take itself for granted? Can the human be thought outside humanism? Has the very idea of *humanitas* lost its meaning? For Martin Heidegger, words like humanism gain a firm foothold only when original thinking has already subsided. Humanism, in other words, may represent the greatest obstacle we face to reinventing the human. Heidegger's philosophical rejection of humanism does not rest on a repudiation of the human; on the contrary, "humanism is opposed because it does not set the *humanitas* of man high enough."[4] But even Heidegger is compelled to wonder whether such an approach still warrants the title "humanism," or whether a more dramatic disturbance is required, one that would, by completely refusing a humanism that is no more than a metaphysics, more thoroughly and significantly radicalize our notion of the human.

This book risks just such a disturbance, disorienting and dislocating our received notions of the human by persistently querying the presumed self-evidence of the term. Any reexamination of the human places us immediately inside an ever-widening field of alterity: animate and inanimate, natural and artificial, living and dead, organic and mechanistic. These and other boundary confusions at the frontiers of the human are the subject of this volume, as each essay takes up one of three disputed border identities: animals, things, or children. The vigilance with which the demarcations between humans and animals, humans and things, and humans and children are watched over and safeguarded tells us much about the assailability of what they seek to preserve: an abstract notion of the human as a unified, autonomous, and unmodified subject. It is as if the alienness of these borderlanders lies not in their distance from the human, but in their proximity. Sameness, not difference, provokes our greatest anxiety (and our greatest fascination) with the "almost human."[5] Indeed, whenever we are called to become "more human" we are reminded that the human is never adequate to itself, and may be defined more by its likeness to these alien others than by its unlikeness.

We take our title from Nietzsche's *Human, All Too Human*,[6] where the "all too" syntactically locates at the center of the human some unnamed surplus—some residue, overabundance, or excess. The doubling of the human that embraces the "all too" suggests that this excess may be internal to the very definition of the human, an exteriority embedded inside the human as its condition of possibility. If humanness constitutes itself through its own superfluity, then to be human is already to be, in some profound sense, nonhuman. Put another way, our title implies that the only way to reach the human may be to overreach it, to exceed the boundaries that fundamentally delimit and define the human.

This book examines the cultural, historical, social, and political borders where the human becomes "all too," and seems to emerge from or slip into another register: animal, thing, child. We begin with the borderline between human and animal, where cultural anxieties over species categorizations put the whole notion of what is "proper" to the human under suspicion. What is going on when we naïvely project our own eccentricities, desires, and ideals onto animals? How do we explain the familiar custom of continually challenging, through the ubiquitous practice of anthropomorphism, the rigid species distinctions that we ourselves have so painstakingly fashioned? The essays in this volume by Marjorie Garber and Harriet Ritvo examine not only the continually shifting boundaries between humans and animals, but also the many and various motivations for breaching them. Human fascination with hybridity in the animal world—with mongrelization, miscegenation, telegony, pedigree, and generation—works through, in displaced form, the more disquieting concerns about hybridity in the human domain. The language that we use to talk about (and to) the animals tacitly encodes the tensions and discriminations that characterize contemporary social discourse on racial, class, and sexual stratification.[7] These essays also suggest that, in a post-Darwinian culture that ceaselessly recalls us to our own status as animals, demarcating just where the human begins and the animal leaves off may be a difficult enterprise. The borders between human and animal are as much social as they are natural, a point that poses rather interesting problems for the classical representation of the human as *animal rationale*.

The taxonomic disorder between humans and things presents similar challenges to traditional conceptualizations of the human, albeit in more muted form. If Heidegger, in his famous essay on "The Thing," concludes rightly that the human has persistently refused to attend to the nearness of things, then what precisely accounts for this neglect?[8] Karl Marx, one of the earliest thinkers to recognize humanism as an ideology, was also one of the first to posit more than a merely instrumental connection between humans and things. Marx's theorization of what he calls the social relations between things uncovers yet another kind of anthropomorphism at work at the very base of commodity culture.[9] But even here, in the most serious intellectual inquiry we have into the interaction of humans and things, we are still left to wonder exactly what a thing is, and how the human might be said to embody it. The essays by Rey Chow, Nancy Armstrong, Barbara Johnson, and David Wills all pursue this particular philosophical line of questioning, asking us to consider where and why things appear *as* things, and how the imputed integrity of the human may already be compromised by them. In the intimacy of its everyday proximity to things, the human registers the shock of its own synthetic nature—its own radical articulation in the lifeless, the inanimate, the mechanical, and the foreign.

Of our three selected border identities, children seem at first glance to have a much more secure affiliation to the human than either animals or things. But as the essays by Cora Kaplan, James Kincaid, and Drucilla Cornell attest, the child, by its very closeness to the human, may pose the most contested limitcase of all. Variously idealized, demonized, eroticized, patronized, and publicized, the child emerges as a highly mystified figure whose claim to the category "human" is, from the very start, governed and circumscribed by political ideology, cultural mythology, legal doctrine, and social policy. The three essays on the child begin with a common set of questions: How are children conceived of in the minds of adults? How, where, and when is the idea of "the child" produced? When does the institution of modern childhood begin? When is a child not a child? What is the meaning of the changeable and ambiguous boundaries between adult and child?[10] Nietzsche once aphorized that "the tragedy of man is that he was once a child." But what, finally, is a child?

Let me conclude with a lingering thought on this introduction's epigraph from *On the Genealogy of Morals*: "one thing is necessary above all if one is to practice reading as an *art*," Nietzsche muses, "something for

which one has almost to be a cow and in any case *not* a 'modern man':
rumination." What does a cow have to tell us about thinking, let alone
the art of reading? Why is a cow closer to rumination than a human?
Why, for that matter, a cow? Is it because the cow—that solid, powerful,
slow-moving beast—provides a better model for deliberate and unhur-
ried thought than the restless and irritable figure we call "modern man"?
Or is Nietzsche asking us to ponder more than simply the anthropomorphic notion that cows may think but also the far more disarming
possibility that thinking may itself be a bovine activity—a slow, halting,
difficult labor? I am reminded of René Descartes' model of human
knowledge in *La dioptrique*, where Descartes recommends that objective
representation be tested by disembodying "the dead eye of a newly dead
person (or, failing that, the eye of an ox or some other large animal)."[11]
This extracted bovine eye, so seamlessly substituted for the human eye,
turns the classical interpretation of the Cartesian *cogito* on its ear. Far from
distinguishing us from the animals, these philosophers of the all-too-
human suggest, the capacity to think or to ruminate may take the very
fullest measure of our own animality.

NOTES

I would like to thank Thomas Keenan, Rey Chow, and Joel Sanders for helpful preliminary discussions of some of the issues raised in this introduction.

1. Friedrich Nietzsche, *On the Genealogy of Morals*, trans. Walter Kaufmann (New York:
   Vintage, 1989), p. 23.

2. Jean-François Lyotard, *The Inhuman* (Stanford, CA: Stanford University Press, 1991).

3. Carolyn Forché, *The Angel of History* (New York: Harper Collins, 1994).

4. Martin Heidegger, "Letter on Humanism" (1947), in *Basic Writings*, ed. David Farrell
   Krell (San Francisco: Harper Collins, 1993), p. 234.

5. I take this phrase from Donna Haraway's impressive work on *Primate Visions: Gender,
   Race, and Nature in the World of Modern Science* (New York and London: Routledge,
   1989). Haraway's *Simians, Cyborgs, and Women: The Reinvention of Nature* (New York:
   Routledge, 1991) continues the project of interrogating the boundary confusions
   between human and animal, human and machine, human and nature.

6. Friedrich Nietzsche, *Human, All Too Human: A Book for Free Spirits*, trans. R.J.
   Hollingdale (Cambridge: Cambridge University Press, 1986).

7. For more on this subject, see Harriet Ritvo's *The Animal Estate: The English and Other
   Creatures in the Victorian Age* (Cambridge: Harvard University Press, 1987).

8. Martin Heidegger, "The Thing," *Poetry, Language, Thought*, trans. Albert Hofstadter (New York: Harper and Row, 1975), pp. 165–182.

9. See, for example, Marx's and Engels's *The German Ideology*, ed. C. J. Arthur (New York: International Publishers, 1947).

10. Jacqueline Rose addresses some of these same questions in *The Case of Peter Pan or the Impossibility of Children's Fiction* (Philadelphia: University of Pennsylvania Press, 1992).

11. René Descartes, *The Philosophical Writings of Descartes*, vol. 1, trans. John Cottingham, Robert Stoothoff, and Dugald Murdoch (Cambridge, 1984), p. 166. Cited in Jonathan Crary, *Techniques of the Observer: On Vision and Modernity in the Nineteenth Century* (Cambridge: MIT Press, 1990), p. 47.

ANIMAL

MARJORIE GARBER

IN LITERATURE and popular culture, psychology, animal behavior, and fashion, 1994 was clearly The Year of the Dog. The success of best-selling books like Elizabeth Marshall Thomas's *The Hidden Life of Dogs* (1993), Stanley Coren's *The Intelligence of Dogs* (1994), and Vicki Hearne's *Animal Happiness* (1994) coincided with the renewed interest in dog movie and TV stars, and with a general fascination with putting on the dog.

HEAVY
PETTING

A remake of *Lassie* by Paramount Pictures and a celebrity biography of the eight (male) collies from Pal to Howard who have starred in the (female) title role has provoked a series of new "Lassie" articles and clothing tie-ins ("win a trip to meet Lassie in 'person' at Bloomingdale's").

A front-page article on Max, the Jack Russell terrier in *The Mask*— "already signed for the sequel"[1] —appeared in the Arts and Leisure section of the *New York Times*. Another telegenic Jack Russell, "Frasier's Pal Eddie," made the cover of *Entertainment Weekly* as "TV's Top Dog— He's Hot. He's Sexy. He's Purebred."[2] *EW* also featured in another issue a page of dog-celebrity look-alikes, or "dogs that do celebrity impersonations": a Shar-Pei as John Goodman, a Chinese Crested Hairless as Joan Rivers, and so on.

What is behind the current cultural obsession with crossover relationships between human beings and their dogs?

Books by William Wegman and Thierry Poncelet feature dogs dressed in human clothes, embodying human foibles, and illustrating the classics of "human" childhood. Poncelet buys ancestral family portraits from the eighteenth and nineteenth centuries, paints out the human faces, and replaces them with dogs.[3] Wegman's Bettina stars as Cinderella and Little Red Riding Hood (where, in a dramatic and reflexive encounter, she meets the wolf). The title of an earlier Wegman volume, *Man's Best Friend*, draws attention to the exchange of properties: the "man" of the title is in fact the dog (Wegman's first Weimaraner, Man Ray, named after the surrealist), while the "best friend," by the process of elimination, must be photographer Wegman, the man. Man (the dog) himself was originally to be named "Bauhaus"—a *great* dog name—but his new owner decided the puppy "didn't look like a Bauhaus"—a Bauhaus, he thought, should be black, white, and square. Fay Wray, Man Ray's successor, was named for the movie actress whose classic encounter with King Kong raised questions about pathos, the human/animal boundary and the ineluctable mysteries of desire.

Meantime, all over New York, pampered pets and bandana-wearing free spirits are stepping out in dogwear that apes human fashion. "Dog owners like to dress up their dogs," said an expert at Dog-O-Rama on Seventh Avenue South. "They have a sense that they're a person and should dress up like a person." "You feel stupid buying dog clothes when people are homeless," admitted the owner of two well-dressed poodles, "but I do other things for charity."[4]

Sometimes the dogs don't wear the fashion items—they are the fashion items. "Dogs make the perfect accessory," declared the *New York Times Magazine*. "At least one English sheepdog . . . has been mistaken for a pillow on a chintz couch. Dalmatians are always at home on a black-and-white checkered kitchen floor."[5]

Or—for a touch of "hair of the dog"—consider a new book called *Knitting with Dog Hair*. "Stop vacuuming and start knitting," urge the authors. The projects they recommend include a golden retriever scarf, a cardigan sweater made of Samoyed hair, and the ultimate in self-referential recycling, a dog sweater for a pet pug made of yarn spun from a Newfoundland.

But if dogs are sharing some of the pleasures of human society, they are also sharing some of its problems. According to the Animal

Veterinary Medical Association, dogs are now taking Prozac.[6] It seems they, too, suffer from anxiety, depression, extreme shyness, aggression and obsessive-compulsive disorders. Dog phobias, from separation anxiety to "high-rise syndrome" (they fall out of unscreened windows), can be found in a hefty classification of animal behavioral disorders analogous to the Diagnostic and Statistical Manual.[7]

A recent spate of dog movies, such as *Homeward Bound* and *Look Who's Talking Now*, have featured the ventriloquized voices of humans playing the parts of dogs: Danny DeVito and Diane Keaton as the mutt and the poodle in *Look Who's Talking*; and in *Homeward Bound* the boyish Michael J. Fox as the mutt, Sally Field as the cat, and Don Ameche as the film's wise elder, the golden retriever Shadow.

Jokes about dog language, a topic addressed earnestly by philosophers and psychologists, are not infrequent in these films: in *Look Who's Talking Now*, the rambunctious mutt Rocks is sure his name is "No!" because that's what is constantly being shouted at him, and there is a wonderful little scene in which the poodle, Daphne, and the little girl, Julie, are each convinced that they are training each other ("Daphne, paw." "Julie, paw.") The same mutual misunderstanding takes place in *Homeward Bound*, where the effect, as so often in dog films, is one of pathos. When at the close the aged and sore-footed Shadow finally limps onto the scene, there is a joyous reunion between dog and boy, and it is Shadow's voice we hear: "Oh Peter, I worried about you so. Peter, you're OK."

As is clear from its title, *Homeward Bound*, like *Lassie Come Home*, draws both literally and liberally on the quality of "nostalgia"—a bittersweet longing for things, persons, or situations of the past, a kind of cultural homesickness, from the Greek word *nostos*, a return home. Home is where the dog is. Reflecting on this phenomenon in nineteenth-century France, Kathleen Kete has analyzed "the exaggerated place of canine affect as an idea within bourgeois culture."[8]

The *canis classicus* here, of course, is Argos, the faithful dog of Odysseus, who recognizes his disguised master after twenty years—and promptly dies:

> There, full of vermin, lay Argos the hound. But directly he became aware of Odysseus' presence, he wagged his tail and dropped his ears, though he lacked the strength now to come nearer his master. Odysseus turned his eyes away, and ... brushed

away a tear. . . . As for Argos, the black hand of Death descended on him the moment
he caught sight of Odysseus—after twenty years.[9]

Not for nothing is "Fido" (faithful) the pet name of man's best
friend. That "home" is the same as "death" is a lesson we do not need
to learn from Freud.

Paul Monette strikes the same somber note of pathos and return
by using the concept of "dog years" in an essay called "Puck," in which
he meditates on his lover's death from AIDS. "Even though we were
all living our lives in 'dog years' now, seven for every twelvemonth, I
still couldn't feel my own death as a palpable thing," he writes. "So don't
tell me I had less time than a ten-year-old dog."[10] In this case the transfer of properties is manifest. The dog with the Shakespearean name is
asked, like his namesake, to bless the threshold.

Perhaps most strikingly, a new pack of dog writers has captured the
popular imagination, performing in a genre that might be called "etho-
humanism." Discussing "happiness," "intelligence," and a "hidden life,"
these widely marketed, best-selling books explore the once-forbidden
terrain of canine consciousness, with the objective of finding out not
only whether dogs think, but (the question is always palpably deci-
pherable beneath the anecdotes) what they think about *us*.

These are "crossover" books in the publishers' sense, books with
one foot—or paw?—in a learned or scholarly field and another in the
domain of the popular. Elizabeth Marshall Thomas, the author of *The
Hidden Life of Dogs*, is described on the jacket flap as a "novelist and
anthropologist." Stanley Coren, author of *The Intelligence of Dogs*, is a
"renowned psychologist and award winning dog trainer," and Vicki
Hearne is "a poet and philosopher" who has taught college English and
"trains dogs professionally."

The border-straddling nature of these works is underscored by the
difficulty bookstores have in deciding where to display them: *The
Intelligence of Dogs*, for example, is marked on the book jacket as
"Pets/Psychology," and defines "intelligence" as a version of "obedience."
It is no exaggeration to say that such books in fact constitute a respectable
new form of pop psychology and self-help, the flip side of a subgenre
more directly aimed at that market niche, like Clarissa Pinkola Estes' best-
selling *Women Who Run with the Wolves*, or its sardonic send-up, Barbara

Fig. 1.1 Untitled (Cinderella in Evening Gown), 1992.
Photo: William Wegman.

Graham's *Women Who Run with the Poodles*. *Poodles* cheerfully offended Jungian feminists by including a section on "Reclaiming Your Sacred Inner Bitch." But unlike *Poodles*, which sees the inner bitch in the woman, *Hidden Life, Intelligence,* and *Happiness* all see the inner woman in the bitch—or, more usually, the inner man in the dog.

"The dread practice of anthropomorphism," as science correspondent Natalie Angier pointed out in the *New York Times*, has long been a "sin" among researchers who study the behavior of nonhuman animals: "to ascribe to the creature under scrutiny emotions, goals, consciousness, intelligence, desires, or any other characteristics viewed as exclusively human." Traditionally, such a view has been regarded as unscientific: "the truly objective biologist will refrain from projecting personal feeling onto the animal"; "a scientist should never presume that an animal has intentions, or is aware of what it is doing, or even that it feels pain."[11]

But lately a new wave of "neoanthropomorphists" has arisen: animal behaviorists who believe that anthropomorphism can actually help them "do their science," as scientists like to say. "Anthropomorphism is really just another word for empathy,"[12] they claim. "For many biologists," said a Berkeley scientist who studies pit vipers, "the major reason they study animals . . . is that they really wonder what' it's like to be that animal."[13]

Why, these new "critical anthropomorphists"[14] ask, should science insist that there is a fixed boundary between human beings and the rest of the living world? Indeed, as one researcher points out, the desire to establish a firm borderline somewhere, anywhere, between humans and other beasts—a desire inherited from both Judeo-Christian religion and the philosophy of Descartes—has resulted in a kind of scientific gerrymandering, a constant redrawing of boundaries to suit the intellectual politics of the time. The "sine qua non of humanness," rather than residing in any particular property, is constantly being revised—the borderline keeps moving. The definition of humanness, said one animal psychologist, "keeps getting pushed away to preserve human exclusivity."[15]

But if biologists are now embracing anthropomorphism, the new ethohumanists are still skittish, and shy away from the concept even as they deploy it. They are, we might say, *conditioned* to do so by the scorn that traditional behavioral scientists (and some philosophers and linguists) have heaped on the idea. Notice the defensiveness (and defiance) with which Elizabeth Marshall Thomas begins *The Hidden Life of Dogs*:

> This is a book about dog consciousness. To some people, the subject might seem anthropomorphic simply by definition, since in the past even scientists have been led to believe that only human beings have thoughts or emotions. Of course, nothing could be further from the truth. . . .
>
> After all, thoughts and emotions have evolutionary value.[16]

So Thomas's approach is, she contends, *more* "scientific" than that of some scientists. Vicki Hearne, too, is both defensive and aggressive about anthropomorphism. The dog trainers she knows, she says, have the habit of "talking in highly anthropomorphic, morally loaded language,"[17] a practice that offends some "academics," among them philosophers or psychologists who think that only people can "love."

Where Thomas draped herself in the banner of science to defend anthropomorphism ("after all, thoughts and emotions have evolutionary value"), Hearne wraps herself in the flag of the humanities. "Having something to say about what animals are like—about the problem of animal consciousness," says Hearne, has become a "ubiquitous . . . way of providing a rhetorical and conceptual frame for investigations of human consciousness."[18] "The family of tropes damned as 'anthropomorphic' points us to the places where the greatest secrets of animal thinking, and thinking in general, begin to be revealed."[19]

If we use the word "humanist" to describe someone who believes that literature tells the truth about human nature, Hearne may be the last humanist of the American mid-century—or, perhaps, the first humanist of the new millennium (Humanist, all too humanist.) In her books about dog training, the names of poets and philosophers serve as frequent reference points, illustrating (and propping up) homely anecdotes about dogs and their owners.

Poems or lines of poetry by Milton, Sidney, Shakespeare, Wordsworth, and Byron, by John Hollander, Donald Davie, Wallace Stevens, and James Merrill are constantly cited, together with those philosophers on which she so straightforwardly depends—Wittgenstein and Stanley Cavell.

"Many people think Airedales are the best dogs, as did the poet and critic Yvor Winters,"[20] she will say. The performance of Sam, a pointer, strikes her as "an illustration of what T. S. Eliot called 'the eternal struggle between art and education.'"[21] She imagines her Airedale Drummer "by himself, meditating," and wonders whether he is "hoping that I would, in Matthew Arnold's phrase, overhear his meditation."[22]

Perhaps the most symptomatic development in the new cultural permission to anthropomorphize is the wide currency of the term "marriage" to describe a relationship between two canines, and the insistent description of them in recent books as "husband" and "wife."

In *The Hidden Life of Dogs*, described on the flyleaf of the book as "a sort of deeply truthful ethological poem," novelist and anthropologist Elizabeth Marshall Thomas describes in affecting terms what she repeatedly calls the "marriage" of the husky dogs Misha and Maria. Misha "had married my daughter's husky, the beautiful Maria,"[23] says Thomas. Maria "would wait near the door for her husband."[24] As Harriet Ritvo cogently pointed out in the *New York Review of Books*, Thomas "evidently wishes to imply that the range of canine behavior includes the highest kind of mutual devotion and fidelity," but the result is both distracting and coy.[25]

Significantly, in this account of a dog marriage Thomas once again rather defensively addresses the question of anthropomorphism:

> Popular prejudice might hold that romantic love, with its resulting benefit of fidelity, sexual and otherwise, is not a concept that can be applied to dogs, and that to do so is anthropomorphic. Not true. Fully as much as any human love story, the story of Misha and Maria shows the evolutionary value of romantic love. The force that drove Romeo and Juliet is no less strong or important if harbored by a nonhuman species, because the strength of the bond helps to assure the male that he, instead of, say, Tybalt or Bingo, is the father of any children born and that both parents are in a cooperative frame of mind when the time comes to raise those children.[26]

Notice that Shakespeare is evoked as the humanistic "evidence" of an emotional standard: "the force that drove Romeo and Juliet" appears here as a fact, not a fiction, while the beguiling fantasy of a litter of baby Montagues sired by Romeo on his Capulet "mate" serves to corroborate the "evolutionary value of romantic love." In fact any analogy here would break down on the level, so to speak, of the breed: presumably the genetic purity and continuation of the Capulet line would profit more directly from marriage—or "mating"—between Juliet and her cousin Tybalt than from the transgressive Montague-Capulet cross. *Romeo and Juliet*, in fact, is in this regard less like Misha and Maria than it is like *Lady and the Tramp*.

As it happens, Shakespeare's *Romeo and Juliet* is also employed to code a relationship between dogs as a love story in Ivan Reitman's film *Beethoven's Second*, a popular family movie featuring a romance between two Saint Bernards that has more than a little in common with *The Hidden Life of Dogs*. Missy, the Saint Bernard, imprisoned by her wicked step-owners on a first-floor apartment house balcony, is wooed by the love-struck Beethoven, and—in a move Juliet might have envied—she leaps over the railing to join him for an afternoon on the town. Once again the reference to Shakespeare—considerably more accurate in the film than in Thomas's book—is cited as shorthand for "romantic love."

The appearance of puppies some weeks later confirms the carnal nature of their relationship (Beethoven's introduction to his new brood is less traumatic than Misha's, and results in a longer-term parental commitment), but the affair is presented in distinctly romantic and manifestly "anthropomorphic" terms. (The filmmakers appear to have wrestled with the problem of how to make this pair of beefy canines look heterosexual, and have solved it by giving Missy a pink hair ornament. Lesson: If the bitch looks butch, put on a bow.) Rather than sniffing one another's rear ends in doggy style, the two Saint Bernards go out together for a hot dog, take a ride in a bicycle buggy, and wind up necking (or should we call it petting?) at a drive-in movie.

To talk about dog "husbands" and "wives" is not, of course, a new practice among ethologists. Konrad Lorenz wrote about a similar kind of "animal husbandry" forty years ago in *King Solomon's Ring*, where he described the mixed "marriage" of his alsatian and his wife's chow.[27] "We discovered," Lorenz reports, "as an unexpected hindrance, a new property of Lupus dogs [dogs which, like the chow, were, Lorenz believed, descended from the wolf]: the monogamous fidelity of the bitch to a certain dog."

Now, "Lupus" dogs such as malamutes, huskies, and chows may in fact be more monogamous than "Aureus" dogs like the German shepherd or the golden retriever, but erotic constancy is not, in general, a trait we associate with the canine world. In any case, the discovery of sexual fidelity in a species not particularly known for that trait—despite the generic name "Fido"—is an interesting commentary on another species (homo sapiens) whose track record in marriage is in fact getting worse all the time. If "Fido" (faithful) is a stereotypical dog name, so, after all, is "Rover."

But the recurrence in these accounts of the word "fidelity" can hardly be an accident. As the generic dog name Fido suggests, "popular prejudice" does associate dogs with fidelity, but of a slightly different kind. We expect dogs to be faithful to human beings, not to each other. They are supposed to be *our* "best friends."

Can all this enthusiasm for marriage between dogs possibly be covering over something else?

In *Sexual Behavior in the Human Male* (1948), and a few years later in *Sexual Behavior in the Human Female* (1953), Alfred Kinsey forthrightly discusses both the phenomenon of sexual "petting" ("physical contacts which involve a deliberate attempt to effect erotic arousal") between male and female humans and the frequency of "animal contacts," that is, sex between male or female human beings and animals, barnyard or domestic.

In an observation I particularly cherish for its lack of affect—always a hallmark of the Kinsey style—America's pioneer sex researcher noted that "Petting provides somewhat fewer orgasms than nocturnal emissions, and only animal intercourse is less important as a source of outlet."[28]

Petting and animal intercourse: Why does the signifier "petting" implicitly join these two activities, which common usage so rigorously keeps apart? Why is "petting" *called* "petting"? What, if anything, does it have to do with pets?

Petting, it turns out, was in Kinsey's time largely a middle- and upperclass activity, more prevalent among the college-educated than among those without higher education. "Petting is the particular activity which has led many persons to conclude that college students are sexually wild and perverted," Kinsey says. It marks a conflict of values "between two systems of mores. . . . With the better educated groups"—says Kinsey—"intercourse versus petting is a question of morals. For the lower level, it is a problem of understanding how a mentally normal individual can engage in such highly erotic activity as petting and still refrain from actual intercourse." "Petting," says historian Paul Robinson, "is a word that has virtually disappeared from our sexual vocabulary."[29]

On the question of "animal contacts," Kinsey has this to say: "No biologist understands why males of a species are attracted primarily, even if not exclusively, to females of the same species. . . . There is a considerable literature on this subject, but it needs to be analyzed with caution because so much of it is anthropomorphic, arriving at the sort of interpretation that a human intelligence would expect to find if intraspecific mating were the only possibility in nature [intraspecific here means within a single species]."[30] "In light of the above, it is particularly interesting," he says in his typically mild-mannered away, "to note the degree of abhorrence with which intercourse between the human and animals of other species is viewed by most persons who have not had such an experience."[31]

Yet animal contacts, as Kinsey shrewdly observed, have had a long and honorable history in sexual *fantasy life*—which is to say, in high culture and popular culture as well as in pornography. Human *females* (Kinsey never says "women") have long featured in those foundational cultural fantasies we call folklore and mythology: "Females have sexual relations with bears, apes, bulls, goats, horses, ponies, wolves, snakes, crocodiles, and still lower vertebrates." "Classical Greek and Roman mythology," he points out, "had accounts of lovers appearing as asses, Zeus appearing as a swan."[32]

Thus, and not for the first time, behavior that appears (in practice) as a primary violation of boundary between humans and animals turns out to be (in figure) foundational to received notions of "culture" and civilization. Not only the ancients found these couplings attractive: in the modern literary canon, "Leda and the Swan" is taught to every English major—as, indeed, is *A Midsummer Night's Dream*. These images of cross-species sexual encounters are among the texts on which we found our culture: from Zeus to Xaviera Hollander to Madonna to Woody Allen's *Everything You Always Wanted to Know About Sex*.

Now Kinsey, as I have said, was a zoologist (his early research was on the gall wasp). His evaluation of behavior was based upon what had precedence among animal species, and not on what was prescribed, or proscribed, by religion or the Church, and his "naturalism" was, in Paul

Robinson's phrase, "responsible for a good deal that humanists found objectionable in the reports."[33]

"The elements that are involved in sexual contacts between the human and animals of other species are at no point basically different from those that are involved in erotic response to human situations,"[34] Kinsey wrote. What he calls, in his section on "Techniques in Petting," the "French kiss or soul kiss, in the college parlance,"[35] for example, is traced to the activities of the reptiles, birds, and mammals. He therefore "found it entirely credible," as Robinson notes, "that a man might fall passionately in love with his dog, and that the affection could be returned in kind."[36]

"That a man might fall passionately in love with his dog, and that the affection could be returned in kind." Consider now this description of a relationship that flourished in the 1940s and '50s, just when Kinsey was issuing his reports.

> I don't believe there was anything special about her, except that she was rather a beauty. In this context it is not she herself but her effect upon me that I find interesting. She offered me what I had never found in my sexual life, constant, single-hearted, incorruptible, uncritical devotion. . . . She placed herself entirely under my control. From the moment she established herself in my heart and home, my obsession with sex fell wholly away from me, my single desire was to get back to her, to her waiting love and unstaling welcome. . . . I sang with joy at the thought of seeing her. I never prowled the London streets again, nor had the slightest inclination to do so. On the contrary, whenever I thought of it, I was positively thankful to be rid of it all, the anxieties, the frustrations, the wastage of time and spirit. It was as though I had never wanted sex at all, and that this extraordinary long journey of mine which had seemed a pursuit of it had really been an attempt to escape from it. I was just under fifty when this animal came into my hands, and the fifteen years she lived with me were the happiest of my life.[37]

The voice here is that of the brilliant novelist and writer J. R. Ackerley, and the beloved he writes about so feelingly is his Alsatian dog Queenie, also known to his readers as the title character in Ackerley's *My Dog Tulip* and as Evie, the desirable (and well-named) bone of contention in the novel *We Think the World of You.*

"Seldom has a loved animal—seldom has any lover—been so completely rendered in literature," wrote Felice Picano about *My Dog Tulip.*

Ackerley's own quest for the elusive Ideal Friend, "the One, the Charmer, the Long Sought-For & Never Found Perfect Friend to Be, instantly recognizable, instantly responsive, the Destined Mate,"[38] whom he imagined as a heterosexual, working-class man, thus culminated in his relationship with a female dog. More than one longtime associate evinced consternation that Ackerley had wound up, as he says, not with a boy but with a bitch.[39]

Given the evident ardor of his passion, and the sexual adventurousness of his early life, it is perhaps not surprising that Ackerley's friends were curious about the specific nature of his relationship to Queenie, a dog E. M. Forster coolly described as "that unnecessary bitch."

Fig. 1.2   J. R. Ackerley with his dog Queenie (Tulip in *My Dog Tulip*). Photo: Francis King.

One of my friends, puzzled by the sudden change in my ways, asked me whether I had had sexual intercourse with her. It may be counted as something on the profit side of my life that I could now receive such a question intelligently. I said no. In truth, her love and beauty when I kissed her, as I often did, sometimes stirred me physically; but although I had to cope with her own sexual life and the frustrations I imposed upon it for some years, the thought of attempting to console her myself, even with my finger, never seriously entered my head. What little I did for her in her burning heats—slightly more than I admitted in *My Dog Tulip*—worried me in my ignorance of animal psychology, in case, by gratifying her clear desires, which were all addressed to me, I might excite and upset her more than she was already excited and upset.[40]

Ackerley, like the ethologists, writes of seeking a "husband" for his beloved Alsatian bitch, and of supervising her various attempts at "marriage."[41] In his tone, however, we hear not the idealization of a human institution, but a commentary on its folly. Tulip's first suitor, Max, had "never been married before," and when Tulip is brought for a "formal introduction to her betrothed,"[42] the mutual inexperience of the pair proves disastrous.

Then the recently married owner of a male dog confides to Ackerley that he has been wondering if his dog "mightn't settle down better if I found *him* a wife, too."[43] But this courtship is likewise doomed to failure, as is the suit of the aristocrat Mountjoy, whose owner, Mrs. Tudor-Smith, was "Frightfully keen on the marriage,"[44] but who turns out to have a physiological problem that impedes the sexual act.[45] "Mountjoy's owners, . . . who had never offered him a wife before, were totally ignorant" of this fact, Ackerley notes with some quiet pleasure.

In any case, Tulip clearly prefers her master: "when she had me back to herself, [she was] in her most disarming mood, and as soon as we were home she attempted to bestow upon my leg and my overcoat all the love that the pusillanimous Max had been denied."[46] And as for Ackerley: "I felt, indeed, extremely sympathetic toward Tulip's courtiers," he confides. "(I would have been after the pretty creature myself, I thought, if I had been a dog.)"[47]

When a young female veterinarian diagnoses the cause of Tulip's chronic misbehavior in the doctors' office, she speaks a self-evident truth that nonetheless comes as a surprise to both master and reader:

> "Tulip's a good girl, I saw that at once. You're the trouble."
>
> I sat down.
>
> "Do tell me," I said.
>
> "Well, she's in love with you, that's obvious. And so life's full of worries for her. She has to protect you to begin with; that's why she's upset when people approach you: I expect she's a bit jealous, too."[48]

In Ackerley's novel *We Think the World of You*, the dog Evie is the central figure in not one but two erotic triangles, and the risible as well as poignant triangulation that inevitably developed among Ackerley and his human and animal dependents is exemplified in a note left by his sister Nancy at the time of her (apparent) attempted suicide. "She seems to have been jealous of your wife as well as your aunt," a police constable tells Ackerley. He explains that he is not married, and the constable persists: "Well, another woman is mentioned. Someone called Queenie."[49]

Author Rosamond Lehmann said of *My Dog Tulip* that it was "the only 'dog book'" she knew "to record a human-animal love in terms of *absolute equality* between the protagonists."[50] "It is necessary to add that she is beautiful," Ackerley says of Tulip in the early pages of that book. Affectionately recording some of Tulip's foibles, he remarks without emphasis that "the events I have related took place many years ago when she was young and a shade irresponsible, and our love was new."[51]

"Love" is a term that is often used by children, and sometimes by adults, to describe their relationship with beloved pets. "I love dogs so much that I want to marry one," declared a five-year-old I encountered when I was walking my own dog. Her elders looked tactfully away, as if she had said something improper. (My own response was equally unacceptable, I'm afraid—all I could think was, "you can't have this one, he's *mine*.")

The fact is that we are as a society quite comfortable with *children* who say they "love" dogs, but we are much less tolerant of adults who do the same thing. This "developmental fallacy" in our common descriptions of dog love, as a way station rather than an end point, devalues passions that are among the most strongly felt, and establishes without critique a "norm" of maturity and adulthood that is, to use Kinsey's term, unreflectively intraspecific.

"Love" is the word invariably used by both Ackerley and his friends to describe his and Queenie's relationship. Indeed part of Forster's discomfort was his conviction, shared by a large proportion of the post-Freudian population, that "people love animals because of sex-repression."[52] The spectacle of an adult person, male or female, whose chief emotional ties are with a pet animal tends to elicit from many observers responses ranging from pity to condescension. The frequently heard "substitution" theory, the idea that love for a dog (or other pet) is a sign of failure rather than success in emotional or erotic relations, is often linked to a kind of pity or contempt, and is directed, more often than not, toward women and gay men.

Thus Nobel prize-winning ethologist Konrad Lorenz, often praised—as those who study animal behavior so often are—for his "warm humanity"[53] and "deep sympathy for the human condition,"[54] discusses the overbreeding of dogs, "like the Pekinese and the pug, with which childless women express their need for love and affection. It is, of course,

Fig. 1.3 Sigmund and Anna Freud with Wolf.
Photo: Freud Museum, London.

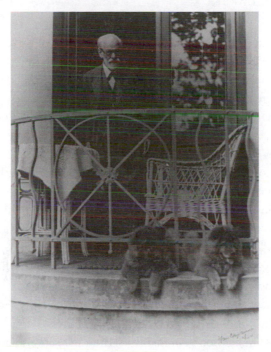

Fig. 1.4 Freud with Jo-Fi's pups Fo and Tattoun, Hohe Warte, 1933.
Photo: Freud Museum, London.

Fig. 1.5 Freud and his chow Lun Yi at the home of Princess Marie Bonaparte, en route from Vienna
to London, June 1938.
Photo: Freud Museum, London.

a sad side effect that these poor dogs are also unusually overfed and made neurotic."[55] Like their owners, he (just) forbears to say.

An article on former movie star and "sex kitten" Brigitte Bardot noted "there were still those who sniped that she chose to love animals because she had been so let down by men."[56] But Ackerley almost suggests that, on the contrary, sex with men was a substitute for or a forerunner of love for a dog. The point is perhaps not to argue about whether dog love is a substitute for human love, but rather to detach the notion of "substitute" from its presumed inferiority to a "real thing." Don't all loves function, in a sense, within a chain of substitutions?

Lorenz's condescending dismissiveness and Forster's notion of "sex-repression" are part of a vulgar Freudian interpretation of developmental stages. In Freud's own life and family, however, the question of dog love was more complex and far more interesting.

"A lot of rubbish has been spoken about the psychoanalyzing of dogs in the modern world," declares "walkies" "dog lady" Barbara Woodhouse in her book *No Bad Dogs*. But the relationship between dogs and psychoanalysis is a long, honored, and indeed foundational one.

Wolf, a black Alsatian, was Freud's gift to his daughter Anna in 1925, the same year that his student Jeanne de Groot, a Dutch psychoanalytic trainee, became engaged to Hans Lampl, a suitor Anna (and her father) had rejected. "Lampl got his Jeanne and Anna got her Wolf," joked a gossip columnist for a Vienna newspaper. The equation was not unjust.

Freud, Anna Freud, and Lampl had once formed an uneasy triangle from which the suitor Lampl eventually dropped out. Anna wrote to her father after the end of the romance "to confirm our judgment of him from last year and to rejoice that we judged correctly."[57] Was Wolf a Lampl substitute? Or was he that which enabled Anna Freud not to leave her father? The two Freuds, Sigmund and Anna, began to develop a dog family of their own. (That the first dog was called "Wolf" has, in view of Freud's career, a certain satisfying insistence of signification.)

In 1927 Freud was presented with a chow, Lin Yug (or Lun Yi), by Anna's friend Dorothy Burlingham. This first chow died in an accident some fifteen months later, and was shortly replaced by another, the beloved Jo-Fi (or Yofi). A succession of chows became in his later years Freud's closest companions.

As Freud aged, as his children married and left home, and as he suffered a series of family bereavements (his precious daughter Sophie; his beloved grandson Heinerle, Sophie's younger son), the dogs began to occupy more of his time and attention. "Wolf . . . has almost replaced the lost Heinerle," he wrote to Jeanne Lampl-de Groot.[58] But, as soon became clear, it was as much a matter of transference as of substitution. In an essay on transference love, written long before he actually had a dog, Freud described the restraint necessary for the analyst in terms of an analogy.

> For the doctor, ethical motives unite with the technical ones to restrain him from giving the patient his love. . . . He must not stage the scene of a dog-race in which the prize was to be a garland of sausages but which some humorist spoilt by throwing a single sausage on to the track. The result was, of course, that the dogs threw themselves upon it and forgot all about the race and about the garland that was luring them to victory in the far distance.[59]

Freud's analogy, which restages the story of Atalanta (the story of how a fleet-footed woman lost a race and became a wife), also recalls a letter he wrote to Sandor Ferenczi cautioning him against kissing and having sex with his patients, a practice Freud describes as part of Ferenczi's analytic "Technique." Here is Ernest Jones' translation of Freud's letter:

> A number of independent thinkers in matters of technique will say to themselves: why stop at a kiss? Certainly one gets further when one adopts "pawing" as well, which after all doesn't make a baby, . . . and soon we shall have accepted in the technique of analysis the whole repertoire of . . . petting parties, resulting in an enormous increase of interest in psychoanalysis among both analysts and patients.[60]

"You have compelled me to be quite blunt," he concluded—an instance of Freud calling a dog a dog.

For Freud, the household dogs offered a new and gratifying preoccupation at a time when he was becoming increasingly restive with the competitiveness and perceived disloyalties of his human disciples. "What Freud prized in his dogs," Anna observed, "was their grace, their devotion and loyalty; what he often commended—as a marked advantage in comparison to people—was the absence of any ambivalence. 'Dogs,' as he used to say, 'love their friends and bite their enemies, quite unlike people who are incapable of pure love and always have to mix love and hate in their object relations.'[61]

On his birthday, May 6, the dogs—assisted by Anna and others in the household—presented him with gifts, and were decked in bows and ribbons for the occasion. This scenario is captured in some Freud family home movies, in which the dogs appear with poems tied around their necks. In these films, Anna Freud is clearly more interested in the dogs and their gifts than in the human members of the psychoanalyt-ic community gathered to place tributary bones at the master's feet.[62] But the dog was not merely an ornament; she was a part of the process (the petting cure?).

"The dog would sit quietly at the foot of the couch during the analytic hour," writes Peter Gay.[63] How quietly she sat, however, is a matter of some small dispute. Anna Freud says that "Yo-Fie . . . patient-ly participated in all analytic hours,"[64] but Freud's son Martin suggested that Jofi helped Freud determine when a session was up by unfailing-ly beginning to stir at the end of the hour,[65] and the poet H.D., who was in analysis with Freud, recalled that "I was annoyed at the end of my session as Yofi would wander about and I felt that the Professor was more interested in Yofi than he was in my story."[66]

When Yofi becomes pregnant, "the Professor" remarks that if there are two puppies, one will go to the owners of the sire, "but if only one, 'it stays a Freud.'"[67] So in a way Freud himself is the real father of the imagined chow pups. He had at one time promised a puppy to H.D.'s lover Bryher, whose nickname was Fido—but only a single puppy sur-vived of that litter, and Freud, as promised, kept him.[68] Perhaps H.D. was right in her suspicion that his interest in Yofi competed with his interest in her.

In the last years of his life, Freud collaborated with his daughter Anna in the translation of a remarkable little book by his pupil and benefactor, Princess Marie Bonaparte: *Topsy, the Golden Haired Chow.* *Topsy,* written between March 1935 and June 1936, describes Bonaparte's distress at discovering a cancerous growth on the lip of her chow Teaupi or Topsy, and chronicles her X-ray treatments and her subsequent cure. The chapter titles are indicative of the style of the whole: the book is divided into two sections, "Topsy is Ill" and "Topsy is Healed" and the chapters include "The Sentence," "Poor Topsy!" "Topsy Beneath the Magical Rays" (the X-rays at the Curie Institute in Paris), "Respite from Things Human," and, perhaps inevitably, given the humanistic scope of the whole. "Topsy and Shakespeare." In that chapter, Topsy's indifference to literary fame is contrasted to the "illusion" of authors like Homer, Shakespeare, and indeed, Princess Marie Bonaparte herself, who "strive[s] laboriously to trace vain signs on this paper" while Topsy "simply inhales the scented June air."[69]

This is a point that Virginia Woolf makes more effectively by looking at it from the dog's point of view in her wonderful biography of Flush, Elizabeth Barrett Browning's cocker spaniel: "Flush was at a loss to account for Miss Barrett's emotions."

Fig. 1.6 Marie Bonaparte, Princess George of Greece (1882–1962), with the chow, Topsy. Late 1930s. Photo: A.W. Freud et al.

There she would lie hour after hour passing her hand over a white page with a black stick; and her eyes would suddenly fill with tears; but why?"[70] The contrast between (human) writing and (animal) living is a constant theme throughout Topsy. "The growth under Topsy's lip seems once more to be dissolving and disappearing," writes Bonaparte at one point. She may be "recovered in spite of my mournful poems. And I think that, up to now, it is only with ink and paper that she had been killed."[71] When the news is good, she exults, "Topsy, Topsy, little healed dog, looking at you I am prouder to have almost magically prolonged your little life, than if I had written the Iliad."[72]

But there is, of course, a comparison implicit in Topsy more compelling than that between Bonaparte and Homer or Shakespeare, and that is the comparison between Topsy and Freud. The "sentence" of oral cancer could only remind Marie Bonaparte, and doubtless her translators

Anna and Sigmund Freud, of the illness of the "master," Freud, likewise suffering from a tumor on the right side of the oral cavity, and likewise treated with surgery, X-rays, and radiation.[73] In the last pages of the book, Bonaparte sees both herself as Topsy's savior ("Topsy . . . thanks to me, has probably recovered from a terrible ailment") and Topsy as a "talisman that conjures away death" for her human owner.

In writing about Topsy, Marie Bonaparte not only found a way to express her own grief and fear about losing Freud, but also literally pro-vided a way for Anna and Sigmund Freud to "translate," displace, and work through their own emotions. As Freud's benefactor, she would also help to "translate" him from Vienna to London to escape the Nazis. There it was dog, not master, who was (temporarily) imprisoned, by the strict British quarantine laws. Freud visited his chow faithfully in the state kennel throughout the summer and winter of 1938.[74]

A recent book on "Freud's discourse" claims that both Freud and Bonaparte manifested symptoms of a syndrome barely hinted at in his works: what the author of the study called "caninophilia."[75] Whether it is a symptom of caninophilia or not, Topsy is a clear sign of something else, something that could be called "caninization." Recall that Alfred Kinsey linked "animal contacts" with the breaching of that other anthro-pomorphic borderline, that between humans and gods, and thus with the foundations of Western culture. The almost compulsive return in these canine narratives of the great figures of the literary canon—Shakespeare, The Iliad, The Odyssey—marks the place of a literary and cultural nostalgia that feels it no longer has a home to go to: a nostalgia, that is, for the canon itself, and for humanism as it is used to be.

Anthropomorphism is itself a kind of transference. It transfers human properties onto dogs, and, in the process, finds in the dog an idealized, improved humanity—human, more than human, showing signs of "intelligence," "happiness," and a "hidden life." Indeed, if you want to make a man appear more human, show him with a dog—a lesson learned by Presidents from Roosevelt to Nixon to Bush. The dog becomes the repository of those idealized human properties that we have cynically ceased to find among humans. ("The word "cynic," of course, comes from a Greek word meaning "dog.")

In penetrating into the hidden life of dogs, we recover notions of fidelity, family, marriage, beauty, romance, pathos, and unambiguousness—

the very notions that underlie the humanism contemporary literary critics have gone to such pains to demystify. Of course, as in that humanism, hierarchy is central, and pack-order (canonicity and canon formation) well understood. Where today can we find the full panoply of Bill Bennett's *Book of Virtues*, from Courage, to Responsibility, to Loyalty and Family Values, but in Lassie, and Beethoven, and Millie, and Checkers, and Spot?

To say you love dogs is like saying you love literature. But of these two sentiments, the second has become the more taboo.

What I want to suggest, then, is that the renewed, even obsessive, popularity of anthropomorphism in science and popular culture is a sign of a desperate nostalgia for humanism. Even among the most die-hard postmodernists and deconstructors, that nostalgia can only be gratified by a transferential displacement—a displacement onto the figure we so blithely and presumptuously describe as "man's best friend."

NOTES

1. *The New York Times*, Arts and Leisure, August 7, 1994, section 2, p. 1.

2. *Entertainment Weekly*, December 3, 1993.

3. Alessandra Stanley, "Great-Grandpa is Now a Great Dane." *The New York Times*, January 12, 1994. Theirry Poncelet, *Sit! The Dog Portraits of Theirry Poncelet*, text by Bruce McCall (New York: Workman Publishing, 1993).

4. Emily Prager, "Fashion Unleashed," *The New York Times*, February 20, 1994, section 9, p. 1, 8.

5. Julie V. Iovine, "Animal House," *The New York Times Magazine*, January 16, 1994.

6. "Pills for Pet Peeves," *Boston Globe*, August 15, 1994, p. 10.

7. Janny Scott, "High-Rise Cat Syndrome: Summer Heat Brings an Increase in Urban Pet Afflictions," *The New York Times*, July 10, 1994, pp. 21, 27.

8. Kathleen Kete, *The Beast in the Boudoir: Petkeeping in Nineteenth-Century Paris* (Berkeley: University of California Press, 1994), p. 38.

9. Homer, *The Odyssey*, Book 17, ll. 290–326, trans. E. V. Rieu, rev. trans. C. H. Rieu (London: Penguin, 1991), pp. 263–264.

10. Monette, "Puck," in *Last Watch of the Night* (New York: Harcourt, Brace & Co., 1994), p. 2.

11. Natalie Angier, "Flouting Tradition, Scientists Embrace an Ancient Taboo," *The New York Times*, August 9, 1994, C1.

12. Angier, C7.

13. Dr. Harry Greene, University of California, Berkeley, quoted in Angier, C7.

14. The term was coined by Gordon Burghardt, who teaches animal behavior at the University of Tennessee. Viva Hardigg, "All in the Family?" *U.S. News & World Report*, November 1, 1993, pp. 69–70.

15. Dr. Frans de Waal, Yerkes Primate Center in Atlanta, quoted in Angier, C7.

16. Elizabeth Marshall Thomas, *The Hidden Life of Dogs*, pp. vi–viii.

17. Vicki Hearne, *Adam's Task: Calling Animals by Name* (New York: Knopf, 1987, p. 6.

18. *Adam's Task*, p. 10.

19. Vicki Hearne, *Animal Happiness* (New York: Harper Collins, 1994), pp. 193–194.

20. *Animal Happiness*, p. 82.

21. *Animal Happiness*, p. 71.

22. *Animal Happiness*, p. 201.

23. Thomas, p. 6.

24. Thomas, p. 57.

25. Harriet Ritvo, "A Dog's Life," *The New York Review of Books*, January 13, 1994, pp. 3–4.

26. Thomas, p. 57.

27. Lorenz, *King Solomon's Ring: New Light on Animal Ways* (1952), trans. Marjorie Kerr Wilson (New York: Mentor, 1991), p. 139. Lorenz writes of the mixed "marriage" of an Alsatian and a chow. The Alsatian, "a son of" his bitch Tito, "married the chow bitch Pygi. This happened quite against the will of my wife [Pygi's owner] who, naturally enough, wanted to breed pure chows." The "true love of Pygi for her enormous and good-natured Booby" frustrated her mistress's desire to breed her with another chow: "she only wanted her Booby and she got him in the end." Here is the marital fidelity of Thomas's Misha and Maria (both, as huskies, also lupus dogs), in this case dryly painted against the backdrop of (human) marital strife: Lorenz's claim for the superiority of Aureus dogs, like the Alsatian (German shepherd), and his wife's claim on behalf of the chow.

    Canadian Farley Mowat described, in *Never Cry Wolf* (1963), his relationship to a wolf named George and his "beautiful," "passionate," and "devilish" "wife" Angeline. "I became deeply fond of Angeline," writes Mowat, "and still live in hopes that I can somewhere find a human female who embodies all her virtues."

28. Alfred Kinsey, *Sexual Behavior in the Human Male* (Philadelphia: W.B. Saunders, 1948), p. 667.

29. Paul Robinson, *The Modernization of Sex* (1976) (Ithaca: Cornell University Press, 1989), p. 63.

30. Kinsey, *Human Male*, p. 539.

31. Alfred Kinsey, *Sexual Behavior in the Human Female* (Philadelphia: W. B. Saunders, 1953), p. 503.

32. Kinsey, *Human Male*, p. 668.

33. Robinson, p. 56.

34. *Human Male*, pp. 676–677.

35. *Human Male*, p. 540.

36. Robinson, p. 56.

37. J. R. Ackerley, *My Father and Myself* (London: Bodley Head, 1968), p. 217.

38. Diary, June 30, 1950. Cited in Peter Parker, *Ackerley* (New York: Farrar, Straus and Giroux, 1989), p. 262.

39. Forster, in Parker, p. 263.

40 Ackerley, *My Father and Myself*, p. 218.

41. J. R. Ackerley, *My Dog Tulip* (New York: Poseidon Press, 1965), p. 57.

42. *Tulip*, p. 60.

43. *Tulip*, p. 69.

44. *Tulip*, p. 96.

45. Ackerley documents his own sexual problems, in this case with premature ejaculation, in the appendix to *My Father and Myself*.

46. *Tulip*, p. 67.

47. *Tulip*, p. 88.

48. *Tulip*, p. 21.

49. Ackerley diary, January 9, 1949. Parker, p. 292.

50. Lehmann, jacket of *My Dog Tulip*, 2nd edition, cited in Parker, p. 264.

51. Ackerley, *My Dog Tulip*, pp. 54–55.

52. Forster, 1934 *Time and Tide*, 23.6.34.

53. *The New Yorker*, review of *On Aggression*, from the back cover of Konrad Lorenz, *On Life and Living* (New York: St. Martin's Press, 1990).

54. *The New York Times Book Review*, review of *On Aggression*, quoted on back cover of *On Life and Living*.

55. Konrad Lorenz, *On Life and Living*, p. 49.

56. Alan Riding, "And God Created an Animal Lover," *The New York Times* March 30, 1994, p. C8. "I always screw it up [with men], but I'm incredibly good with dogs," says comic writer Cynthia Heimel, a columnist for the *Village Voice* and for *Playboy*, the author of books like *Sex Tips for Girls* and "*Get Your Tongue Out of My Mouth, I'm Kissing You Goodbye*."

57. Anna Freud, letter to Sigmund Freud, July 7, 1921.

58. Michael Molnar, *The Diary of Sigmund Freud, 1929–1939. A Record of the Final Decade* (London: The Hogarth Press, 1992), p. 214 [Thursday, January 14].

59. Sigmund Freud, "Observations on Transference-Love." (1914; 1915) *The Standard Edition of the Complete Psychological Works of Sigmund Freud*, trans. James Strachey (London: The Hogarth Press, 1960), 12:169.

60. Ernest Jones, *The Life and Work of Sigmund Freud*. Ed. and abridged by Lionel Trilling and Steven Marcus (New York: Basic Books, 1961), p. 487.

61. Quoted in Molnar, p. 260.

62. Molnar, p. 98. In 1930 the favored poem was from Jofi ("the nicest thing is a poem in Jofi's name, from Anna of course, in the company of a live little tortoise," he wrote), and a year later, in Freud's seventy-fifth birthday, the poem declared itself to be from "the union of quadrupeds—Wolf-Jofie-Tattoun." Tattoun was Jofi's "son." The tradition of the birthday poem presented by the dogs dates from 1926, when Wolf offered a greeting in rhyme, and continued through his eightieth birthday, when the latest Yofi (the one to whom poet H.D. became attached) wandered "into my bedroom to show her affection in her own fashion, something she has never done before or after. How does a little animal know when a birthday comes around?" he wondered to H.D. in H.D., *Tribute to Freud* (New York: New Directions, 1956), Appendix, p. 193.

63. Peter Gay, *Freud: A Life for Our Time* (New York: Norton, 1988), p. 540.

64. Anna Freud, "Foreword to Topsy by Marie Bonaparte," *The Writings of Anna Freud*, Vol. VIII (New York: International Universities Press, 1981), p. 360.

65. Jennifer Stone, "A Psychoanalytic Bestiary: The Wolff Woman, the Leopard, and the Siren," *American Imago* 49./1 (1992): 141.

66. HD (Hilda Doolittle), *Tribute to Freud*, p. 162.

67. *Tribute to Freud*, p. 166.

68. Barbara Guest, *Herself Defined: The Poet H.D. and Her World* (Garden City: Doubleday, 1944), p. 213.

69. Marie Bonaparte, *Topsy, the Story of a Golden-Haired Chow* (New Brunswick: Transaction Publishers, 1994), p. 151.

70. Virginia Woolf (1933), *Flush: A Biography* (Harmondsworth: Penguin, 1983), pp. 27–28.

71. *Topsy*, p. 105. When Bonaparte is about to depart on a vacation in the south of France, she writes elegiacally, "In a few weeks, Topsy, I shall come back from over there with a tanned skin and a book you cannot read, ... when I return ... you will, doubtless, either be healed or doomed." p. 109.

72. *Topsy*, p. 123.

73. Topsy's victory over cancer "must have expressed" for both the Freuds and Bonaparte "the wish that Freud would yet recover," thinks Lynn Whisnant Reiser ("Topsy—Living and Dying: A Footnote to History," *Psychoanalytic Quarterly* LVI/4 (1987: 687), while allowing all the human participants to "keep some distance" from their suffering.

74. Gary Genosko, introduction to *Topsy* (New Brunswick: Transaction Publishers, 1994), p. 25.

75. Patrick J. Mahoney, *On Defining Freud's Discourse* (New Haven: Yale University Press, 1989, pp. 62–63.

HARRIET RITVO

VICTORIAN SCIENTISTS usually accounted for their fascination with hybrids by their concern with species. As Charles Darwin pointed out in *On the Origin of Species*, the existence of discrete, independent species was inconsistent with his theory of descent with modification—or, indeed, with any evolutionary theory, whether its mechanism was natural selection or not.[1] If species changed slowly but markedly through time—if no precise boundaries separated living forms from their extinct forebears—then the lines between similar living species correspondingly paled in significance. He summarized this argument in the final chapter of the *Origin*:

BARRING THE CROSS

MISCEGENATION AND PURITY IN EIGHTEENTH- AND NINETEENTH- CENTURY BRITAIN

> On the view that species are only strongly marked and permanent varieties, and that each species first existed as a variety, we can see why ... no line of demarcation can be drawn between species, commonly supposed to have been produced by special acts of creation, and varieties which are acknowledged to have been produced by secondary laws.[2]

Darwin's assertion was welcomed by colleagues apparently only too happy to dispense with the species, at least in its most rigid and uncomfortable reification, which could, as Charles Lyell pointed out, cause embarrassment as well as intellectual confusion. He referred particularly to "the difficulty of defining ... the terms 'species' and 'race', . . . [and to] the surprise of the unlearned . . . when they discover how wide is the difference of opinion" among experts.[3] Soon after the publication of the *Origin*, George Henry Lewes, explaining to a general audience why "the zoologist sometimes . . . will class two animals as of different species, when they only differ in colour . . . [while] at other times he will class animals as belonging to the same species, although they differ in size, colour, shape, instincts, [and] habits," triumphantly revealed that "the reason is that the *thing* species does not exist."[4] By the end of the century, such debunking of previous orthodoxy was fit even for the eyes and ears of children. Thus the author of one volume of "The Library for Young Naturalists" forewarned his juvenile readers that "It is . . . for reasons of convenience that men have invented species. Nature knows no such distinction."[5]

The energy of these rejections, as well as their reiteration over a period of half a century, suggests that their target nevertheless retained some of its prestige and power, even at the end of the Victorian period. And this surviving attractiveness was only a shadow of its former self. The notion that, as one English interpreter of Buffon put it, "the most constant and invariable thing in Nature is the image or model allotted to each particular species"—that species had been divinely created and could not be altered by any other agency—was among the most cherished dogmas of Enlightenment natural history.[6] The conviction that species were somehow real—that in labeling a group of organisms with a latinate binomial, taxonomists were identifying an entity that had an existence independent of that naming process—flourished in spite of a striking absence of consensus about the nature of the entity in question, even among those who did not reject it in principle.[7]

For it did not take the further heresy of evolution to raise awkward questions about the species category. Some of these issues emerged in the rarefied reaches of philosophy or theory. For example, immutable and impermeably bounded species could seem inconsistent with one of the other cherished dogmas of Enlightenment natural history—that is, the subtly graduated chain of being.[8] But the problems that most bedeviled naturalists arose on a very practical level, where the assumption that species were essential and unchanging did not greatly assist in identifying them on the wing or on the hoof. Although, as Darwin later conceded, many species were "tolerably well-defined objects"—that is, like humans or hippopotami, they were relatively easy to distinguish from all other creatures—many species demonstrably were not.[9] On the contrary, like mice, horses, and weasels, they bore an incontestable and confusing resemblance to numerous other animals.

The confidence of even the most orthodox naturalists in the essential reality of species was thus constantly challenged by the profusion and variety of the world. But although human beings had a difficult time drawing the line between similar animals, as was frequently asserted, their confusion was not shared by their fellow creatures, whose concerns transcended mere intellectual curiosity. In the most important transactions of their lives, those involving the selection of reproductive partners, animals could be relied on to identify members of their own species and to avoid members of other species. Not only could they see through the spurious similarities that confounded human investigators, but they were particularly sensitive to the boundaries separating their own groups from those which seemed most closely akin. They obeyed a rule starkly formulated by the Victorian racial scientist Robert Knox as, "Nature produces no mules; no hybrids, neither in man nor animals."[10] In making these fine discriminations, animals were forwarding a higher purpose. As Thomas Bewick put it:

> Nature has providently stopped the . . . propagation of these heterogeneous productions, to preserve, uncontaminated, the form of each animal; without which regulation, the races would in a short time be mixed with each other, and every creature, losing its original perfection, would rapidly degenerate.[11]

Works of natural history offered voluminous testimony to the desire of animals to avoid miscegenation, often citing a mutual repulsion between apparently similar creatures as persuasive evidence of specific difference. According to the zoologist John Fleming, "in a natural state, the *selective attribute* of the procreative instinct unerringly guides the individuals of a species towards each other, and a *preventive aversion* turns them with disgust from those of another kind."[12] Such reasoning allowed, for example, the confident recognition of a species boundary between domestic cattle and the buffalo of the Old World because, "they will not copulate together, neither will the female buffaloes suffer a common calf to suck them; nor will the domestic cow permit the same from a young buffalo."[13] The celebrated London menagerist Edward Cross, who had successfully bred both leopards and jaguars, had for this reason observed "no instance of sexual intercourse between the transatlantic species and that of the old world, notwithstanding their great similarity, and though every opportunity has been afforded them."[14] Similarly, although:

> no two animals can make a more near approach to each other than the stag and the fallow-deer, . . . yet no two animals keep more distinct, or avoid each other with more fixed animosity; they never herd or intermix together, and consequently never give rise to an intermediate race.[15]

The closer the apparent resemblance, often the greater the ascribed aversion, as though nature needed to deploy more stringent psychological barriers in physical cases that were particularly ambiguous or liminal. Thus, "the wolf both externally and internally so nearly resembles the dog, that he seems modeled upon the same plan; and yet . . . so unlike are they in disposition that no two animals can have a more perfect antipathy to each other."[16] The Edinburgh Natural History Society was informed that one particularly punctilious "African wild boar . . . refused to copulate with a common sow and presently tore it to pieces."[17] And naturalists frequently remarked that "notwithstanding the general resemblance between . . . [the rabbit] and the hare, their habits and propensities are very different, . . . and they . . . seem to have a natural aversion for each other," to the extent that "a rabbit will live upon more friendly terms with a cat than a hare."[18]

These demonstrations were spectacular and, in their way, conclusive. But aversion was only a first barrier, and, as experience readily demonstrated, not invariably reliable. If it was breached, there were other barriers to reinforce it. The conditions of artificial constraint and proximity under which captive and domesticated animals lived provided ready opportunities for matings between ostensibly unlike creatures. As one late-eighteenth-century agricultural expert observed, "when animals are domesticated, many intermixtures take place, . . . that never would have been experienced had they retained their native freedom. . . . A state of nature . . . [tends] to keep each variety aloof from every other, and thus to preserve them uncontaminated."[19] Even if the animals were themselves loathe to take advantage of these anthro-pogenic opportunities, they might receive strong encouragement to do so from their owners, and not all animals faithfully resisted such force-ful, if unnatural suggestions. Sometimes, even if they succumbed, the lack of consequences only confirmed the point made by their initial reluctance. In support of his contention that "it was beyond the reach of human ability to exceed the limits prescribed by nature, by uniting two distinct species of aboriginal animals, and thereby producing a fac-titious one, capable of re-production," a contributor to the *Hippiatrist and Veterinary Journal* reported on his repeated attempts to cross a buck rabbit and a doe hare. Although he was so far successful in overcom-ing their natural antagonism that "in one instance . . . the sexual intercourse actually took place, . . . there was no issue."[20]

Such unambiguous confirmation of the separation of similar species could not, however, invariably be counted on. Indeed one kind of hybrid, far from being impossible or unlikely, had been intentionally and reliably produced by crossing horses and asses or donkeys for thou-sands of years.[21] But those seeking corroboration in nature for the existence of essential species had to understand even such ordinary workaday creatures as exceptional. Thus a mid-Victorian agricultural encyclopedia grouped the parents of mules with apparently less fre-quent hybridizers in their innate reluctance to couple outside of their species: "the wolf and the dog will not breed *freely* together; not more so than will the horse and ass—the lion and the tiger—the sheep and goat—the hare and rabbit."[22] And even if such couplings took place, and were fruitful, their products were characterized as significantly dif-ferent from those of intraspecies mating. The union of horses and donkeys might be predictably fertile, but it was often claimed that the hybrid issue of such unions were forbidden by divine and natural law to produce further offspring by mating with each other. As the Victorian creationist Philip Gosse explained, species were

distinct forms which are believed to have proceeded direct from the creating Hand of GOD. . . . We know of no fixed principle on which to found our decisions [about the difference or identity of species], except the great law of nature, by which spe-cific individuality is preserved,—that the progeny of mixed species shall not be fertile *inter se*.[23]

For this reason the zoological, veterinary, and agricultural literature dealing with equine mules contained endless reassurances to the effect that "male and female mules and hinnys are absolutely sterile."[24]

If horse-donkey crosses could be confidently relied upon to be sterile (although not to be celibate—their readiness to copulate inspired repeated musings on the nonfunctional in nature), some other hybrids between recognized species proved unnervingly prolific. Faced with such an apparent anomaly, naturalists committed to fertile reproduction as the determinant of species boundaries might repudiate the previously accepted boundary, no matter how hallowed by tradition, rather than abandon their theory. As George Garrard suggested, "there are not so many species as some have imagined; but all . . . are of one species, which propagate with each other."[25] More colorfully, John Jones denounced those who adduced the vigorous and prolific produce of cock pheasants and domestic hens to "prove the falsity of the received opinion that mules will not breed," asserting that "this case proves no more than that pheasants and dung hill fowls are of the same species, like the fox and the dog."[26]

The wish to understand full hybridization—that is, the ability to produce offspring whose own mixed strain would be indefinitely prolific—as a natural or divine guarantee that the two original parents belonged to the same species, was not, however, universal. Some scientists, who were less committed to the concept of inflexibly defined and divided species, contented themselves with describing the phenomena of hybridity, rather than interpreting them. In general, their observations were consistent with the grander claims of their essentialist colleagues, but they were more willing to note apparent anomalies, and less eager to explain them away. Nor was such judicious detachment the only alternative perspective on hybridization. A large audience of naturalists and others interested in the animal kingdom found apparent violation of the laws of nature attractive rather than (or as well as) dismaying or repellent. They energetically sought out exceptions at every level of the neatly layered formulation by which animals readily recognized conspecifics, preferred to mate only with them, and, if they were forced or induced to violate this preference, produced no offspring or, in the worst case, sterile offspring.

When any creature conceived an affection for one of different species—and the more different, the better—it was therefore always news. Naturalists reported that a female zebra had been deceived by "a common Jack-ass" painted with stripes, and had as a result "admitted its embraces"; without benefit of any human hoax, a male "Mongooz" became "fond of she cats; and even satisfied his desires."[27] And humans themselves could be the objects or the originators of passions that transcended or violated the species barrier, although accounts of this kind were carefully distanced by skepticism or censure. Indeed, the most common such breaches, those involving farmyard animals, were much more frequently noticed in a legal context than in works devoted to natural history or animal husbandry.[28] More remarkable events figured more prominently in the zoological literature. At the end of the eighteenth century, Charles White reported that orangutans "have been known to carry off negro-boys, girls and even women . . . as objects of brutal passion"; more than sixty years later the Anthropological Society republished Johann Friedrich Blumenbach's summary of travelers' accounts that "lascivious male apes attack women" who "perish miserably in the brutal embraces of their ravishers."[29] A late-Victorian colonial administrator reported that the "notion amongst the natives of the jungle-tracts in Mysore that solitary male bears will carry off women" was "I need hardly say groundless," but he nevertheless included it in his memoirs.[30]

Authors who reported romantic human-beast encounters were circumspect about the possibility of progeny, although the idea clearly exerted a certain unacknowledged appeal. White recorded rumors "that women have had offspring from such connection," and proposed that, "supposing it to be true, it would be an object of inquiry, whether such offspring would propagate, or prove to be mules."[31] Blumenbach, still more cautious, asserted "that such a monstrous connection has any where ever been fruitful there is no well-established instance to prove."[32] In his pathbreaking anatomy of a chimpanzee, Edward Tyson had gone out of his way to assure his readers that "notwithstanding our *Pygmie* does so much resemble a *Man* . . . : yet by no means do I look upon it as the Product of a *mixt* generation."[33] But the issue of other transspecific amours, even between primates, could be reported with frank appreciation. Thus, for example, a dead baby monkey, half Cape baboon and half pig-tailed macaque, claimed as "the first instance of a *hybrid monkey* on record," was displayed at a meeting of the Asiatic Society of Bengal in 1863.[34] In 1878 the secretary of the Zoological Society of London proudly announced that a male macaque was the father of the hybrid offspring recently borne by a female mandrill, and would also have been the father of a half-mangabey infant, except that the expectant mother had unfortunately fallen to her death before she had delivered.[35]

So great was the fascination exerted by hybrid creatures, that many impossible mixes were reported as fact, or lingered over regretfully as persistent superstitions. Thus Renaissance reports of crosses between bears and dogs were repeated (if only to be dismissed) throughout the nineteenth century, and Aristotle's account of "a hybrid race between the dog and the tiger" was similarly elaborated, before being characterized as "inadmissible" in "The Naturalist's Library."[36] But skepticism was hardly the invariable rule in such matters. At one time or another, nineteenth-century British readers were assured of the existence of "a hybridous race . . . between the domestic cat and the pine marten," a pair of puppies "the produce of a lioness and a true English mastiff," a stuffed animal in the Keswick museum "said to be between a racoon [sic] and a sheep," a ram with antlers about which "the presumption is that it is a mule, got between two animals often found together in our parks," and "an animal between a stag and a mare."[37] On the face of it, after all, such creatures appeared as probable as the incontestably real hybrids of horse and donkey, sheep and goat, cow and bison, and lion and tiger that could be seen more or less readily on exhibition or in the streets.

It is difficult to account for the intensity of this interest, sustained as it was through the eighteenth and nineteenth centuries, solely as a consequence of theoretical differences within the scientific community. Earnest as antiessentialist scientists may have been in their search for counterexamples, their fascination with hybrids transcended intradisciplinary partisanship, and merged with that of the larger public. Indeed, while the accumulation of well-attested examples of fertile interspecific hybrids undermined the essentialist position, the very characterization of such animals as crosses tended to reify the category of species by acknowledging that the parents represented two different entities. Conversely, the insistence of essentialists on explaining away or debunking apparent hybrids implicitly emphasized their significance and magnetism. But hybrids resonated with other Victorian preoccupations of more general concern than the species question. The most broadly based appeal of hybrids depended on the fact of mixture, not the degree of difference. In a culture that valued boundaries of all kinds between people, and that devoted great energy to establishing and defending them, taxonomic border areas and the intermediate animals that inhabited them had very interesting implications, both pragmatic and symbolic. And even those scientists most strongly convinced of the conventional nature of wild species might feel differently about the lines that divided animals more closely connected with human society.

Thus the fascinating influence exerted by hybrids was compounded of horror as well as pleasure, in parts that varied with the mood and predilections of the observer. The range of reaction was often signalled by choice of vocabulary. Hybrids between more or less distinct species, whether wild or domesticated, were described by some observers with breathless appreciation as "extraordinary" and "remarkable."[38] Others characterized them more matter-of-factly as a "mule race," a "heterogeneous production," or a "mixed breed."[39] Partisans at the negative extreme invoked the language of moral disapprobation, identifying hybrids as the source of "deterioration," "disturbing effects," and "a confused chaos of mongrelism."[40] And naturalists were not the only ones to take positions. The transposition of this discussion to the subspecific sphere of domestic animal breeds, where the potential crosses were all demonstrably similar, and where infertility was not an issue, might have been supposed to moderate its tone. But if the intellectual stakes diminished with the scientific prestige of the categories, the financial ante rose, and with it the temper of the debate. Decades of painstaking segregation and improvement, it was feared, could be undone with a single cross. Breeders stiffly defended the elaborately documented labor represented by pedigreed livestock, as if their enthusiastic verbal reification of breed distinctions could compensate for the rather subtle differentiation displayed by their animals in the flesh. And their defense was made more energetic by the latent realization, seldom directly acknowledged although often only thinly veiled, that the maintenance of high genealogical standards was an issue for the breeders as well as the bred. Whether the analogy was explicit or unstated, the resonance between animal pedigree and the stratification of human society was difficult to ignore.

Even the temperate Darwin revealed a sense of the special moral valence of intraspecific crosses. In the middle of his argument that species and varieties were indistinguishable, he consistently denominated the offspring of parents of different species as "hybrids" while denigrating the offspring of parents of different varieties as "mongrels."[41] This choice of word was not merely descriptive; the disparaging connotation was much stronger than any compensatory denotative precision. As Darwin's contemporary W. C. Spooner argued in a slightly different context:

> although the term *mongrel* is probably correct as referring to a mixed breed, yet, as it is generally used as a term of reproach, it should not be fairly applied to those recognized breeds which, however mixed or mongrel might have been their origin, have yet by vigilance and skill become . . . almost as marked and vigorous and distinctive as the Anglo-Saxon race itself, . . . whose mixed ancestry no one is anxious to deny.[42]

And those with greater investments in the elaborately celebrated but somewhat insubstantial technology of animal breeding expressed themselves more forcefully. The results of unions that compromised their rigorous standard of isolation by what could be called "the ill-judged and unscientific introduction of alien blood" were excoriated in no uncertain terms.[43] One agricultural expert described crossing as "a national evil and a sin against society," especially if the crossbred animals were themselves used for breeding what he called "a generation of mongrels."[44] "Blood" that would have been perfectly acceptable, even admirable or desirable, in its proper place became reprehensible when transposed into a different genealogical context. Thus a prominent breeder of shorthorn cattle considered what was euphemistically referred to as "alloy blood" in a rival strain as "a stain in the pedigree of shorthorns" and "a disgrace to the breed."[45]

This aggressive insistence on purity may have reflected some unacknowledged uneasiness about the claims symbolized by pedigree. Even the most elaborately documented breed was wreathed in indeterminacy at every stage of its descent. Its remote wild ancestors were as elusive as the parentage of the individual animals recorded in its early breed books. And between these two stages, little could be confidently asserted about the original subgroup of domesticated animals, the unsung and unsingable founders of the breed, who had somehow become detached from the rest of their kind. Most breed advocates admitted that attempts to identify the forebears of contemporary improved varieties were "more amusing than profitable or instructive."[46]

Committed champions of this ambiguous and unreliable ground may well have seen a good offense as their best defense. Thus both animals and people whose behavior threatened the carefully drawn boundaries that defined breeds came in for severe criticism. Since the chain of responsibility in the breeding enterprise was not long, it was easy to identify potentially weak links. The general rule for the human participants in the process was that "on no account should a cross be permitted," and breeders who "tampered with" a pure strain were castigated as "reckless" or even "radical."[47] The animal role was, of course, less complicated, but ensuring that the animals kept up their end was not always easy. They might succumb to the hazards of illness and accident, or they might, still more annoyingly, exert their own wills in contradiction to those of their proprietors. That is, they might not wish to copulate with the mates chosen for them, preferring instead to follow the dictates of their own hearts or minds.

For several reasons, concern about this kind of insubordination focused on female animals.[48] Female reproductive capacity was more limited and vulnerable than that of males, so any wastage was more of a loss. Because females produced the young, their proprietors were stuck with the fruit of their indiscretions; the consequences of wild male oats were someone else's problem. And, at least among otherwise healthy animals, it was only females who expressed reluctance to copulate. In any case, the most persistently troublesome avenues of compromise and contamination exposed highly bred females to the physical or mental influence of unsuitable rival males. In consequence of such exposure, females could absolutely obstruct the realization of their proprietors' grand genealogical designs. As in human families, it was up to them to maintain both their own purity and the purity of their lineage. In the view of breeders, indeed, as in that of paterfamiliases, to compromise the one was to compromise the other. The literature of animal husbandry brimmed with compulsive worrying about the undesirable hybrids or mongrels that might be produced even by females subject to the most careful confinement and control.

Misdirected affiliations were feared to produce protracted, even ineradicable consequences. For example, the concept of telegony, which was almost universally believed by nineteenth-century breeders and fanciers and widely accepted within the scientific community, attributed to the "previous sire"—usually understood as the father of a female's first child—the power of influencing her subsequent offspring. The first public discussion of this subject occurred in 1820, when the original owner of the animal thereafter eponymously designated as "Lord Morton's mare" wrote the the President of the Royal Society about her remarkable reproductive career.[49] She was a chestnut of seven-eighths Arabian blood, whose first foal had been sired by a quagga and predictably resembled both parents. The fact that the mare's next two foals, both sired by a "very fine black Arabian horse," also bore "a striking resemblance to the quagga" was more surprising.[50] Although the chestnut mare and her offspring were the most frequently adduced, perhaps because the best documented and most reliably attested, instances of this kind of time-lapse hybridization, they were far from the only ones to be publicized.[51] For example, a domestic sow first mated with a wild boar continued in subsequent litters to produce piglets "easily distinguished by their resemblance to the wild boar."[52] It was similarly reported that the grandchildren by other grandsires of a shorthaired domestic cat still sported the long silky fur of the Persian tom who had sired her first litter.[53]

Most breeders therefore strove vigorously to eliminate or contain the contamination that could result from miscegenation. The literature of animal husbandry was full of simple and straightforward prescriptions. When a bitch formed "an undesirable connection . . . breeders . . . at once put the strayed bitch down, or discard her from their kennels." The purveyor of this ostensibly draconian counsel, however, then showed rather inconsistent flexibility, suggesting that, since telegony was "not absolutely certain" to operate in every case, a "much valued" bitch could be bred again, to a suitably pedigreed dog, on the chance that the puppies would not reveal any mongrel taint.[54] The risk that their colleagues would exercise such ill-considered forbearance prompted other breeders "never . . . [to] commence a herd by breeding from a purchased cow," no matter how good she seemed on her own merits. She might have "been accidentally or otherwise served" by a crossbred bull or a bull of a different pure breed, in which case "the risk is always there that she may throw calves with a crossbred strain."[55]

If the ideology of purity was compelling in the abstract, however, it could prove problematic in the real world to which breeders belonged. Principled abhorrence of mongrelization was nearly universal among those concerned with the business of animal husbandry, but their practical applications of that principle varied widely. Interpreted literally, it prescribed a standard of segregation that even the most fastidious breeders would have found difficult to satisfy. Indeed, too rigid a demand for purity would have threatened not only the reputation of well-regarded and long-established breeds, but also the very reification expressed in the term "breed" itself. Although they might denounce contamination, taint, and bastardization with frequency and vigor, most realistic breeders knew that their chosen strains could not endure stringent scrutiny on these grounds. It was impossible to demonstrate the historic genealogical purity of even the most distinguished animals, but the mingled origins of some well-regarded and long-established breeds were readily apparent. Indeed, the aficionados of breeds with the most ancient pedigrees were most likely to argue that past mongrelization did not preclude present purity. As a prolific authority on sporting dogs and horses asked in 1881, if such transformations were not possible, "where are we to find a certainly pure breed of dog, excepting perhaps the Bulldog and the Mastiff?"[56] The frequently rehearsed mythology of the thoroughbred horse, which stressed the three foreign founding sires, made clear its origin in "an Eastern cross on native mares."[57] Paradoxically, the only reliable protection against such deconstruction was the absence of documentation. Thus the origins of the Yorkshire terrier were likely to remain "most obscure; for its originators—Yorkshire-like—were discreet enough to hold their own counsel."[58]

If pure descent had a practical value, in addition to its manifest rhetorical appeal, it was as a guarantee that the offspring of pedigreed animals would inherit the desirable characteristics of their parents.[59] As David Low, professor of agriculture at the University of Edinburgh, commented, with reference to a cross between Zetland and Orkney sheep, "mixed races are rarely equal to those of pure descent.... If we breed solely from [pure breeds] ... we calculate securely on obtaining those varieties ...; but if we produce a mixed race, we can predicate nothing certainly regarding ... the mongrel progeny."[60] Low's final claim was an understatement, since the concentrated reproductive force symbolized by breed status and pedigree was supposed to ensure that purebred sires and dams exercised a disproportionate influence over the resulting offspring, even when they were mated with more ordinary animals.

This heightened power to shape offspring was called prepotency. It was, of course, essentially comparative. That is, it offered a way to discriminate among breeds, as well as between pedigreed and non-pedigreed animals. Thus it could be used as a measure or confirmation of breed quality, especially since it could be tested in practice. The workings of prepotency seemed often simply to confirm the value of unsullied descent—to exemplify the rule by which "the most inbred parent generally influences the offspring to the greatest extent."[61] Indeed, in some lineages it was alleged to operate so powerfully as completely to repel the taint of an injudicious cross. For example, a dealer in highly bred ponies boasted that one of his fillies was "so prepotent that, though she were sent to the best Clydesdale stallion in Scotland, she would throw a colt showing no cart-horse blood."[62]

Victorian breeders and fanciers ambitious to develop or consolidate a strain were routinely encouraged to follow the example of Robert Bakewell and other heroes of the eighteenth-century age of improvement. Without the guarantees that pedigree provided to their successors, they had discovered that persistent inbreeding—referred to as "in and in"—provided the quickest method of fixing a strain's characteristics and getting it to breed true. Exponents of this system were extremely fastidious in excluding alien blood that might contaminate their nascent breeds. Low noted that Bakewell "did not scruple to connect together animals the nearest allied in blood."[63] If blood relationship was necessary to ensure breed purity, then even a very slight degree of difference could produce mongrelization. One enthusiastic Victorian adherent warned that "crossing even 'in the line' is a speculative, if not a dangerous proceeding."[64] That is, a breed might be compromised by the blood of remote relatives. It was safer to stick to close kin. In the course of the nineteenth century, such advice became more pointed and forceful, urging that very radical measures be taken to avoid contamination: "mate sire to daughter and son to dam, [although] never if you can avoid it brother to sister."[65] So satisfactory were the results of such close inbreeding in animals that they were repeatedly urged as justification for similarly hygienic practices among people—at least marriages between first cousins, if not between members of the same nuclear family—so long as "the parties" were not "both predisposed to the same disease."[66] The "extraordinary fear" with which people had traditionally regarded such unions was disparaged as the result of "ignorance" and "delusion."[67]

The more narrowly in-and-in advocates defined the universe of mates whose introduction within a strain would not vitiate its purity, however, the more resistance they provoked within the breeding community. From the beginning, some resisters had taken a high moral line, reversing the argument that suggested human incest taboos be abandoned by applying them rigorously to animals. One of Bakewell's earliest disciples thus complained that "some have imbibed the prejudice so far as to think it *irreligious*."[68] But most dissenters relied on pragmatic rather than theological arguments, blaming inbreeding for a panoply of defects observed to afflict elaborately pedigreed animals. As Everett Millais put it, after protracted and exclusive inbreeding "the breed rapidly goes downhill, loses constitution, . . . becomes unable to withstand disease, and eventually becomes sterile."[69] Such declines, as with inbred human families, were apt to involve mental as well as physical problems, including loss of "true courage and bottom" in hounds, diminution of "virility" in bulls and of "sexual appetite" in cows, as well as the complete disappearance of "sagacity" in dogs of all kinds.[70]

Although they were outnumbered among high-end breeders, critics of in-and-in breeding were as vociferous in their criticism as advocates were in their defense, and as generous in their proffering of salutary advice. The invariable prescription for problems caused by inbreeding, whether dire or superficial, was "the introduction of fresh blood"—that is, a cross from outside the overbred line.[71] But in making this suggestion, whatever their opponents might think, critics of in-and-in breeding did not mean to advocate mongrelization. They shared the appreciation for genealogical purity that had been intensifying throughout the nineteenth century, along with a consequent strong commitment to the defense of reasonably defined boundaries. Thus the author of a late Victorian horse-breeding manual, who felt that "consanguineous intercourse has developed more imbecility in the human race than . . . any other cause," also asserted that "purity of blood is another essential, and perhaps the most important of all."[72] The compilers of the first herd book of the British Goat Society proposed "to enable breeders desirous of introducing fresh blood into their herds to know where to go to . . . preserve the blood of a certain strain without breeding too closely 'in and in'."[73] In *The Book of the Pig*, James Long similarly advocated scrupulous attention to lineage—even "the pedigree of an animal is not alone sufficient to distinguish it as being one of a great race"—while asserting that "of all things in connection with stock breeding there is none . . . more necessary to avoid than . . . in-breeding."[74]

Thus what inbreeders perceived as an issue of kind, crossers perceived as one of degree. Their argument was not about whether like and unlike animals should be mated, but about the point at which likeness became unlikeness, or, to put it a different way, the point at which unlikeness stopped enhancing and began to threaten. As with the scientific debate about interspecific hybrids, at stake was not only where boundary lines should be drawn, but also the rationale for drawing them; and in the case of breeds, the definition of such artificial categories could plausibly be ascribed neither to nature nor to its author. Their creation clearly expressed human will and ingenuity, and their alleged violation was a matter of human policy and interpretation. Whether expressed in terms of hybridization or crossbreeding, discussions of animal miscegenation inevitably connected general zoological matters with more narrowly human concerns. Indeed, in a period of global empire and rising nationalism, the zoological and agricultural discussion of these matters—involving mixture and separation, constructed boundaries and carefully analyzed distinctions—may have derived much of its structure, as well as its heated tone, from its easy compromise of the taxonomic barrier that ostensibly separated animals from people.

NOTES

1. A variety of evolutionary theories had been current in some radical or advanced circles since the end of the eighteenth century. For the best discussion of pre-Darwinian evolutionary debate in Britain, see Adrian Desmond, *The Politics of Evolution: Morphology, Medicine, and Reform in Radical London* (Chicago: University of Chicago Press, 1989).

2. Charles Darwin, *On the Origin of Species: A Facsimile of the First Edition*(1859), ed. Ernst Mayr (Cambridge, MA: Harvard University Press, 1964), pp. 469–470.

3. Charles Lyell, *The Geological Evidences of the Antiquity of Man, with Remarks on Theories of the Origin of Species by Variation* (London: John Murray, 1863), p. 388.

4. George Henry Lewes, *Studies in Animal Life* (London: Smith, Elder, 1862), pp. 128–129.

5. F. G. Aflalo, *Types of British Animals* (London: Sands, 1909), p. 4.

6. Georges Louis Leclerc, Comte de Buffon, *Barr's Buffon. Buffon's Natural History. Containing a Theory of the Earth, a General Theory of Man, of the Brute Creation, and of Vegetables, Minerals, &c.* (London: H. D. Symonds, 1797), VI, p. 48.

7. This debate is far from over, and it has generated an enormous amount of commentary. For recent historical accounts, see Peter F. Stevens, "Species: Historical Perspectives," in *Keywords in Evolutionary Biology*, ed. Evelyn Fox Keller and Elisabeth A. Lloyd (Cambridge, MA: Harvard University Press, 1992), pp. 302–311; Scott Atran, *Cognitive Foundations of Natural History: Towards an Anthropology of Science* (Cambridge: Cambridge University Press, 1990), ch. 6; and Ernst Mayr, *The Growth of Biological Thought: Diversity, Evolution, and Inheritance* (Cambridge, MA: Harvard University Press, 1982), ch. 6.

8. Henri Daudin, *De Linné à Lamarck: Méthodes de la classification et idée de série en botanique et en zoologie* (Paris: Librairie Félix Alcan, 1926), p. 229.

9. Darwin, *Origin*, p. 177,

10. Robert Knox, *The Races of Men* (London: Henry Renshaw, 1862), p. 65.

11. Thomas Bewick, *A General History of Quadrupeds* (Newcastle upon Tyne: T. Bewick, 1824), p. 16.

12. John Fleming, *The Philosophy of Zoology; or A General View of the Structure, Functions, and Classifications of Animals* (Edinburgh: Archibald Constable, 1822), I, p. 429.

13. Thomas Pennant, *History of Quadrupeds* (London: B. and J. White, 1793), I, p. 29.

14. Edward Griffith, *General and Particular Descriptions of the Vertebrated Animals Arranged Conformably to the Modern Discoveries and Improvements in Zoology. Order Carnivora* (London: Baldwin, Cradock, and Joy, 1821), p. 67.

15. Buffon, *Barr's Buffon*, VI, p. 64.

16. Buffon, *Barr's Buffon*, VI, pp. 146–147.

17. James Watson Roberts, "Of the Degeneration of Animals," Society for Investigating Natural History/Natural History Society, *Papers Delivered* IV (1785–1786), p. 107. Manuscript in Special Collections, Edinburgh University Library.

18. John Bigland, *Letters on Natural History: Exhibiting a View of the Power, Wisdom, and Goodness of the Deity* . . . (London: Longman, Hurst, Rees and Orme, 1806), p. 230; John French Burke, *Farming for Ladies; Or, a Guide to the Poultry-Yard, the Dairy and Piggery* (London: John Murray, 1844), p. 324.

19. James Anderson, *Recreations in Agriculture, Natural-History, Arts, and Miscellaneous Literature* (London: T. Bensley, 1799), vol.I, pp. 57–58.

20. John Fry, "On Factitious or Mule-Bred Animals," *Hippiatrist and Veterinary Journal* 3 (1830), p. 113, 115.

21. Juliet Clutton-Brock, *Horse Power: A History of the Horse and the Donkey in Human Societies* (Cambridge, MA: Harvard University Press, 1992), pp. 43–44. Indeed, the general vernacular term for hybrid had been generalized from the ancient term for these mixed creatures. For a discussion of the shades of meaning attached to the French cognate and related terms, see Jean-Louis Fischer, "Sens, contre sens et

synonymie dans l'emploi des termes 'mulet', 'métis' et 'hybride' en zoologie de 1749 à 1860," in *Documents pour l'histoire du vocabulaire scientifique*, No. 2 (Paris: Editions Klincksieck/Centre National de la Recherche Scientifique, 1981), pp. 23–35.

22. H. D. Richardson, "Dogs," in John C. Morton, ed., *A Cyclopedia of Agriculture, Practical and Scientific; in which the Theory, the Art, and the Business of Farming, are Thoroughly and Practically Treated* (Glasgow: Blackie and Son, 1855), I, p. 665.

23. Philip Gosse, *An Introduction to Zoology* (London: Society for Promoting Christian Knowledge, 1844), I, p. xv.

24. William Bernhard Tegetmeier and C.L. Sutherland, *Horses, Asses, Zebras, Mules, and Mule Breeding* (London: Horace Cox, 1895), p. 80. A mule is the offspring of a female horse and a male donkey; a hinny is the offspring of a female donkey and a male horse.

25. George Garrard, *A Description of the Different Varieties of Oxen, Common in the British Isles* (London: J. Smeeton, 1800) n.p.

26. John Jones, *Medical, Philosophical, and Vulgar Errors, of Various Kinds, Considered and Refuted* (London: T. Cadell Jun. and W. Davies, 1797), p. 101.

27. *The Animal Kingdom, or Zoological System of the Celebrated Sir Charles Linnaeus; Class I, Mammalia . . .*, trans. Robert Kerr (London: J. Murray, 1792), p. 346; "Mongooz," *The Naturalist's Pocket Magazine* 2 (1799), n. p.

28. E. P. Evans(1906), *The Criminal Prosecution and Capital Punishment of Animals: The Lost History of Europe's Animal Trials* (London: Faber and Faber, 1987), 174–153; see also Jonas Liliequist, "Peasants against Nature: Crossing the Boundaries between Man and Animal in Seventeenth- and Eighteenth-Century Sweden" in John C. Fout, ed., *Forbidden History: The State, Society, and the Regulation of Sexuality in Modern Europe* (Chicago: University of Chicago Press, 1993), pp. 57–88.

29. Charles White, *An Account of the Regular Gradation in Man, and in Different Animals and Vegetables; and from the Former to the Latter* (London: C. Dilly, 1799), p. 34; Johann Friedrich Blumenbach, *The Anthropological Treatises . . .*, ed. and trans. Thomas Bendyshe (London: Longman, Green, Longman, Roberts and Green/The Anthropological Society, 1865), p. 73.

30. George P. Sanderson, *Thirteen Years Among the Wild Beasts of India: Their Haunts and Habits from Personal Observation* (Edinburgh: John Grant, 1907), p. 377.

31. White, *Account of the Regular Gradation in Man*, p. 34.

32. Blumenbach, *Anthropological Treatises*, pp. 80–81.

33. Edward Tyson, *Orang-Outang, sive Homo Sylvestris. Or, the Anatomy of a Pygmie Compared with that of a Monkey, an Ape, and a Man* (London: Thomas Bennet, 1699), p. 2.

34. Rajendra Mallika, "Exhibit of a Dead Hybrid Monkey," *Proceedings of the Asiatic Society of Bengal* 32 (1863), pp. 455–456.

35. P. L. Sclater, "Notice of Some Hybrid Monkeys," *Proceedings of the Zoological Society of London* (Nov. 5, 1878), p. 791.

36. H. Scherren, "Some Notes on Hybrid Bears," *Proceedings of the Zoological Society of London* (1907), p. 432; Charles Hamilton Smith, *The Natural History of Dogs. Volume II. Canidae or Genus Canis of Authors. Including Also the Genera Hyaena and Proteles* (Edinburgh: W. H. Lizars, 1840), p. 98.

37. Edward Griffith, *General and Particular Descriptions of the Vertebrated Animals . . . Order Carnivora* (London: Baldwin, Cradock, and Joy, 1821), p. 58; George R. Jesse, *Researches into the History of the British Dog, from Ancient Laws, Charters and Historical Records* (London: Robert Hardwick, 1866), I, pp. 337, 338; "Curious Ram," *Annals of Sporting and Fancy Gazette* 1 (1822), p. 198; "Remarkable Hybrid," *Farrier and Naturalist* 1 (1828), p. 86.

38. Poster in Cambridgeshire Collection, Cambridge Central Library; A. D. Bartlett, "On Some Hybrid Bovine Animals," *Proceedings of the Zoological Society of London* (1884), pp. 399, 401.

39. Charles Lyell (1832), *Principles of Geology*, ed. Martin Rudwick (Chicago: University of Chicago Press, 1991), II, p. 49; Bigland, *Letters on Natural History*, p. 69; Peter Simon Pallas, *An Account of the Different Kinds of Sheep Found in the Russian Dominions and among the Tartar Hordes of Asia* (London: T. Chapman, 1794), p. 79.

40. Charles Hamilton Smith, *The Natural History of Horses. The Equidae or Genus Equus of Authors* (Edinburgh: W. H. Lizars, 1841), p. 344; Richardson, "Dogs" in Morton, *Cyclopedia of Agriculture*, I, p. 665.

41. Darwin, *Origin*, ch. 8, especially pp. 272–276.

42. W. C. Spooner, "On Cross Breeding," (London: W. Clowes, 1860), pp. 21–22. (Offprint from *Journal of the Royal Agricultural Society of England* 20, Pt. 2).

43. William Ridgeway (1905), *The Origin and Influence of the Thoroughbred Horse* (New York: Benjamin Blom, 1972), p. vii.

44. W. C. Spooner, "Breeding, Principles of" in Morton, *Cyclopedia of Agriculture*, I, p. 338.

45. Thomas Bates and Thomas Bell, *The History of Improved Shorthorn or Durham Cattle, and of the Kirklevington Herd* (Newcastle-upon-Tyne: Robert Redpath, 1871), p. 194.

46. "Cecil" [Cornelius Tongue], *Hints on Agriculture, Relative to Profitable Draining and Manuring; also the Comparative Merits of the Pure Breeds of Cattle and Sheep* (London: Thomas Cautley Newby, 1858), p. 118.

47. J. Rogers, *The Dog Fancier's Guide: Plain Instructions for Breeding and Managing the Several Varieties of Field, Sporting and Fancy Dogs* (London: Thomas Dean, n.d. [ca. 1850]), p. 26; W. F., "The Points of the Gordon Setter," *Kennel Gazette* 8 (1889), p. 39; "The Great Peterborough Hound Show," *Kennel Gazette* 2 (1881), p. 328; "Pillars of the Stud Book.—No, 11. The Irish Water Spaniel," *Kennel Gazette* 4 (1883), p. 469.

48. For further discussion of the sexual politics of eighteenth- and nineteenth-century animal breeding, see Harriet Ritvo, "The Animal Connection," in *The Boundaries of Humanity: Humans, Animals and Machines*, ed. James J. Sheehan and Morton Sosna, (Berkeley: University of California Press, 1991), pp. 68–84.

49. It seems likely that this idea emerged into the light of print and science after and as a result of a long history of popular acceptance. Thus, according to John Aubrey, the seventeenth-century doctor William Harvey had claimed that "he that marries a widow makes himself Cuckold." Quoted in Alan MacFarlane, *Marriage and Love in England, 1300–1840* (Oxford: Basil Blackwell, 1986), p. 232.

50. Lord Morton to W. H. Wollaston, August 12, 1820, quoted in J. C. Ewart, *The Penycuik Experiments* (London: Adam and Charles Black, 1899), pp. 165–166.

51. The story of Lord Morton's mare was endlessly rehearsed in the literature of animal breeding, with only occasional variation in such details as the number of affected foals, the extent to which they resembled their nonparent, and the species of the sire (sometimes he was a zebra).

52. G. H. Lewes, "Hereditary Influence, Animal and Human," *Westminster Review* 66 (1856), p. 85.

53. George M. Gould and Walter L. Pyle (1896), *Anomalies and Curiosities of Medicine* (New York: Bell, 1956), p. 87.

54. Hugh Dalziel, *The St. Bernard: Its History, Points, Breeding, and Rearing* (London: L. Upcott Gill, 1889), p. 109.

55. "Scotus," "Polled Angus or Aberdeenshire Cattle" in John Coleman ed., *The Cattle of Great Britain: Being a Series of Articles on the Various Breeds of the United Kingdom, their Management, &c.* (London: "The Field," 1875), p. 103.

56. Vero Shaw, *Illustrated Book of the Dog* (London: Cassell, Peter, Galpin, 1881), p. 275.

57. Vero Shaw, *British Horses Illustrated. With Brief Descriptive Notes on Every Native Breed* (London: Vinton, 1899), p. 5.

58. Shaw, *Illustrated Book of the Dog*, p. 155.

59. On the development and acceptance of this understanding of pedigree, see Harriet Ritvo, "Possessing Mother Nature: Genetic Capital in Eighteenth-Century Britain," in John Brewer and Susan Staves, eds., *Early Modern Conceptions of Property* (London: Routledge, 1995), pp. 413–426.

60. David Low, *The Breeds of the Domestic Animals of the British Islands* (London: Longman, Orme, Brown, Green and Longmans, 1842), I, pp. 9–10.

61. C. J. Davies, "Fallacies of Breeding," *The Dog Owner's Annual for 1901* (1901), p. 109.

62. Arthur Shipley, "Zebras, Horses, and Hybrids," *Quarterly Review* 190 (1899), p. 416.

63. Low, *The Breeds of the Domestic Animals of the British Islands*, II, p. 26.

64. Robert Smith, "Report on the Exhibition of Live Stock at Chester," *Journal of the Royal Agricultural Society of England* 19 (1858), pp. 399–400.

65. Vero Shaw, *How to Choose a Dog and How to Select a Puppy*, (London: W. Thacker, 1897), p. 81.

66. Alfred Henry Huth, "Cross-Fertilisation of Plants, &c.," *Westminster Review* 108 (1877), pp. 467, 483; George Henry Andrews, *Modern Husbandry: A Practical and Scientific Treatise on Agriculture* (London: Nathaniel Cooke, 1853), p. 162.

67. Huth, "Cross–Fertilisation of Plants," p. 467; G. W. Child, "Marriages of Consanguinity," *Westminster Review* 80 (1863), p. 89.

68. George Culley, *Observations on Live Stock, Containing Hints for Choosing and Improving the Best Breeds of the Most Useful Kinds of Domestic Animals* (London, 1786), p. ix.

69. Everett Millais, "Basset Bloodhounds. Their Origin, Raison D'Etre and Value," *The Dog Owner's Annual for 1897* (1897), p. 17.

70. Robert T. Vyner, *Notitia Venatica: A Treatise on Fox-Hunting. Embracing the General Management of Hounds and the Diseases of Dogs* (London: R. Ackerman, 1847), p. 24; George Tollet to Charles Darwin, May 10, 1839, quoted in R. B. Freeman and P. J. Gautrey, "Darwin's *Questions about the Breeding of Animals, with a Note on Queries on Expression,*" *Journal of the Society for the Bibliography of Natural History* 5 (1969), p. 322; W. D. Fox to Charles Darwin, ca. November 1838, *Correspondence of Charles Darwin,* II, p. 110; An Old Sportsman, "On Breeding Race Horses; With Remarks on Mr. Lawrence's History of the Horse," *Annals of Sporting and Fancy Gazette* 2 (1822), p. 2.

71. John Downing, *Private Catalogue of the Ashfield Herd of Pure-Bred Shorthorns* (London: Vinton, 1872), p. iii.

72. William Day, *The Horse: How to Breed and Rear Him* (London: Richard Bentley, 1890), pp. 141, 137.

73. *British Goat Society Herd Book and Prize Record from 1875 to 1885,* I, Part I (1886; reprint 1918), p. 2.

74. James Long, *The Book of the Pig: Its Selection, Breeding, Feeding, and Management* (London: L. Upcott Gill, 1886), pp. 22, 24.

THING

REY CHOW

THESE DAYS we have become complacent about our ability to criticize the racist and sexist blunders inherent in the stereotypical representations of our cultural "others." "Our" here refers to the community of intellectuals, East and West, who have absorbed the wisdom of Edward Said's *Orientalism*, and who are on the alert to point out the discriminatory assumptions behind the production of cultural artifacts, in particular those that involve Western representations of the non-West. But Said's work, insofar as it successfully canonizes the demystification of Western cultural pretensions, is simply pointing to a certain direction in which much work still waits to be done—namely, the direction in which we must examine in detail the multifaceted psychical and philosophical implications of the conflict, confusion, and tragedy arising from "cross-cultural exchange" when that exchange is conditioned by the inequities and injustices of imperialist histories. This work that needs to be

THE DREAM OF A BUTTERFLY

love is of such a nature that it changes man into the things he loves.

—Martin Heidegger
(citing Meister Eckhart), "The Thing"

. . . inescapably, I passed beyond the unreality of the thing represented, I entered crazily into the spectacle, into the image, taking into my arms what is dead, what is going to die . . . .

—Roland Barthes, *Camera Lucida*

The mystical is by no means that which is not political. . . . What was tried at the end of the last century . . . by all kinds of worthy people . . . was an attempt to reduce the mystical to questions of fucking.

—Jacques Lacan,
"God and the *Jouissance* of The Woman"

done cannot be done simply by repeating the debunking messages that Said has already so clearly delivered in his book. Rather, we need to explore alternative ways of thinking about cross-cultural exchange that exceed the pointed, polemical framework of "antiorientalism"— the lesson from Said's work—by continually problematizing the presumption of stable identities, and also by continually asking what else there is to learn beyond destabilized identities themselves. In this essay, I read the 1993 film *M. Butterfly* (directed by David Cronenberg, screenplay by David Henry Hwang) as an instance of such a badly needed alternative approach to the problematic of orientalism.[1]

Let me emphasize at the outset that I am not discrediting or de-emphasizing the continual need for the criticism of orientalism. Far from it: I am saying that precisely because orientalism has many guises—both decadent and progressivist, in the form of sexual adventures and textual devotion, *and also* in the form of political idealization, fascination with subaltern groups and disenfranchised classes, and so forth—what we need to examine ever more urgently is fantasy, a problem which is generally recognized as central to orientalist perceptions and significations.

My task is made all the more challenging because the problem of fantasy, even though it is a predominant consideration of the stage play on which the film was based, is usually dismissed moralistically, in this case also by playwright Hwang. In responding to the real-life story of the French diplomat whose affair with a Chinese male opera singer gave him his inspiration for the play, for instance, Hwang writes confidently: "I . . . concluded that the diplomat must have fallen in love, not with a person, but with a fantasy stereotype."[2] Hwang's interest in this bizarre story is, one might say, primarily didactic, as he expresses it clearly in these remarks:

> *M. Butterfly* has sometimes been regarded as an anti-American play, a diatribe against the stereotyping of the East by the West, of women by men. Quite to the contrary, I consider it a plea to all sides to cut through our respective layers of cultural and sexual misperception, to deal with one another truthfully for our mutual good, from the common and equal ground we share as human beings.
>
> For the myths of the East, the myths of the West, the myths of men, and the myths of women—these have so saturated our consciousness that truthful contact between nations and lovers can only be the result of heroic effort. Those who prefer to bypass the work involved will remain in a world of surfaces, misperceptions running rampant.[3]

And yet, because the question of fantasy as stated here is already part of a conclusive understanding, of a plea for truthful human contact devoid of "misperception," there is something inherently superfluous about the representation of the story: if these layers of cross-cultural "misperception" are a fact of such crystal clarity, why not simply state it as such? Why, in other words, do we need to have a play in the first place? As a moral fable that was designed to preach a lesson well understood in advance—the lesson about the laughable "fantasy" and ludicrous "false consciousness" of the imperialist Western man—Hwang's play, it would seem, is a gratuitous act. Is the play's overwhelming success in the West due perhaps precisely to this gratuitous, stereotypical, and thus absolutely safe mockery of fantasy and false consciousness? But this success—this approval received by an Asian-American playwright in the West for correctly reprimanding Western imperialist fantasies—is it not itself a sign and a warning, not of how the West has finally learned its lessons, but rather once again of the very orientalism that Hwang intends to criticize, and to which non-Western peoples nonetheless continue to be subjected today?[4]

My interest in the film *M. Butterfly* begins where Hwang would have us stop. Rather than being my conclusion, fantasy is the beginning of my inquiry, which is framed by two major questions.

First, if fantasy is not simply a matter of distortion or willful exploitation, but is rather an inherent part of our consciousness, our wakeful state of mind,[5] what are the possibilities and implications of achieving any kind of sexual and racial identification in a "cross-cultural" exchange? Further, if the most important thing about fantasy is not the simple domination of an other but, as J. Laplanche and J.-B. Pontalis argue, the variable positionality of the subject, whose reality consists in a constant shifting between modes of dominance and submission,[6] what could be said about the relations between East and West, woman and man, that is perhaps alternative to the relations they are assumed, in anti-orientalist discourse, to have?

The second major question that concerns me, after fantasy has been sufficiently understood to be a kind of structuring and setting that is indispensable to any consideration of subjectivity, is how the film *M. Butterfly* also moves *beyond* subjectivity to philosophical issues of phenomenology and ontology. What is of particular interest is the manner in which the film relates the question of "cross-cultural" fantasy not simply to homosexuality, heterosexuality, or race, but also to the larger, open-ended question of the limits of human vision. As I will attempt to demonstrate, the film probes this other question by exploring the phenomenological effects of the image and the gaze.

"EAST IS EAST AND WEST IS WEST, AND NE'ER THE TWAIN SHALL MEET"

For me, what is most remarkable about the *M. Butterfly* story is, to put it in the simplest terms, the fact that it is a stereotype, in which a Western man believes he is romantically involved with an oriental woman. The story goes briefly as follows. It is 1964 in Beijing, China. René Gallimard, an accountant working at the French Consulate, has just been to a performance of excerpts from Giacomo Puccini's opera *Madama Butterfly* (1904), staged at one of the foreign embassies. Gallimard finds himself drawn to the Chinese opera singer, Song Liling, who plays the role of Madame Butterfly. When he relates his fascination to his wife, who dismisses the Chinese with the familiar attitude, "East is East and West is West, and never the twain shall meet," he finds that she does not share his enthusiasm. In the rest of the film she is to become less and less significant as he embarks on a clandestine relationship with the opera singer. Song later tells Gallimard she has become pregnant; eventually she shows him a baby boy who is supposedly his son. As the Cultural Revolution progresses, the lovers are separated: Gallimard is sent back to Paris and Song put in a labor camp. Just as he is abandoning all hope, she shows up again unexpectedly in Paris outside his apartment. The lovers are happily reunited until they are arrested for passing secret information of the French government to China. But for Gallimard, the most devastating consequence of this exposure is the revelation by the French government that Song, who has all these years been his "Butterfly," is actually a male spy whose involvement with him has been for the purpose of extracting information for the Chinese government.

Precisely because of its stereotypical structure, the relationship between Gallimard and Song allows us to approach it as a kind of myth. In this myth, Gallimard occupies the role of the supposedly active and dominant white male, and Song, the role of the supposedly passive and submissive oriental female. The superimposition of the racial and sexual elements of this relationship creates the space in which the story unfolds.

In order to heighten the story's mythical quality on film, director Cronenberg dispenses with many of the complexities that characterize both the real-life story and the stage play. For instance, while in the real-life story the "Chinese woman" the French diplomat fell for always appeared as a man but told his beloved that he was really a woman, in the film Song always appears as a woman until the final scenes. And while the stage play contains many farcical moments that present the Frenchman as an obvious object of ridicule, the film trims away such moments, preserving the story instead in an elegant mode, against an often hazy and darkish background and frequently melancholic music. In thus stripping and reducing the story, Cronenberg makes its macabre structure stand out starkly. In the same vein, the usual elaborate manner in which a leading "feminine" character is fetishized is kept to a minimum. Instead of filling the movie screen with lavish physical, cosmetic, and sartorial details—such as is the case in the film with which *M. Butterfly* is often compared, *Farewell My Concubine*, by Chen Kaige—the portrayal of Song is low-key and unglamorous. Her singing and her stage performance, in both Western and Chinese theaters, are presented only briefly and appear to have been rather unremarkable. Some critics, predisposed toward a sensational and extravagantly colorful approach whenever a non-Western culture is represented, are quick to criticize *M. Butterfly* on the basis of verisimilitude: they point out disparagingly that, for instance, John Lone, who plays Song, does not look like a woman, that he and Jeremy Irons are unconvincing as lovers, and so forth.[7]

In thus missing the significance of the purposefully restrained design of the film, such critics also miss its status as the uncluttered sculpting of a stereotypical story, the artful experimenting with a familiar myth. What they have utterly failed to grasp is that, as in the case of the Beijing opera, what we see are not so much realistic props as suggestive ones, which are meant to conjure and signify rather than resemble an entire ambiance.

As the effects of verisimilitude give way to those of simplified plot, sparse detail, and minimalist characterization, the object of the story—fantasy itself—becomes intensified. The film becomes literally the *setting* that typifies fantasy.[8] With little sensational visual detail to distract us, we are compelled to focus on the absurd question: What happens when a man falls in love, not with a woman or even with another man, not with a human being at all but with a thing, a reified form of his own fantasy?[9] In the context of this film, this question is mapped over the question of orientalism, so that it becomes: What happens when a Western man falls in love with a reification of the orient, with that mysterious thing called the "oriental woman"?

In many ways, we can say that the film teaches the lesson that is summarized in that platitudinous phrase repeated by Mme. Gallimard: "East is East and West is West." The conclusion that "never the twain shall meet" could, obviously, be interpreted according to the argument against orientalism, with *M. Butterfly* serving as a piece of didacticism. This argument would go something as follows: Gallimard, a Frenchman working in the exotic East, harbors the typical Western male fantasy about the East and in particular about submissive oriental women. He is so enamored of this fantasy that he cannot tell a fake oriental woman from a real one. This fantastical relation to "the other" could then be said to be symptomatic of a deep-rooted racist, sexist, and homophobic imperialism; and Gallimard could be called a symbol of the West, with a downfall that is well deserved, and so forth.

This kind of moral is, as I have already suggested, indeed what the stage play tries to point at explicitly. For Hwang, the significance of fantasy is that of a content that needs to be changed; it needs to be changed because, by using other people as objects and things, fantasy dehumanizes them. Cronenberg, on the other hand, refuses this approach to fantasy and, as in the case of most of his other films, notably *Videodrome*, *The Fly*, *Dead Ringers*, and *Naked Lunch*, explores instead the possibilities and implications of fantasy precisely as a process of dehumanization—of deconstructing the human.[10] Instead of entirely dispensing with the antiorientalist didacticism, however, Cronenberg's film makes it part of its dramatization of the Gallimard-Song relationship. In this dramatization, the film no longer simply offers a diatribe against the stereotyping of the East by the West, or of women by men, but rather raises questions about the fundamental misrecognition inherent to processes of identification, *which the encounter between an oriental woman and a Western man magnifies and thus exemplifies.* The didactic, antiorientalist criticism of the West, then, remains a significant part of the story, but it is no longer its central focus.

Consider, for instance, the scene of the lovers' first encounter, where Song, instead of acting flattered, reprimands Gallimard for thinking that the story of Madame Butterfly is a beautiful one. It is only because he is so grossly ignorant of the history of the atrocities committed by Japan in China, Song says, that he could think that a Chinese actress playing a Japanese woman could be convincing. Further, if the races of the roles had been reversed—if it had been a Western woman sacrificing herself for an unattractive Japanese man—the judgment would most likely be that the woman is deranged rather than beautiful.

> SONG: It's one of your favorite fantasies, isn't it?—the submissive Oriental woman and the cruel white man.
>
> GALLIMARD: Well, I didn't quite mean. . .
>
> SONG: Consider it this way: what would you say if a blonde homecoming queen fell in love with a short Japanese businessman? He treats her cruelly, then goes home for three years, during which time she prays to his picture and turns down marriage from a young Kennedy. Then, when she learns he has remarried, she kills herself. Now, I believe you would consider this girl to be a deranged idiot, correct? But because it's an Oriental who kills herself for a Westerner—ah!—you find it beautiful.

While Song's words are undoubtedly historically astute, they also serve to fuel Gallimard's imagination of the "oriental woman" rather than cure it. In other words, the fact that this piece of antiorientalist criticism is inserted in the film as part of the first dialogue between Gallimard and Song means that the film has a relationship to the didactics of antiorientalism that is not direct but mediated. Rather than simply endorsing such a didactics, the film explicitly stages orientalism as a psychic, interpersonal structure that unfolds with a specific logic. The Western man caught in a fantasy about oriental women is here portrayed as a version of Pavlov's dog: conditioned to respond according to certain artificially induced stimuli, such creatures can, at the mere ringing of a bell or the mere appearance of an oriental woman, be expected to behave in a predictable manner—so predictable, in fact, that their behavior cannot be altered simply by an explicit exposure of the conditions that enable it. These creatures would salivate and come alive *for real* even if the stimulus had nothing "real" behind it. In Gallimard's case, the stimulus is the stereotype of the "inscrutable oriental" in the female form—and the more inscrutable she is, the more charmed he is. Simply by playing "herself," by playing her stereotypical, inscrutable role, the "oriental woman" sets the Western man's mind afire.

There is, however, another twist that makes the film decidedly different from the play. Even though she may be the relentless scheming "woman" working for the Chinese Communist Party, and even though she is fully capable of giving Gallimard lectures about the political incorrectness of his "imperialist" fantasies, Song is, as Lone plays the part, herself attracted to Gallimard. As she tells him at the end of their second encounter before saying good-bye, "sometimes, the fascination could be mutual." Is this a response spoken from her heart? Or is it also part of her role-playing? We have no way of knowing until the very end. What is crucial, nonetheless, is that this suggestion of mutual fascination takes the film beyond the one-sided antiorientalism "message" that Song verbally enunciates. And what is mutuality here if not precisely the problematic of the "meeting" between East and West, and between woman and man? As I will go on to argue, mutuality in this film occurs exactly in the form of nonreciprocity, so that together, mutuality and nonreciprocity constitute a symbiotic process of fantasy which, as it draws the lovers together, also ensures that they will never meet.

"THE BEAUTY . . . OF HER DEATH.
IT'S A . . . PURE SACRIFICE."

Why is Gallimard so fascinated by the Madame Butterfly character? He explains: he is moved by the beauty of her death. It's a pure sacrifice, he says, for even though the man she loves is unworthy, she sacrifices herself for him. To this Song responds, as I mentioned, by pointing out the imperialist implications of his fascination. But there are other possibilities of understanding this "pure sacrifice" of the "oriental woman."

At the most immediate level, this "pure sacrifice" describes exactly the role that Song plays even as she speaks. In the course of their amorous relationship, Song does, we may say, sacrifice herself for Gallimard, a man who is not worthy of her love, by living up to his fantasy. In this instance, the "pure sacrifice" of the "oriental woman" has the status of what Lacan calls lure—that lack of a coincidence between the eye and the gaze, a lack of coincidence that, however, is often what constitutes love:

From the outset, we see, in the dialectic of the eye and the gaze, that there is no coincidence, but, on the contrary, a lure. When, in love, I solicit a look, what is profoundly unsatisfying and always missing is that—*You never look at me from the place from which I see you.*

Conversely, *what I look at is never what I wish to see.*[11]

In this well-known passage, Lacan shows that the essential ingredient in love is misrecognition—a circular pattern of wishing, solicitation, frustration, and desire which stems from the belief that there is something more behind what we see (in the beloved). What Lacan calls lure, Jean Baudrillard calls, in a slightly different manner, seduction. To seduce, Baudrillard writes, is to divert the other from his own truth, from the secret (of himself) that escapes him.[12] In the film, by giving Gallimard the lure, the illusion of the self-sacrificing "oriental woman," Song leads Gallimard astray from his own truth. (I will specify what I think this truth is toward the end of this essay.) But this process of seduction is, as Song says, mutual: while she successfully lures Gallimard, Song herself is also being seduced by Gallimard, in that she has been drawn into his area of *weakness*—his weakness precisely for the beauty of the self-sacrificing Madame Butterfly. As Baudrillard writes, comparing seduction and challenge:

Challenge and seduction are quite similar. And yet there is a difference. In a challenge one draws the other into one's area of strength, which, in view of the potential for unlimited escalation, is also his or her area of strength. Whereas in a strategy (?) of seduction one draws the other into one's area of weakness, which is also his or her area of weakness. A calculated weakness; an incalculable weakness: one challenges the other to be taken in. . . .

To seduce is to appear weak. To seduce is to render weak. We seduce with our weakness, never with strong signs or powers. In seduction we enact this weakness, and this is what gives seduction its strength.[13]

If Song seduces Gallimard with the artifice/sacrifice of the submissive "oriental woman," Gallimard seduces Song with his naïveté, his capacity for fascination, and ultimately his gullibility. In spite of her real status as a spy for the Chinese government, therefore, she too seems to have genuinely fallen in love with him.

What seduces, in other words, is not the truth of the other—what he or she really is—but the artifact, the mutual complicity in the weaving of a lure, which works as a snare over the field of encounter, ensuring that the parties meet at the same time that they miss each other, in a kind of rhythmic dance.

Furthermore, because the "pure sacrifice" of the "oriental woman" is the thing that propels and sustains the lure, the act (such as Song's in the earlier scene) of pointing out that it is a *mere* imperialist fantasy does not only not succeed in destroying this lure; it actually enhances it—makes it more alluring. Meanwhile, if the point of the film is not a straightforward antiorientalism, it is not simply homosexual love either: as in the case of the criticism of imperialist fantasy, the lure cannot be destroyed by pointing out that Gallimard is really a bisexual or closeted gay man.

A "homoerotic" reading intent on showing Gallimard's real sexual preference would run a parallel course with the "antiorientalist" reading, in the sense that both readings must rely on the belief in a kind of repressed truth—repressed homosexuality or repressed racism—for their functioning. In both cases, the assumption would be that we need to look beyond the surface structure of the lure in order to locate what is "behind" or "beneath" it. In effect, critics who read this story as the story of a confused sexual identity would lend themselves to the lure set up by the film itself, in that they would be seduced into going after the real penis, the visible body part, the "fact" of Song being a male; their re-search would echo the re-search of the antiorientalist critics, who are seduced into going after the real penis, the visible body part, the "fact" of Gallimard being a white man. Be it through the route of race or the route of sexual preference, such critics would be trapped by their own desire for a secret—the secret of cross-cultural exploitation or the secret of homosexual love—which they might think they are helping to bring to light, when in fact it is they themselves who have been seduced. In each case what seduces (them) is, shall we say, the "purity" of a secret—an indubitable orientalism or an indubitable homoeroticism—the way the indubitable love, the pure sacrifice, of an "oriental woman" seduces Gallimard.[14]

The film *M. Butterfly*, on the other hand, is much more cunning. We can see this, for instance, in the interesting scene in Song's bedroom where she is confronted by a party cadre about her decadent behavior. Dressed in a beautiful traditional Chinese woman's jacket, reclining on her bed by herself, and reading girlie magazines featuring oriental women, Song is surprised by the visit of Comrade Chin, her connection to the party authorities. Comrade Chin contemptuously reprimands Song for indulging in "decadent trash." This scene reveals for the first time that Song is working for the Chinese Communist Party and that her relationship with Gallimard is a means to uncover American military plans in Indochina. Is Song not merely playing a role for the sole purpose of getting information from Gallimard? So why, Comrade Chin demands, is she behaving in such a degraded manner when Gallimard is not even present? Song's response to these moralistic charges are remarkable:

> SONG: Comrade, in order to better serve the Great Proletarian State, I practice my deception as often as possible! I despise this costume, yet, for the sake of the Great Helmsman, I will endure it along with all other bourgeois Western perversions!
>
> COMRADE CHIN: I am not convinced that this will be enough to redeem you in the eyes of the Party.
>
> SONG: I am trying my best to become somebody else.

Significantly, deception, as it is described by Song, has shifted from the status of dishonesty to that of honor: the seductive "oriental woman," as we are now given to understand, is not only a romantically but also a politically self-sacrificing figure, who gives up herself—her "real" identity—for the cause of the revolution, so much so that she sacrifices even her private moments in order to immerse herself in this cause entirely, purely. The greatest deception, then, is also the greatest act of loyalty—to the people, to the country, to the "Great Helmsman." Even though, as the audience, we cannot but sense that these words of loyalty are spoken with irony—that Song's loyalty to the party is dubious precisely because she is so eloquent about it—this scene reveals that the myth of the self-sacrificing "oriental woman" far exceeds the "imperialist fantasy" that has been commonly used to decode it, and that in her artificial role, Song is faithfully serving in the intersection of two cultural symbolics—the nationalistic as well as the erotic, the intracultural as well as the intercultural.

Song does not rebel against her intended and prescribed role in either situation; rather she plays it, indeed lives it, with her truest emotions. In the relationship with Gallimard, the disguise, lure, and veil of the "oriental woman" serve the purpose of gaining access to the realm that is his trust, love, and imagination. In Gallimard's words, thus, her love is pure: she performs her artificial role to the hilt, and thus sacrifices herself—gives up her "real" identity—for a man who, as he notices in the story of Madame Butterfly, is unworthy of that love. At the same time, with the revelation of Song's relationship with the Party, a supplementary dimension of the myth of Madame Butterfly unfolds. In this supplementary dimension, we see for the first time that the Song-Gallimard story, which plays on the stereotype of "imperialist male fantasy," is itself the mere instrument of espionage, a means of gaining access to the forbidden realm of another country's military secrets. Gallimard's words about Madame Butterfly, then, were an unwitting description of Song's role-playing in this other political realm as well: for is not the "man unworthy" of her love not only Gallimard, her imperialist aggressor, her foreign enemy, but also her Party leader, the Great Helmsman himself?

If, as we already said, the fascination between Gallimard and Song is mutual, we see now how this mutuality is simultaneously structured as a nonreciprocity. While the "oriental woman" remains an erotic object on the side of Gallimard, on the side of Song it is much more complex. For Song, the "oriental woman" is a means to exploit a foreigner as part of her service to the party. Gallimard, then, is not simply an erotic object or subject; rather he has been identified as a political object, a plaything that would unconsciously help Song give the party what it wants.

THE FORCE OF BUTTERFLY; OR, THE "ORIENTAL WOMAN" AS PHALLUS

The foregrounding of this supplementary, political dimension of our Madame Butterfly story enables us to read the Gallimard character in a very different manner from the one originally intended by Hwang and followed by most critics. The fateful encounter between East and West takes place at a critical moment of twentieth-century world politics.

For France, it is the end of the imperial empire, when Indochina has been recently lost and Algeria has become independent. The emptiness of diplomatic life in Beijing is clear: officials cheat on expense accounts; women have illicit affairs; dinner parties and other gatherings are perfunctory and boring. Like a character from a Kafka novel, Gallimard has an uninspiring, low-ranking job as an accountant, but it is a job that he takes seriously, so seriously that his corrupt colleagues become annoyed with him for continually exposing them. The high point of this rationalistic bookkeeping existence is tracking down the documentation from people who try to falsify their expense accounts. While we may say that Gallimard is the perfect example of the disciplined individual whose body and mind have, as Michel Foucault shows us in a work such as *Discipline and Punish*, been produced for the efficient, utilitarian functioning of his society, it is equally important to note that Gallimard is clearly a "flunky" in terms of the unspoken rules of political society. His tireless efforts to track down documentation for dubious expense accounts mean that he is out of tune with the smooth debaucheries that constitute the substance of the bureaucratic world. Precisely because he takes his job of accounting seriously, he reveals himself to be someone who does not know how to play the game. At a dinner gathering, as Gallimard sits down at the same table with his colleagues, they sneer and remind him: "You are nobody. You are worse than nobody: you are an accountant. If you are not careful we'll break all your pencils in half." To this Gallimard responds by leaving the table, clumsily dropping his silverware as he does so.

In terms of his relation to the cultural symbolic that is the world of politics, therefore, Gallimard occupies a place that is not dissimilar to that of Song, in that he, too, is a bureaucratic informant, a submissive "woman" to the "man not worthy of her love"—the French government, to which he gives his loyal service. The affinity between Gallimard and Song lies in the fact that both are manipulable and useful instruments of their respective political orders, and both respond to these orders with dedication. Gallimard's political usefulness is soon recognized by the ambassador, who sees in him the qualities of a head servant who is not smart enough to cheat, and who can therefore be entrusted with the task of "coordinating a revamped intelligence division," that is, of policing the other employees. But it is obvious that in this world of complex political "intelligence," Gallimard is not at home at all as *a person in command*. As he receives, in the ambassador's office, the surprising news of his own promotion to vice-consul, we can see that he does not possess the suave body language to respond appropriately; instead his posture remains awkward and stiff, marking his destiny as someone who will remain marginal and insignificant in French diplomatic culture. When he finally sits in his office as vice consul, he lacks the presence to command the respect of those who are supposedly working for him. Instead of speaking to them with the air of mastery, he reads woodenly from a prewritten script as if he were someone being cross examined.

It is into this impersonal but overpowering world of bureaucracy, which is echoed by a routine domestic life complete with an uncomprehending wife, classic pajamas, and bedtime tooth-brushing, that "Butterfly" intrudes with an irresistible force. Gallimard, we remember, stumbles upon "Butterfly" unexpectedly. Before the performance of the aria "Un bel dì" from Puccini's opera begins, Gallimard tells his neighbor, Frau Baden, with whom he will later have a casual affair, that he has never seen *Madama Butterfly*, although his lack of culture is unsuspected by most people.[15] In the position of an outsider to his own European culture, then, Gallimard's eyes catch the "oriental woman" on stage, even though the situation—of a contemporary Chinese opera singer performing the role of a fetishized Japanese heroine from an Italian opera—cannot be more bizarre. If the "entrance of Butterfly" (as printed on the musicians' scores) represents a decisive marking of cultural identity and its concomitant confusion, what it marks first of all is in fact Gallimard's alienation from his own culture. Rather than simply notice the foreignness, the exoticness, of the spectacle in front of him, Gallimard finds in "Butterfly" a kind of anchorage for *himself*. (This is why his behavior takes on a noticeably greater air of self-assurance from this point on.)

Because it is not fully attainable even as it is consumed through sexual contact, the fantasy of the "oriental woman" keeps the Frenchman *afloat with life* by inscribing in him an unanswerable lack. Song exists for Gallimard as the phallus in Lacan's sense of the term— that is, as the Other that is always assumed to be more than it appears, and that has the power to give us what we want and also to take it away.

Lacan, we remember, emphasizes that the phallus functions only when it is veiled and that, once revealed, it becomes shame.[16] Song's tactic, however, includes precisely this "unveiling" of shame by deliberately calling attention to it in a letter to Gallimard: "What more do you want?" she writes. "I have already given you my shame." By feigning loss of dignity, thus, Song preserves her power as phallus, while the "shame" that has been revealed—the oriental woman's love—continues to be a sham veiling the male body that is beneath it.

The manner in which the "oriental woman" functions as a phallus is made even more clear by the fact that Gallimard seems content in love without ever experiencing Song completely naked. (Later in court, responding to the inquiry about this incredible fact, Song will describe Gallimard as a lover who has been very responsive to his "'ancient oriental ways of love,' all of which I invented myself—just for him.") The one time Gallimard comes dangerously close to stripping her, Song tells him at the crucial moment that she is pregnant, thus shifting his sexual desire into a more paternal frame. Meanwhile, Gallimard can have what he calls an "extra extramarital affair" with Frau Baden without its intruding into his fantasy. In the scene where he and Frau Baden are in their hotel room, Gallimard, coming out of the bathroom in his hygienic-looking undershirt, is shown to be somewhat taken aback by the sight of Frau Baden sitting casually naked on the edge of the bed. Instead of the typical sexual excitement one would expect with an illicit affair, the following matter-of-fact exchange takes place between the would-be copulants:

GALLIMARD: You look . . . just like I thought you would under your clothes.

FRAU BADEN: What did you expect? So come and get it!

While Gallimard's remark highlights the complete coincidence between the eye and the gaze, and therefore the lack precisely of a lure in his relationship with this other woman, Frau Baden's notion of "getting it" complements his observation by containing sex entirely within the satiable and short-term realm of physical need. Sex with her is but a casual meal, in which the physical body, because it is completely available, remains a *mere* body. The force of the phallus—and with it fantasy, the lure, and seduction—does not come into play at all.

"UNDER THE ROBES,
BENEATH EVERYTHING, IT WAS ALWAYS ME"

One of the most moving and unforgettable scenes in this film is the one in which, after the costume farce in the French courtroom, Song and Gallimard, both in men's suits, sit face to face alone in the police van taking them to prison. As the two men stare at each other, Song is the first to break the silence: "What do you want from me?" he asks. In psychoanalytic terms, this question is an indication of the fundamental issue in our relationship with an other—demand. However, even though Song has brought up this fundamental issue, he has, nonetheless, posed his question imprecisely, because he still thinks in terms of Gallimard's wanting something *from him*. Instead, as Lacan has taught us, the significance of demand is never simply what can be effectively enunciated by way of what the other can literally give us; rather, it is what remains resistant to articulation, what exceeds the satisfaction provided by the other.[17] To pose the question of demand with precision, therefore, Song would have had to ask: "What do you want, by wanting me? What is your demand, which you express through me?"

Gallimard, on the other hand, responds to (the philosophical implications of) this question precisely: "You are my Butterfly."

With this exchange, what takes place between the former lovers is now a new kind of nonreciprocity. If, in the past, their nonreciprocity was a matter of their playing their respective roles in the game of erotics and politics, a nonreciprocity that enabled them to meet through the lure, the new nonreciprocity has to do rather with Song's attempt to change the very terms of their relationship. Instead of playing "Butterfly" the way he has for Gallimard all these years, Song does something he has never done before: he undresses, challenging Gallimard to see for the first time what he has always wanted but somehow always failed to see. Kneeling completely naked in front of Gallimard, Song pleads for a rekindling of the affection that once existed between them. As he gazes tenderly up at his former lover, Song says, in a manner that reveals that he has indeed loved the Frenchman all along: "Under the robes, beneath everything, it was always me."

If, until this tragic moment, the lure has been kept intact because it is upheld on both sides, Song, by the very gesture of undressing with which he tries to regain Gallimard's love, has destroyed that lure forever. While Song intends by this brave and defiant gesture a new beginning for their relationship—a beginning in which they can face each other honestly as they really are, two men physically and emotionally entangled for years—what he actually accomplishes is the death of that relationship. Song fails to see that what Gallimard "wants" is not him, Song, be he in the definitive form of a woman or a man, but, as Gallimard says, "Butterfly." Because Gallimard's desire hinges on neither a female nor a male body, but rather on the phallus, the veiled thing that is the "oriental woman," Song's candid disclosure of his physical body can only be lethal. Like Frau Baden, who, having dis-clothed herself, invites Gallimard frankly to "come and get it," Song's gesture of undressing serves not to arouse but extinguish desire.

The naked body destroys the lure once and for all by demonstrating that what lies under the veil all these years is nothing, no thing for fantasy. With the veil lifted, the phallus shows itself shamefully as merely a man, a penis, a pathetic body in all its banal vulnerability, which Gallimard rejects in abhorrence. (As many have pointed out, this moment in *M. Butterfly* is comparable to a similar one in *The Crying Game*, in which the man, in love with a transvestite whom he supposes to be a female, vomits at the sight of his beloved's actual genitalia. What has to be thrown up literally is the repugnant reality of the physical.) Song's naked body must therefore be understood ultimately as the traumatic Real that tears apart the dream of "Butterfly," forcing Gallimard to wake up in the abyss of his own self. In the two men's *parting* conversation, we see how, instead of rescuing Gallimard, Song's sincere love finally brings about the nonreciprocity that is their absolute parting of ways:

GALLIMARD: You, who knew me so well—how could you, of all people, have made such a mistake?

SONG: What?

GALLIMARD: You've just shown me your true self—when all I loved was the lie. A perfect lie—it's been destroyed.

SONG (genuinely hurt): You never really loved me?

GALLIMARD: I'm a man who loved a woman created by a man. And anything else— simply falls short.

"IT'S NOT THE STORY; IT'S THE MUSIC"

From Gallimard's perspective, the disappearance of that "lie" he loves, that very thing in which he has found a means of anchoring his identity, means a traumatic self-awakening that is the equivalent of madness. Before examining this awakening/madness closely, I think it is necessary to discuss one more aspect of this "thing"—the music from *Madama Butterfly*—which, as much as the fetishized "oriental woman," serves as Gallimard's anchorage.

It is possible to think of the operatic music as a kind of big Other, to which the human characters submit in such a manner as to create their "fate." This fate is predicted by a remark made by Song in an early conversation with Gallimard, in regard to his fascination with the Madame Butterfly story: "The point is," she says, "it's not the story; it's the music." Indeed, one could argue that, as much as the "oriental woman," the music is the agent that engenders the plot of the story, so that it is the story which follows the lead of the music rather than the reverse. From the initial performance at the foreign embassy of "*Un bel dì*," which establishes contact between Gallimard and Song, we move through scenes in which the music of *Madama Butterfly* continues to haunt the characters, as if always to recall them to the primal moment of their fateful encounter. For instance, even Gallimard's wife, when she hears about his captivation by Song's performance, bursts into a spontaneous performance complete with hand gestures. In the mirror reflection that follows, we see Gallimard looking bewildered and uneasy at his wife's uncanny mimicry of the "other woman." He goes on to place a special order of the record album of the opera, noticing, upon its arrival, its cover illustration of the "oriental woman" in a submissive posture to her Western lover.

Crucially also, Gallimard's amorous relationship with "Butterfly" takes place at a time when both *Madama Butterfly* and Chinese opera singers are considered to be relics of the past.

In the China of the mid-1960s, not only were imported items such as Western operatic music considered bourgeois and imperialist; even indigenous traditional art forms such as the Beijing opera were deemed feudal and corrupt. The revolution demanded that all such ideologically suspect relics be purged and replaced by new, progressive practices. The second time Gallimard visits the Chinese theater where Song used to perform, a Maoist "model play" is being staged with a different kind of dramatic semiotics and a noticeably different didactic sentience. Such ostensible state intervention in aesthetic forms, together with the massive burning of traditional artifacts, the forced trial and punishment of intellectuals, writers, and artists, and the coerced surrender of personal ideals for the common good, made up the new reality of Chinese political life. In the film, the Communist Revolution establishes itself in Chinese society as a new big Other with its power to interpellate ordinary citizens with the call to repudiate the past and labor for the future. As Gallimard is finally sent back to France (since, as he is told, his foreign-policy predictions about Vietnam and China were all wrong), Song is seen working with other intellectuals in a labor camp, where loudspeakers blare away with "reeducation" messages to cleanse people's souls.

If the loudspeaker of a labor camp is the apparatus for a new type of fantasy—the fantasy of revolutionized subjectivity, of proletarian agency, of nationalist progress—it is shown to compete rather weakly with that other, older, and "corrupt" apparatus of interpellation, the operatic music of *Madama Butterfly*. As Song looks up strained and exhausted from her labor, she seems to hear another voice from afar, which gradually takes over the audible space hitherto occupied by the loudspeaker. As this voice becomes louder, we recognize it to be the familiar music from *Madama Butterfly*, and the grayish backdrop of the labor camp changes into Paris, 1968, when Gallimard is watching a performance of *Madama Butterfly*, with tears slowly trickling down his face, at the Paris Opera. Song and Gallimard are thus, we might say, reunited through this persistent, "corrupt," big Other of "Butterfly," which was what brought them together in the first place.

This dream of a Butterfly, of an unforgettable erotic and emotional experience, inserts itself in a Paris that, as Gallimard's acquaintance in a bar tells him, is looking more like Beijing, with students shouting Maoist slogans and rioting in the streets. The juxtaposition at this point of the erotic and the political, the "personal" and the "historical," raises a question that *M. Butterfly* merely hints at, but that nonetheless is crucial to any consideration of fantasy: is "revolution" itself, the film seems to say, not simply another type of "fantasy stereotype"—the fantasy stereotype that exploits in the name of the collective, the people? If we mobilize, as we must, criticism against Western "orientalist" and "imperialist" fantasies about the East, then should the cruelties committed by way of this other fantasy stereotype not also be under attack? The pro-Chinese Communist fervor in France of the 1960s—is it an awakening from Western imperialism and orientalism, or is it not simply the other side of that dream called Butterfly, which fetishizes the East this time not in the form of an erotic object but in the form of a political object, not in the form of the beautiful "oriental woman" but in the form of the virile oriental man, the Great Helmsman, Mao Zedong?

In his indifference to the political revolution, Gallimard will listen again to the music from *Madama Butterfly* in his own private space, away from the clamor of the streets. An evening alone in his minimalist orientalist apartment, where a meal consists of mere bread and soup, he sits forlornly, accompanied by the "Humming Chorus" played on his MCA record. As if by miracle, "Butterfly" again enters: in the midst of the melancholic music, Song has mysteriously reappeared.

MADAME BUTTERFLY, C'EST MOI

After this scene of reunion, the music from *Madama Butterfly* will be heard one final time—as an accompaniment to Gallimard's performance in jail. Played on a cassette, the music has by this time become a portable object, very much like the other things that Gallimard consciously displays *on himself* in this scene. How then are we to bring together the music, the "pure sacrifice" of the "oriental woman," and Gallimard's gory suicide?

In this final one-man show, which progresses as Song is meanwhile released and sent back to China, Gallimard begins by commenting on his own "celebrity," and then proceeds to tell the story that led up to it. Gradually but steadily, as he describes his vision of the slender "oriental women" in "cheongsams and kimonos, who die for the love of unworthy foreign devils," Gallimard performs a transformation into Madame Butterfly herself. The camera shows him putting on the sash for his kimono, followed by white foundation across his face, eyeliner, shiny red lip gloss, and finally a wig. As his transformation becomes complete, the transvestite pronounces: "At last, in a prison far from China, I have found her. . . . My name is René Gallimard! Also known— as Madame Butterfly!"

This scene of dramatic transformation offers, I think, one of the most compelling and complex moments in cinematic history. Because of this, I must emphasize that the readings I provide below function more as experimental explorations than as exact renderings of its significance.

1. First, what is effected in these last moments of the film seems to be a merging of two separate identities. This merging returns us, once again, to the theme of the self-sacrificing "oriental woman" discussed above, with a new twist. If Gallimard is Madame Butterfly, then this performance of his transformed identity should perhaps be described as a retroactive enactment, a slow-motion replay, of a story whose meaning has become visible only now—for the first time. In this story, Gallimard the "oriental woman" has been sacrificing himself (herself) for a man (Song) who, as Gallimard points out, is not worthy of his (her) love. This merging and swapping of identities, through which Gallimard turns into "Butterfly," is what Hwang intends as the basic "arc" of his play: "the Frenchman fantasizes that he is Pinkerton and his lover is Butterfly. By the end of the piece, he realizes that it is he who has been Butterfly, in that the Frenchman has been duped by love; the Chinese spy, who exploited that love, is therefore the real Pinkerton."[18] To return to the point of seduction I made earlier, we may add, paradoxically, that in seducing Gallimard, Song in fact led him temporarily away from his own truth—the truth of a fantasy that is not a fantasy of the other but rather *of himself as the suicidal "oriental woman."* In desiring Song, Gallimard was desiring not exactly to have her but to be her, to be the "Butterfly" that she was playing. While being the setting and structuring of fantasy, therefore, the encounter with Song served in effect to displace and postpone the fulfillment of Gallimard's wish for his own immolation. The "Butterfly" that was Song, in other words, shielded Gallimard from the "Butterfly" that is himself.

But if the relationship with Song has been a screen against the Real by giving Gallimard a conventional anchorage—a relation with a physical other and within the acceptable symbolic of heterosexual sociality—the revelation of Song's banal maleness means that this screen, which protected him but also prevented him from seeing, has evaporated. With the screen also disappear the fixed positions that are usually ascribed to man and woman, occident and orient. In a manner similar to Laplanche and Pontalis's argument about fantasy, what Gallimard's fantasy of "Butterfly" accomplishes in this final scene of monstrous transformation is ultimately a belated staging of a field of relations with multiple entry points, a field where positions of dominance and submission, of male and female, of aggressor and victim, are infinitely substitutable and interchangeable. Gallimard's transformation continues, in tandem, the series of vertiginous transvestite masquerades that began with Song.

2. While the interpretive narrative of interchangeable racial and sexual subjectivities that I have just offered is perhaps the one most likely to be favored by critics who are invested in the utopian potential of destabilized identities, other elements in this transformation far exceed such a narrative. For one thing, the conclusion that Gallimard finally discovers himself to be Madame Butterfly does not explain the power of the *visual* play of this last series of shots. How, in other words, might we understand his transformation in terms of the dynamics, the power structure of vision—the relations between the image and the gaze? What does the interplay between Gallimard the Frenchman, Gallimard the performer, and Gallimard the Madame Butterfly signify *in terms of visuality*? For my own aid, I turn at this point to Lacan's reading of a story that has much genealogical affinity with ours.

I am referring to Lacan's consideration of the Chinese philosopher Zhuang Zi's well-known butterfly dream. Zhuang Zi wrote that, one day, he dreamt that he was a butterfly, happily flitting and fluttering around. He did not know he was Zhuang Zi. On waking up, he was, of course, once again solidly and unmistakably himself, but he did not know if he was Zhuang Zi who had dreamt that he was a butterfly, or a butterfly dreaming he was Zhuang Zi.[19] Lacan's analysis, which foregrounds the relations of visuality, goes as follows:

> In a dream, he is a butterfly. What does this mean? It means that he sees the butterfly in his reality as gaze. What are so many figures, so many shapes, so many colours, if not this gratuitous *showing*, in which is marked for us the primal nature of the essence of the gaze. . . . In fact, it is when he was the butterfly that he apprehended one of the roots of his identity—that he was, and is, in his essence, that butterfly who paints himself with his own colours—and it is because of this that, in the last resort, he is Choang-tsu [Zhuang Zi].[20]

What fascinates Lacan, I think, is that the dream—in which the "I"/eye of Zhuang Zi becomes this Other, the butterfly—returns Zhuang Zi for a moment to a state of nondifferentiation in which the Other exists as pure gaze.[21] In this state of nondifferentiation, one is not conscious of oneself as consciousness, as thought. This dream is so powerful that even when he wakes up, Zhuang Zi is not sure whether "he" is not simply (a lost object) dreamt by the butterfly. For Lacan, Zhuang Zi's butterfly dream is a glimpse into the truth: "it is when he was the butterfly that he apprehended one of the roots of his identity—that he was, and is, in his essence, that butterfly who paints himself with his own colours—and that it is because of this that . . . he is Choang-tsu." The conscious identity of Zhuang Zi, the "I"/eye of waking life, in other words, is the result of the butterfly "causing" him to exist or marking him with the grid of desire.[22] Waking from this dream back into consciousness is therefore an unsettling awakening into the fact that, in one life's as *cogito*, one is a captive butterfly, captivated by nothing but the inescapable law and structure of human cognition.

Lacan's reading of Zhuang Zi's dream brings us one step closer to unraveling the visual dynamics of Gallimard's transformation. Accordingly, we could see Gallimard's transformation as an equivalent to Zhuang Zi's dream, in which he, Gallimard, becomes a "Butterfly." The very image of the "oriental woman" in her strange shape and figure, in her bright colors, is then the gratuitous *showing* that Lacan mentions as the primal nature of the essence of the gaze. This gaze returns Gallimard to the roots of his identity by showing, by giving to the eye, the knowledge that "Butterfly" is what causes him to exist by marking him with desire. As in Zhuang Zi's story, therefore, the question implicit in Gallimard's performance is: how do "I," Gallimard, know that I, with my fantasy, my longing for the "oriental woman," am not merely an object dreamt by "Butterfly," the gaze that I (mis)took for an image? Instead of being Gallimard dreaming of a "Butterfly," might I not myself be the dream of a "Butterfly"?

3. Just as Lacan writes that Zhuang Zi is, in his essence, "the butterfly who paints himself with his own colours," so Gallimard, strictly speaking, does not simply perform but rather *paints* himself into Madame Butterfly—or more precisely, paints himself with her colors. Once this emphasis is introduced, we are able for the first time to view

this scene of transformation as about a process of painting, with philosophical implications to be deduced from the relationships between the act of painting, the painted image, and the gaze.

Lacan, contrary to conventional thinking and following philosophers such as René Caillois and Maurice Merleau-Ponty, writes that painting is not really mimicry or imitation in the sense of creating a secondary, derivative form on the basis of a pre-existing one. Rather, if it is indeed mimicry or imitation in the sense of producing an image, this image is part of a process in which the painter enters a specific relation with the gaze—a relation in which the gaze (especially as embodied by the spectator) is tamed:

> To imitate is no doubt to reproduce an image. But at bottom, it is, for the subject, to be inserted in a function whose exercise grasps it. . . . The function of the picture—in relation to the person to whom the painter, literally, offers his picture to be seen—has a relation with the gaze. This relation is not, as it might at first seem, that of being a trap for the gaze. It might be thought that, like the actor, the painter wishes to be looked at. I do not think so. I think there is a relation with the gaze of the spectator, but that it is more complex. The painter gives something to the person who must stand in front of his painting which, in part, at least, of the painting, might be summed up thus—*You want to see? Well, take a look at this!* He gives something for the eye to feed on, but he invites the person to whom this picture is presented to lay down his gaze there as one lays down one's weapons. This is the pacifying, Apollonian effect of painting. Something is given not so much to the gaze as to the eye, something that involves the abandonment, the *laying down*, of the gaze.[23]

These passages indicate that painting can be described as a process of disarming the Other, of warding off the menace that comes from the Other. The means of disarming the Other is the painted image, which may thus be described as a second-order gaze, an artificial eye, a fetish in the sense of an amulet or talisman that may ward off evil. However, in using this understanding of painting as a way to read Gallimard's transformation, we are immediately confronted by the fact that Gallimard is not only the painter, nor only both painter and image, but painter, image, and spectator, all three at once. This fact considerably complicates the combative relation between the painter and the gaze that Lacan sets forth. By painting himself as Madame Butterfly, is Gallimard simply making an image to fend off the gaze (in which case he would remain in the subjectivity of the painter)? Is he not also the painted image, and is he not, as he looks at himself in the mirror, also the spectator, the one to be tamed? As "Butterfly," Gallimard appears also as a clown—but is the clown mocking us, or is she the object of our mockery, and for what reason? All in all, how are we to describe this ultimate act of Gallimard's *passion*, his *passage* from painter to image to spectator?[24]

This passion/passage that is painting, we might say, is a process of making visible that which could otherwise never be directly seen. Significantly, therefore, painting here rejoins the etymological meaning of the word "fantasy," which means, precisely, "to make visible."[25] But "making visible" at the end of *M. Butterfly* is no longer simply a making visible of the multiple positions available to the subject. Rather, it is a process of throwing off the colors that make up the "self," a process of stripping and denuding that is comparable with processes of change in the natural world: "If a bird were to paint," Lacan writes suggestively, "would it not be by letting fall its feathers? a snake by casting off its scales, a tree by letting fall its leaves?"[26]

As Gallimard looks at the "Butterfly" in the mirror, he is transformed into the spectator who is invited to lay down his own gaze. This laying down of the gaze is the laying down of the weapon, the protective shield that separates us from the Other. What Gallimard finally meets, in the painted picture of himself as Madame Butterfly, is that thing which, in its muteness and absoluteness, renders him—the man Gallimard—obsolete, inoperant, excluded.[27] If the gaze is that which is always somehow eluded in our relation to the world,[28] then what Gallimard meets, in his own Butterfly image, in a manner that can no longer be eluded, is the gaze as it has all along looked at him.

If this scene of transformation could indeed be seen as a performing of enlightenment—of Gallimard's discovery that Madame Butterfly is none other than he himself—it is also enlightenment-as-self-deconstruction. From the perspective of the man with desire, this enlightenment is not progress but a regression, a passage into inertia, into the thing he loves. With this passage and passion, which we call death, the illusory independence that one achieves through the primary narcissism of the "mirror stage," which shows one as "other" but gives one the illusion of a unified "I," disappears. Significantly, therefore, the instrument of death in the film is not simply the *seppuku* dagger in the opera *Madama Butterfly* or the knife in the play *M. Butterfly*, but a mirror—a mirror, moreover, that has lost its reflective function. Being no longer the usual means with which one says, "this is me, myself," the mirror now returns to its material being as a shard of glass with which to terminate life and pass into the inorganic. Gallimard's suicide completes and fulfills the fateful plot of *Madama Butterfly*, but instead of him performing "Butterfly," it is, strictly speaking, "Butterfly" that has been performing him. As the Frenchman "sacrifices" himself and passes into his beloved spectacle, the "Butterfly" that is the character, the story, and the music—in short, the gaze—lives on.[29]

CODA: NEW QUESTIONS FOR CULTURAL DIFFERENCE AND IDENTITY

What I have attempted to show through a more or less Lacanian reading is the ineluctability of a serious consideration of fantasy—and with it, questions of cognition—in a story of exchange that is overtly "cross-cultural." What this reading makes explicit, I hope, is that fantasy is not something that can be simply dismissed as willful deception, as "false consciousness" to be remedied by explicit didactics. Once fantasy is understood as a problem structural to human cognition, all the "cross-cultural" analyses of ideology, misogyny, and racism that are rooted in a denigration of fantasy will need to be thoroughly reexamined.

If, in this fantasy, the orient is associated with femininity itself, then the problem of coming to terms with the orient is very much similar, structurally speaking, to the problem of coming to terms with woman in psychoanalysis—in that both the orient and woman have been functioning as the support for the white man's fantasy, as the representation of the white man's *jouissance*. However, what distinguishes Cronenberg's film from many examples of such representation—one thinks, for instance, of Bernardo Bertolucci's *The Last Emperor*, *The Sheltering Sky*, and *The Little Buddha*—is precisely the manner in which the lavish visible painting of fantasy finally takes place not on the female, feminized body of the other but on the white male body, so that enlightenment coincides with suicide, while the woman, the other, escapes.[30]

What remains unknown, then, is the "supplementary" *jouissance* of woman (and, by implication, of the orient) as spoken of by Lacan, who, in an aptly deconstructionist manner, puts his emphasis on the word "supplementary."[31] What does woman want, and what does the orient want? At no moment in the film *M. Butterfly* does Song's subjectivity and desire become lucid to us—we never know whether she is "genuine" or masquerading, whether her emotions are "for real" or part of her superb playacting—until in the "showdown" scene in the police van. In that scene, we see for the first time that what she "wants" is a complete overturning of the laws of desire that have structured her relationship with Gallimard. In other words, in spite of her love for the Frenchman, what the "oriental woman" wants is nothing less than the liquidation of his entire sexual ontological being—his death.

Even though Song does not get what she wants directly, her wish is vindicated by the ending of the film. Gallimard's transformation into Madame Butterfly indicates that femininity and the "oriental woman" are the very truth of Western Man himself, and because he is traditionally identified with power, he is so far removed from this truth that his self-awakening must be tragic. Gallimard's death shows that Western Man is himself nothing—no-thing—more than a French penis dreaming of (being) an oriental butterfly.

By definition, the death of the white man signals the dawn of a fundamentally different way of coming to terms with the East. The film closes with "Butterfly" flying back to China. This "oriental woman" who existed as the white man's symptom—what will happen to her now that the white man is dead? That is the ultimate question with which we are left.

NOTES

1. I am very grateful to David Cronenberg for providing me with a copy of the shooting script of the film *M. Butterfly*. For related interest, see David Henry Hwang, *M. Butterfly*, with an afterword by the playwright (New York: Plume Books, 1989). For a discussion of the play in terms of the politics of transvestism, see Marjorie Garber, *Vested Interests: Cross-Dressing and Cultural Anxiety* (New York and London: Routledge, 1992), pp. 234–251; for a discussion of the play in terms of its criticism of essentialist identity formed through orientalism and heterosexism, see Dorinne Kondo, "*M. Butterfly*: Orientalism, Gender, and a Critique of Essentialist Identity,"

Cultural Critique, No. 16 (Fall 1990), pp. 5–29. For a discussion of the misogynist implications of Puccini's opera, see Catherine Clément, *Opera, or the Undoing of Women*, trans. Betsy Wing, foreword by Susan McClary (Minneapolis: University of Minnesota Press, 1988), pp. 43–47. For a biography of Bernard Boursicot, the Frenchman whose love affair with the Chinese opera singer Shi Peipu gave rise to the *M. Butterfly* story, see Joyce Wadler, *Liaison* (New York: Bantam Books, 1993).

2. Hwang, *M. Butterfly*, p. 94.

3. Hwang, *M. Butterfly*, p. 100.

4. See Kondo's essay for summaries of the vexed reactions to Hwang's play from some members of the Asian American communities.

5. See, for instance, Freud's well-known discussion in "Creative Writers and Day-Dreaming," *The Standard Edition of the Complete Psychological Works of Sigmund Freud*, vol. ix, trans. James Strachey (London: Hogarth Press, 1959), pp. 141–153. For an authoritative intensive reading of Freud's works on fantasy, see Jean Laplanche and Jean-Bertrand Pontalis, "Fantasy and the Origins of Sexuality" (first published in the *International Journal of Psychoanalysis*, Vol. 49, part 1, pp. 1–17; 1968), in *Formations of Fantasy*, edited by Victor Burgin, James Donald, and Cora Kaplan (London and New York: Methuen, 1986), pp. 5–34. Because I am, in this essay, primarily interested in exploring the social and cross-cultural implications of fantasy, I am not fine-tuning the various modes of conscious and unconscious fantasies, as would be necessary in a more strictly clinical analysis. For the same reasons, I am also using terms such as "fantasy" and "dream" interchangeably.

6. See Laplanche and Pontalis, "Fantasy and the Origins of Sexuality." Two discussions of fantasy that I have found very helpful are Cora Kaplan, "*The Thorn Birds*: Fiction, Fantasy, Femininity," in *Formations of Fantasy*, pp. 142–166, and Elizabeth Cowie, "Fantasia," in *The Woman in Question*, edited by Parveen Adams and Elizabeth Cowie (Cambridge, MA: MIT Press, 1990), pp. 149–196.

7. Examples of these uncomprehendingly dismissive reviews: "Hwang also wrote the misguided movie version of *M. Butterfly* for director David Cronenberg, in which Jeremy Irons and an oddly sullen John Lone act out a straightforward love story devoid of heat or plausibility. The problem is not simply that Lone's drag wouldn't fool a baby. In the magnified intimacy of the camera's eye, it's clear Hwang doesn't really know who these unlikely lovers are." David Ansen, "Much Stranger than Fiction," *Newsweek*, October 18, 1993, p. 84. "The problem with *M. Butterfly*, both play and movie, is that the audience gets the point right away—it's too crude and too facile to miss—and has nothing to do for the rest of the evening except listen to tiresome restatements of it. . . . Cronenberg's treatment of Hwang's material has the effect of exposing it for what it really is: not a pure, incandescent work of art but an extremely ordinary piece of agitprop drama." Terrence Rafferty, "The Current Cinema: Blind Faith," *The New Yorker* 69: 33, October 11, 1993, p. 123. If one were indeed to judge the film on the basis of verisimilitude, one could obviously criticize the improbability of a Cantonese-speaking servant in Song's house, while every

other Chinese character, including Song, speaks in Mandarin, the language most commonly used in Beijing.

8. "Fantasy involves, is characterized by, not the achievement of desired objects, but the arranging of, a setting out of, desire; a veritable mise-en-scène of desire. . . . The fantasy depends not on particular objects, but on their setting out; and the pleasure of fantasy lies in the setting out, not in the having of the objects. . . . It can be seen, then, that fantasy is not the object of desire, but its setting." Cowie, "Fantasia," p. 159.

9. In the early scenes of the film, Gallimard's fascination with "Butterfly" extends even to fly-swatting and dragonfly-gazing. In terms of the genealogy of Cronenberg's films, *M. Butterfly* is similar to its predecessors in that it stages the manner in which a man's imagination infects him like a disease, which gradually consumes and finally destroys him. For extended discussions of this—his favorite—theme, see the director's *Cronenberg on Cronenberg*, ed. Chris Rodley (London and Boston: Faber and Faber, 1992). However, two factors make *M. Butterfly* different from the earlier films. First, the restrained, minimalist design of the film is a major departure from the elaborate special effects and shocking images that are the Cronenberg trademark. Second, the biological and science-fiction modes of Cronenberg's usual film language are here complicated by the story of a cross-cultural encounter, with all its sexual, racial, and political implications. Because of these factors, I am reading *M. Butterfly* as a unique work in Cronenberg's corpus, even though the conceptual affinities with the other films are definitely present. In particular, as I will go on to argue, the significations of visuality in this film are unprecedentedly mind-boggling.

10. Even though Hwang too has used the notion of deconstruction, what he aims at deconstructing is the fantasy, the stereotype, and the cliché, rather than the human *per se*: "The idea of doing a deconstructivist *Madame Butterfly* immediately appealed to me. This despite the fact that I didn't even know the plot of the opera! I knew Butterfly only as a cultural stereotype; speaking of an Asian woman, we would sometimes say, 'She's pulling a Butterfly,' which meant playing the submissive Oriental number. Yet, I felt convinced that the libretto would include yet another lotus blossom pining away for a cruel Caucasian man, and dying for her love. Such a story has become too much of a cliché not to be included in the archtypal [sic] East-West romance that started it all. Sure enough, when I purchased the record, I discovered it contained a wealth of sexist and racist clichés, reaffirming my faith in Western culture." Hwang, *M. Butterfly*, p. 95.

11. Lacan, "The Line and Light," *The Four Fundamental Concepts of Psycho-Analysis*, edited by Jacques-Alain Miller, trans. Alan Sheridan (New York and London: Norton, 1981), pp. 102–103; emphases in the original.

12. See Jean Baudrillard, *Seduction*, trans. Brian Singer (New York: St. Martin's Press, 1990).

13. Baudrillard, *Seduction*, p. 83.

14. On this point—namely, that *M. Butterfly* is not about the conflict of homosexuality and heterosexuality—Hwang is absolutely clear: "To me, this is not a 'gay' subject, because the very labels heterosexual or homosexual become meaningless in the

context of this story. Yes, of course this was literally a homosexual affair. Yet because Gallimard perceived it or chose to perceive it as a heterosexual liaison, in his mind it was essentially so. Since I am telling the story from the Frenchman's point of view, it is more specifically about 'a man who loved a woman created by a man.' To me, this characterization is infinitely more useful than the clumsy labels 'gay' or 'straight.'" Hwang, personal communication, April 30, 1989, quoted in Kondo, p. 21.

15. This is one of the many significant differences between the film and the play. In the play, Gallimard is familiar with the Madame Butterfly story, which he claims to like, but complains that he has only seen it "played by huge women in so much bad make-up" (Hwang, *M. Butterfly*, p. 16).

16. Lacan, "The Meaning of the Phallus," *Feminine Sexuality: Jacques Lacan and the école freudienne*, edited by Juliet Mitchell and Jacqueline Rose, trans. Jacqueline Rose (New York: Norton, 1985), p. 82.

17. See Lacan's discussion in "Feminine Sexuality in Psychoanalytic Doctrine." Responding to Freud's questions in the investigation of feminine sexuality, "What does the little girl want from her mother?" and "what does she demand of her?" Lacan writes (*Feminine Sexuality*, pp. 130–131; emphases in the original):

> "What does the little girl demand of her mother?" But it's easy! She has no shortage of words for telling us: to dress her, to make her hurt go away, to take her for a walk, to belong to her, or to her alone, in short all sorts of demands, including at times the demand to leave her alone, that is, the demand to take a rest from all demand. If, therefore, Freud's question has any meaning, it must signify something else, that is, not so much "What is she demanding *of her*?" as "What is she *demanding*, what is she really demanding, by demanding of her mother all that?"
>
> In other words, Freud's question implies the separating out of demand onto two planes: that of the demands effectively spoken, or enounced, and that of Demand (with a capital D) which subsists within and beyond these very demands, and which, because it remains resistant to articulation, incites the little girl to make those demands at the same time as rendering them futile, both the demands and any reply they might receive.

18. Hwang, *M. Butterfly*, pp. 95–96.

19. I am following Burton Watson's English translation of Zhuang Zi's text, which appears in *Qiwulun* [a treatise on equalizing (with) all things]. See *The Basic Writings of Chuang Tzu*, trans. and ed. Burton Watson (New York: Columbia University Press, 1964), p. 45.

20. Lacan, "The Eye and the Gaze," *Four Fundamental Concepts*, p. 76; emphasis in the original.

21. "When dreaming of being the butterfly, . . . he is a captive butterfly, but captured by nothing, for, in the dream, he is a butterfly for nobody." Lacan, "The Eye and the Gaze," p. 76.

22. "The butterfly may . . . inspire in him the phobic terror of recognizing that the beating of little wings is not so very far from the beating of causation, of the primal stripe marking his being for the first time with the grid of desire." Lacan, "The Eye and the Gaze," p. 76.

23. Lacan, "The Line and Light," pp. 100–101; emphases in the original.

24. See Garber for an interesting discussion of "passing" in her reading of the play *M. Butterfly*: "'What passes for a woman.' And what passes for a man. Passing is what acting is, and what treason is. Recall that the French diplomat Boursicot was accused of passing information to his Chinese contacts. In espionage, in theater, in 'modern China,' in contemporary culture, embedded in the very phrase 'gender roles,' there is, this play suggests, only passing. Trespassing. Border-crossing and border raids. Gender, here, exists only in representation—or performance." *Vested Interests*, p. 250. As my reading throughout this essay indicates, my reading of passing—and hence of crossing, role-playing, representation, and performance—is quite different from Garber's.

25. See Cowie's discussion in "Fantasia," p. 154.

26. Lacan, "What is a Picture?" *Four Fundamental Concepts*, p. 114.

27. The passage indicated by the previous footnote continues with these lines: "What it amounts to is the first act in the laying down of the gaze. A sovereign act, no doubt, since it passes into something that is materialized and which, from this sovereignty, will render obsolete, excluded, inoperant, whatever, coming from elsewhere, will be presented before this product." Lacan, "What is a Picture?" p. 114.

28. "In our relations to things, in so far as this relation is constituted by the way of vision, and ordered in the figures of representation, something slips, passes, is transmitted, from stage to stage, and is always to some degree eluded in it—that is what we call the gaze." Lacan, "The Eye and the Gaze," p. 73.

29. This ending could also be read along the lines of Cronenberg's fascination with the resemblance of fantasy to disease. For instance, even though the vocabulary he uses is predominantly biological rather than visual, the following lines from the director could well serve as a reading of the ending of *M. Butterfly*, once we substitute the word "fantasy" for the words "virus" and "disease":

> To understand physical process on earth requires a revision of the theory that we're all God's creatures. . . . It should certainly be extended to encompass disease, viruses and bacteria. Why not? A virus is only doing its job. It's trying to live its life. The fact that it's destroying you by doing so is not its fault. It's about trying to understand interrelationships among organisms, even those we perceive as disease. To understand it from the disease's point of view, it's just a matter of life. It has nothing to do with disease. I think most diseases would be very shocked to be considered diseases at all. It's a very negative connotation. For them, it's very positive when they take over your body and destroy you. It's a triumph. It's

all part of trying to reverse the normal understanding of what goes on physically, psychologically and biologically to [sic] us. . . . I identify with [the characters in *Shivers*] after they're infected. I identify with the parasites, basically. . . . (*Cronenberg on Cronenberg*, p. 82)

30. In terms of a man "painting" his fantasy, a comparison could also be made between Cronenberg's film and Hitchcock's *Vertigo*, in which the male character, Scotty, attempts to rejuvenate his fantasy world by artificially remaking—by painting—Judy, his new girlfriend, into Madeleine, his supposedly dead one. Once again, in *Vertigo* it is the female body that serves as the canvas for male enlightenment and that is ultimately sacrificed; while in *M. Butterfly* it is the male body that bears the consequences of this cruel and crude act of painting.

31. Lacan, "God and the Jouissance of The Woman," *Feminine Sexuality*, p. 144.

NANCY ARMSTRONG

CITY THINGS

PHOTOGRAPHY

AND THE

URBANIZATION

PROCESS

IN WHAT MAY be considered his most probing examination of history, *Camera Lucida*, Roland Barthes claims that "we have an invincible resistance to believing in the past, in History, except in the form of myth."[1] This claim turns out to rest on two unstated assumptions: (1) that seeing is believing, and (2) that certain images can make things perfectly visible as such, even when they are no longer there in the flesh. For, Barthes continues, "[t]he photograph, for the first time, puts an end to this resistance [to history]: henceforth the past is as certain as the present, what we see on paper is as certain as what we touch. It is the advent of the Photograph—and not, as has been said, of the cinema—which divides the history of the world" (*CL*, pp. 87–88). Where Barthes loves images for their capacity to resurrect the past, Georg Lukács seems to hate them for killing off history. His claim assumes that seeing is believing, but that things obscure the social relations necessary to produce them, especially when those objects appear to be there in the flesh. When images take over the task of representing historical reality, according to Lukács, "genuine historicism—the conception of history as the destiny of the people"—disintegrates: "The more this historicism breaks down, the more everything social appears simply as 'milieu,' as picturesque atmosphere or immobile background."[2] Although Lukács approaches the relationship between image and object from the side of literature, and concludes that history vanishes in the presence of too many images, he implies precisely what Barthes declares, namely, that photography divides the history of the world.

Before 1848, Lukács contends, novels had the "power to give a living and dynamic picture of the essential driving forces of history" (*HN*, p. 206). In novels written after that date, however, this power suddenly dwindled, and the description of objects, "the dead environment of men, overwhelms the portrayal of men themselves" (*HN*, p. 186). No doubt he chose 1848 to mark the point at which fiction first reneged on its promise to represent social reality faithfully, because that was the date of the revolution in France that similarly betrayed the promise of liberal democracy (*HN*, p. 237). By choosing to identify what he calls "the crisis of bourgeois realism" so specifically with a major turning point in the history of the class struggle, Lukács produces what he considers a satisfying explanation for the literary crisis (*HN*, p. 171). When it actually comes to describing this turning point in literary history, however, he switches to English literature and charts the parabolic descent of the history of the novel from its apogee in Scott, to Dickens and the early signs of a decadence that would eventually reduce the world of things to "picturesque atmosphere or immobile background." Turning then to Flaubert, Lukács elaborates the novel's irreversible decline into naturalism in France. By thus shifting back and forth between national literatures, he uses the revolution of 1848 more as an analogue than as a causal explanation for the crisis in literary realism; the cause for that crisis remains implicit.

I want to call attention to the fact that Lukács blames "the principle of the photographic authenticity of description," or prominence of visual details, for propelling the novel into naturalism (*HN*, p. 198). For it was only a couple of years after the oft-cited revolution in France that the calotype process became widely available in England, an impressive number of photographic studios went into business, and still more would-be photographers took up a method of chemically reproducing images that had for a decade been restricted to a select group of amateurs.[3] Lukács consistently and emphatically identifies the destructive element in fiction with a creeping pictorialism that observes the principle of "photographic authenticity." No matter how often he encounters evidence that images had invaded literature, he never grants the production of those images the status of a historical event in its own right. He never even asks where these images came from, and how they might have changed the way in which people experienced the world. As a result, historically new and evidently powerful forms of visual information exist only as an obtrusively negative presence in his argument. In demonstrating that there was in fact such a sudden and powerful encroachment of images, however, his peculiar concatenation of literary evidence actually works against the grain of his argument. If not because of Barthes, then certainly because of a reader as sensitive to history as Lukács, we have to consider whether the rise of photography could have been as much of a shaping force in modern history as was an event such as the revolution in France.

ICONOPHOBIA

Despite the affection Barthes professes for the materials of his study, on the issue of the relative value of images and objects, he is again not so far from Lukács as we might expect. Barthes sifts through any number of photographs in search of details capable of destroying the surface tension of the image in the hope that it will put him back in touch with things themselves. Scanning a Kertesz photograph of a blind gypsy violinist being led by a boy, for example, he fixes on the dirt road: "its texture gives me the certainty of being in Central Europe; I perceive the referent (here, the photograph really transcends itself: is this not the sole proof of its art? To annihilate itself as *medium*, to be no longer a sign but the thing itself)" (*CL*, p. 45). If he is ultimately not so far from Lukács in his desire for a truth that resides on the other side of representation, can the two really differ all that much in their attitude toward images? Does Barthes really adore what Lukács holds in such contempt, or does his reaction to the photograph of the old gypsy not indicate that he actually shares Lukács's hostility toward images? Barthes likes the photographic image best when it "annihilate[s] itself as a *medium*" and disappears into the thing it represents. Just when it appears to be "no longer a sign but the thing itself," however, the photographic image has effectively reduced its referent to an icon, or sign of itself, and whenever Barthes realizes this has happened, he likes the image least.[4] His delight in ordinary photographic images and his refusal to moralize the

modern lust for unmediated access to things themselves seems to defy
the spirit of Lukács and mainstream European thought. But his search
for the detail that will reinstate the object outside the image locates
him squarely within a tradition that considers images bad whenever
they are caught displacing rather than acknowledging their complete
dependency on the things they represent. Like the love of things real
that it accompanies, such iconophobia is a common feature of modern literary and cultural theory.[5]

Foucault offers one of the few explanations for this modern aversion to certain images, when he explains how necessary they are to our
position as modern individuals in an institutional setting. *Discipline and
Punish*, his epic account of nineteenth-century institutional culture,
chronicles the production of a static social space in which individuals
are fixed and framed as visible objects. He attributes the power of the
modern penal institution directly to its visualizing procedures, and
makes the reader feel it is not good to become the object of an institutional gaze. In our culture, as he puts it, "[v]isibility is a trap."[6] Yet
where would this critique be without the image of Jeremy Bentham's
panopticon to make the argument visible? Would Foucault's theory of
discourse have the explanatory power it does without the *mise-en-scène*
of institutional power? Doesn't *Discipline and Punish* render us image-
dependent in order to explain the subordinating power of images? Yes,
behind his intricate accounts of the measures by which institutions
rule by rendering us visible in certain ways, there is the simple diagram
of the panopticon and the illustrations of various buildings built according to that model. Without these images, arguably few of his logical
moves would have been received, much less reproduced in countless
research projects across a range of academic disciplines.

His many detractors are not wrong to charge him with doing precisely what he describes; Foucault certainly does pay more attention to
the procedures of cultural subordination than to the struggles of subordinated groups. His conceptual crime is, according to his critics, very
much the same one for which Lukács blamed "photographic authenticity": a lack of concern for real people and the material conditions they
experienced. But this is not my quarrel with his argument. The more
important problem for my purposes is Foucault's failure to acknowledge
his own image-dependency. Though determined to meet his critics'

charge of culturalism with a more thoroughgoing culturalism, he inadvertently naturalizes the image. True, he enjoins us to think of the panopticon as "a mechanism of power reduced to its ideal form," "a pure architectural and optical system," or "a way of defining power relations in terms of the everyday life of men."[7] But Foucault never considers how the panopticon works as a *visual* mechanism in his own argument, something we see before reading his explanation of its historical formation and disciplinary structure, an image that inserts itself as the referent between his text and the historical reality of Bentham's plan for a penitentiary that never took the form of so many bricks and mortar. The image of the panopticon must have carried on a social life independent of any nineteenth-century institution in order for it to occupy the place it does within his argument. But lavish as he is in spinning out its consequences as a model, Foucault refuses to acknowledge the panopticon's history as an image, a history in which he himself plays such an important part. He collapses the visual properties of the image into those of the social spaces it helped to create and so removes the effects of the image itself from critical consideration. Was Foucault himself too much a product of the culture of the image to see that it was grounding his argument? Or was he too much a part of a critical tradition that denigrated the image to acknowledge its importance in his description of modernity? For whatever reason, he places himself alongside Lukács and Barthes within the mainstream of European critical theory by relocating the advent of mass visuality outside the mainstream of cultural history.

More recently, a growing number of geographers, historians, and social theorists have argued convincingly that the kind of spatial analysis that descends from Henri Lefebvre and Foucault is absolutely essential to understanding the modern city.[8] On the assumption that to analyze space is to abandon the narrative of class relations, historical accounts of capitalism consistently leave out what in David Harvey's opinion is one of its most salient aspects, namely, the urbanization process.[9] To correct this oversight, Edward Soja provides this account of how urbanization not only changed the organization of the social world, but also rendered that organization fundamentally spatial:

> Hidden within the modernity that was taking shape [during the nineteenth century] was a profound "spatial fix." At every scale of life, from the global to the local,

the spatial organization of society was being restructured to meet the urgent demands
of capitalism in crisis—to open up new opportunities for super-profits, to find new
ways to maintain social control, to stimulate increased production and consumption.
This was not a sudden development, nor should it be viewed as "conspiratorial,"
completely successful, or *entirely unseen* by those experiencing it.[10] (my italics)

In his effort to assign the production of social space its rightful part in
modern history, Soja goes up against much the same kind of historicism that once inspired Lukács to blame visual description for obscuring
what is most human about human history, and that today fuels the sense
of outrage in many readers of Foucault.[11]

I am not so interested in discovering a new and better social historical analogue for the flattening and presentism that sweeps away all sense
of linear history in cultural analyses by Lukács and Barthes, however. On
the contrary, I want to call attention to the historical impact of mass visuality, which seems to acquire the stature of an event only indirectly. All
of these accounts—Lefebvre, Foucault, Harvey, Soja—want to put the
production of space at the center of the modernization process, but in
doing so, they displace and marginalize the visual component of the new
social spaces that emerged within the major nineteenth-century European
cities. And yet, as Soja inadvertently acknowledges, the making of the
modern city is not something that could have gone "unseen"; the changes
it brought about would necessarily have been experienced visually. If we
cannot understand this turning point in the history of capitalism without a better account of the urbanization process, then how, I wonder,
can we account for the production of new city spaces as something that
occurred separate and apart from the advent of mass visuality? To read
for the traces of this event in critical theory is to find them everywhere
apparent only in the negative.

To move beyond instances of denial to a point where we can explain
such iconophobia, we must, I contend, return to the period when pictures first began to speak louder than words. Furthermore, we have to
find our way back to the nineteenth century by a route that is not unwittingly hostile to images and thus predisposed to marginalize their
production. For this purpose, I have chosen two studies of nineteenth-
century culture that focus on the sudden development and widespread
impact of new technologies for visual representation. These studies

isolate a cluster of events that occurred around the mid–century and brought about the simultaneous detachment of images from objects and subsumption of objects into images which then became their most telling components. Also important for my purposes, both studies suggest how this change in the relationship between image and object might have transformed the consumer of visual information as well.

THE ADVENT OF VISUALITY

As long as images pointed to things in much the same way that verbal description did, images were relatively unproblematic. And images did indeed represent what the eye could see, according to Jonathan Crary, until sometime during the 1830s and '40s, when the camera replaced the camera obscura as the most accurate method of reproducing visible objects. The camera obscura had been an extremely popular drawing aid for well over a century when the camera was invented, and mainstream art history still describes photographic technology as an effort to improve upon that earlier model. Crary revises this thinking. In his account, the camera obscura carries out the logic of visibility, which is grounded in the natural operations of the human eye and assumes that images originate in objects. Images then enter the mind through an aperture in the eye and project themselves on an interior wall, whereupon the individual recognizes them. A similar aperture in the wall of the camera obscura makes it possible to project the image of that object on the inside surface of the apparatus in much the same way that eye is imagined to project that image on a wall inside the mind. If this is done with any competence, the observer should recognize the object and still know the image is just a copy. When photography transforms visible things into visual images, however, it modifies this relationship between eye and optical apparatus. Crary locates the change historically:

> During the seventeenth and eighteenth centuries that relationship had been essentially metaphoric: the eye and the camera obscura or the eye and the telescope or microscope were allied by a conceptual similarity, in which the authority of an ideal eye remained unchallenged. Beginning in the nineteenth century, the relationship between eye and optical apparatus becomes one of metonymy: both are

now contiguous instruments on the same plane of operation, with varying capa-
bilities and features. The limits and deficiencies of one will be complemented by
the capacities of the other and vice versa.[12]

Although Crary identifies the shift from visibility to what can be called
visuality as a major turning point in cultural history, he is not so good
at explaining what happened as a result of the rupture of the metaphor-
ic relationship of camera to eye: What changes did cultures undergo
as the two ways of seeing suddenly began to exist on the same terrain—contiguously?

In so revising the cultural logic of visibility, I would argue, the
invention of photography did much more than shift the relationship
between apparatus and eye from one of resemblance to one of complementarity. Insofar as it paved the way for the mass reproducibility
of images, the advent of the photograph operated more as a supplement than as a complement to the image of objects that could be seen
with the eye. The new kind of image did something to "the image"—
giving it a capacity to reduce its subject matter to the visible traces of
places, people, or things. This transformed the very being of the object
as well. Rather than the image of an object pure and simple, photography offered the observer the objectification of a glance, neither his
own nor that of the photographer so much as a glance that no one
owns up to, because it is one that belongs to the culture.[13] The reproduction that results cannot be understood simply as another copy. The
photograph confers a new reality on the thing it represents, that of the
already seen. Thus the invention of photography not only placed the
camera on the same terrain as the eye, as something that could see for
itself, it also shifted the camera into a position of potential superiority, where it determined that objects would henceforth be seen just as
photographs had pictured them.[14]

One receives a vivid sense of photography's political objectives and
effects by turning from art history to studies of colonial culture, where
Said, Alloula, Gilman, Sekula, Mudimbe, Chow, Suleri, and others have
described European techniques of visualization as instruments of colonial domination.[15] In demonstrating the means by which Europe
subordinated other cultures, most of these studies regard photography
as one among many such means of cultural domination.[16] Indeed, on

the assumption that photography's enormous popularity was a symptom of the will to dominate, most scholarship neglects to ask why certain images had so much appeal.[17] "In short," as Bourdieu contends, "taking the effect for the cause, [historical accounts explain the rise of] photographic practice, subject to social rules, invested with social functions, and therefore experienced as a 'need', . . .with reference to something that is actually its consequence, namely the psychological satisfaction that it produces."[18]

Particularly helpful in this respect is Timothy Mitchell's analysis of the exhibitions of Islamic culture staged during the nineteenth century in some of the major cities of Europe. Mitchell's account of what he calls "the exhibitionary order" describes the role of the image in nineteenth-century Europe as that of a supplement: a new kind of image that exercised a new kind of power over objects, and changed not only how people saw things but how they felt about them as a result. From poring over their travel accounts, he concludes that Egyptian visitors to late-nineteenth-century Paris or Copenhagen often encountered some kind of exhibit containing certain pieces of their own culture—the false front of a mosque or perhaps a mock casbah—and that encounter inadvertently gave them a kind of insight into their European counterparts. As he explains, "The Europe one reads about in Arabic accounts was a place of spectacle and visual arrangement, of the organization of everything and everything organized to represent, to recall, like the exhibition, a larger meaning."[19]

To see exotic objects within the exhibition, as Mitchell describes it, was paradoxically to understand them in terms of the same epistemology of realism that Lukács accused pictorialism of eroding in his account of the historical novel. The exhibition had the effect of the real because its meaning resided elsewhere, in some ulterior reality. Exhibitions featuring exotic cultures created a double world: one that was merely a picture of the world, and another that was out there somewhere in Africa or Asia, where most Europeans could not see it. By collapsing seeing into knowing, exhibitionary realism used images aggressively to fulfill its promise. The exhibition not only exhibited the world, so as to set the world of objects exhibited apart from the viewer by virtue of its object status; the exhibition also organized and grasped the world, as though it were already on exhibit. Observers came

to expect whatever was outside and other than the European metropolis to look like the system of objects on display there, in much the
same way that the world-as-picture promised and failed to deliver social
reality in fiction. Like the nineteenth-century novel, the exhibition necessarily went back on its promise to the observer. Convinced of the
fundamental difference between text and world, Europeans apparently went looking for the world in other places, and if Mitchell's research
is any indication, they usually found it disappointing. The sense of
emptiness Nerval experienced on nearing the end of a visit to Cairo
is actually quite typical: "Just as well the six months I spent there is
over; it is already nothing, I have seen so many places collapse behind
my steps, like stage sets; what do I have left of them [but an] image as
confused as that of a dream."[20]

When we think of the camera in terms of the exhibition, we get a
more socially textured observer than Crary was interested in giving us,
one who reacts to photographic images in a way that places those images
squarely within the project of colonialism. Where the photograph still
performs a metaphorical substitution of image for object in Crary's analysis, the exhibition actively replaces Cairo with a European system of
objects in Mitchell's. When Egyptians observed one of the great European
spectacles, they knew perfectly well they were looking at objects that
had been selected and arranged on the basis of their visible characteristics. Things, real or fabricated, were not the things themselves. Those
objects already belonged to a complex visual system that determined
how they would be observed. Thus Europe's encounter with those things
was actually an encounter with their visible arrangement, and not with
things at all. Disappointment welled up in the gap between visuality and
visibility; the original was likely to strike the European viewer as nothing but a debased version of the copy; and that viewer responded by
cultivating the illusion there was something yet to be seen that would
indeed live up to its image. But of course the new object of desire was
an image too. European tourists began to supplement the experience of
looking at foreign places by picture-taking. As one Egyptian observed,
"Every year that passes, you see thousands of Europeans traveling all over
the world, and everything they come across they make a picture of."[21]

It should be noted that even such groundbreaking studies as Crary's
and Mitchell's implicitly limit the desire-infusing displacement of objects

to exotic subject matter—namely, to people and things other than "the observer" and his property. Yet neither the class of people who produced and consumed photographic images nor the spaces those people inhabited in Europe were immune to the effects of being visually objectified. The people who consumed photographs also produced significantly more images of themselves, their families, homes, shops, parks, and thoroughfares than they did of other people and exotic habitats.[22] In representing their own environment in certain ways, those who produced and consumed the spectacles of primitive and oriental cultures also divided that environment into "us" and "them" on the basis of rather crude visual distinctions. As they did so, they grew fascinated with life in the squalid neighborhoods, and they made those economically just below them want to occupy the bright spaces of the city, possess the goods, and inhabit the bodies of those stationed luminously above them.[23] As Bourdieu observes:

> Just as the peasant is expressing his relationship with urban life when he rejects the practice of photography, a relationship in and through which he senses the particularity of his condition, the meaning which *petits bourgeois* confer on photographic practice conveys or betrays the relationship of the *petite bourgeoisie* to culture, that is, to the upper classes (*bourgeoisie*) who retain the privilege of cultural practices which are held to be superior, and to the working classes from whom they wish to distinguish themselves.[24]

According to the theories most often used to think about urban life during the nineteenth century, this image–object, the illusive subject of photography, should be classified as idealism pure and simple. But what about the spaces that developed to display things and people both within the city and in the colonies? This means of making social and cultural distinctions cannot be so easily dismissed. Lefebvre has argued that social space is neither a thing among other things nor a product among other products, but "subsumes things produced and encompasses their interrelationships . . . and thus cannot be reduced to the rank of a simple object. At the same time," he also insists, "there is nothing imagined, unreal or 'ideal' about it." Any group that claims to be real must produce a space, its own space, he continues, or else remain trapped within the purely ideological or the strictly cultural domains, which would entail its reduction to the status of folklore.[25] I have already suggested how David Harvey uses this concept of space to describe the urbanization process. More specifically, he contends that in London the class struggle turned into a struggle for land. However, it was not, as we might assume, a struggle that depended on who could possess the most land. To the contrary, it was waged and won by converting land into cultural space. Under these circumstances, one could possess land, only to discover it had been redefined as a space that was either too expensive to rent, on the one hand, or unfit to inhabit, on the other. Victory went to those who possessed the cultural means to divide the city into parcels of private property and so establish the value of certain neighborhoods and commercial areas over others. Victory went, in Harvey's words, to the class who established "the authority of the spaces it could control over the spaces it could not."[26] The next section of this essay will explore the part the photography played in this struggle. The various genres of urban photography provide a record of the transformation of city space into a differential system that put certain kinds of space in charge of others, . . . but is this really all they do?

THE ORDER OF URBAN THINGS

It can be argued that what the exhibitions did to Cairo, the camera could in theory do to virtually anything.[27] Judging from the sheer redundancy of certain kinds of Victorian photographs, however, the camera was in fact just as selective as the exhibition hall, and photographs tended to pile up around a very limited number of sites. These images also converged to form an entire world, much as the objects in the exhibition did. Having gone about as far back into the nineteenth century as I can go by means of contemporary theory, let me turn to photographs taken during the Victorian period, and see how they define their role in the production of the kinds of city space that Harvey describes. To read photographs for this purpose, it is necessary to focus on what Barthes calls "the *studium*." Whenever the *studium* dominates, as he explains, the photograph "emphatically transforms 'reality' without doubling it . . . : no duality, no indirection, no disturbance. [Such a] photograph has every reason to be banal" (*CL*, p. 41). Why does the lack of tension between

Figure 4.1 *London Bridge 1895–1896.*

image and object guarantee that it adheres to an utterly commonplace public meaning? Because the *studium* is photography's way of doing what it is supposed to do—informing, representing, making significant, shocking, being tasteful, and so forth—all the while behaving as if things have been arranged to reveal only what they really are.[28] I am certainly aware of the scholarship that tries to give certain photographic images the same kind of subtlety and sophistication that we expect to find in canonical literature and painting.[29] The half-conscious manipulation of visual information—what just seems to look right at a particular time and place—is more important for my argument than the recalcitrant detail, or *punctum*, that enables Barthes as observer/reader of these images to challenge the generic categories that can subsume most any one or thing.[30]

Nowhere is this principle more evident perhaps than in the panorama (figure 4.1). The panoramic image was created as a novelty in a market for topographical images that was already flourishing by the mid 1860s, when a number of large commercial firms in England, France, and Italy were producing and publishing such photographs on a large scale. At first, photographs of the urban landscape stuck close to the guidelines for drafting city streets and important buildings. But in contrast with those drawings, topographical photography aimed primarily at introducing tourists to the city in a way that would entice them to see it for themselves, and photographic images soon developed their own distinctive way of doing this. Street views were characteristically shot from a second-story window or some other elevated vantage point, the better to capture the spatial character of the modern thoroughfare. During the 1860s, a shorter exposure time and combination printing allowed photographers to maximize this effect in panoramas that could compress and encompass a substantial piece of the city in a single, horizontally extended view. "The emphasis on the notable and the new," writes Eve Blau, "resulted in representations of cities that not only were incomplete and partial collections of major monuments, public buildings, and grand new boulevards—but that also made every city look alike."[31]

The result was to transform the city from a visible space that surrounded the observer into a space that he could step back from and view in much the same way he would a large object. In the panoramic photograph, details become important because there are simply too many for any one of them to count. These details were not supposed to represent things in themselves but rather the volume of things that could be transported rapidly through a rather wide thoroughfare that either spanned the image or cut through it along an imaginary line from front to back. The panoramic photograph transformed that street into a great mechanical belt that distributed people, goods, and information throughout the city, and represented this kind of motion as a sign of vitality.[32] The result was a unitary space capable of controlling the relative motion and inertia of the objects and people imbedded within it. It hardly needs to be said that such a spatial image refers to an object that was not really there to be seen before the popularity of such panoramas. Europeans began looking for it elsewhere in Europe as well as in the Middle East, since it was both a city in which they happened to be located and the city in terms of which they understood their relation to the real. Diaries of tourists visiting Egypt reveal that these tourists immediately sought a position from which to view Cairo panoramically, as if they could not really see it from within its winding streets and crowded bazaars.[33]

By turning from the panorama to a very different kind of photograph, we can begin to understand what these images, dependent as they were on visible things, did to the urban people and things that they pictured and put in circulation. Recalling that Paris doubled and London tripled their populations during the nineteenth century, we can certainly understand why the old city centers might have required renovation. But not so evident is why photographers were routinely commissioned to make a historical record of each plot of land, alleyway, and tenement slated for demolition. The thirty-one photographs of old Glasgow taken by Thomas Annan between 1868 and 1874 record the first major redevelopment scheme in Great Britain, and provide perhaps the most eloquent example of what was in fact a massive enterprise of converting the historic city into a visual record of the past. Empowered to acquire property, pull down buildings, and realign streets, the city government

Figure 4.2 Thomas Annan,
Close No. 193, High Street,
The Old Closes and Street of Glasgow (1868).

put in thirty-nine new streets, widened a dozen more, and cleared a substantial amount of land for sale or lease to private owners. As first arranged in an album, Annan's images were supposed to provide a record of those parts of the city that had not yet been touched by modernization. To do so, Annan began with a shot of a main thoroughfare that obviously belongs to the new city, proudly displayed for tourists by topographical photography. From there, his camera veers sharply onto numerous narrow, dark, and crooked passageways which seem to lead the eye into another city (figure 4.2). Where panoramas display the new city, bursting with people and things, all coursing toward some destination, this kind of photography evacuates the old city centers of both people and things. What in fact Annan records is the intervention of the camera: how it converted these parts of the city into the spectacle of a bygone era in the city's history.

On the one hand, then, these images are historical records pure and simple. In what is perhaps the best single account of this kind of image, Blau reminds us of the original character of Annan's photographs: stark in comparison with more nostalgic photographs of their kind, and bound in a volume designed to support the redevelopment project.[34] Soon after the photographs were taken, this photographic record was all that remained of the wyndes and vennels of medieval Glasgow and stone tenements that had been home to wealthy merchants up through the eighteenth century. At the same time, however, what Annan considered a purely documentary project had a literary counterpart in the most dismal descriptions of the city found in novels by Dickens or Gaskell, and a pictorial counterpart in the popular engravings of Gustave Doré (figure 4.3). Such descriptions can all be called "gothic" for representing the old city as a ruin or memorial to the life that had once animated it; the techniques of tunnel vision, a use of light and darkness that could be said to anticipate the visual effects of *film*

Figure 4.3 Gustave Doré, *Bluegate Fields*.

noir, and the dwarfing and blurring of human figures, even the empty clothes, all indicate that this part of the city is on the verge of disappearing, if not already gone. Photography intuitively exploited the difference between visibility and visuality to define the difference between certain parts of the city and others as a difference between past and present.[35] In doing so, it could be argued, photography overcame the friction that kept people and goods from circulating freely throughout the city. If things in motion sometimes create an opacity in the panoramic shot that makes the traffic appear to flow, then an object's movement in the gothic image renders that object translucent, so that we can see right through it to an emptiness beyond.[36]

Figure 4.4 A Butcher's Shop (c. 1900).

While gothic images depopulated the habitat of the poor, another genre of photography dealt with this population in the manner of the picturesque tradition. In taking up this project, photography joined forces with folklore and ethnography to acquaint the armchair tourist with the curiosities of other cultures. Ultimately, however, this effort was much less concerned with preserving authentic folkways than with displaying the details that would conjure up the type. William Gilpin could be called the founder of what was perhaps the first middlebrow aesthetic doctrine. In 1792, he argued that to see something as a picturesque object, all the observer had to do was select a view that was irregular, highly textured, and composed of things rugged, rustic, or antique, and then strip those things of their utilitarian value. This makes it possible to reduce what we see as "a variety of little parts; on which the light shining shews all its small inequalities, and roughness."[37] The camera brought the principles of the picturesque into the city streets, and broke down their complex and dynamic social organization into its smallest visible components. The photograph of a butchers' stall is one of countless images that could be used to demonstrate what happens to the relationship between people and things as the photograph disperses the gaze across an almost entropically detailed surface (figure 4.4). The reduction of everything within the frame to such information creates a strange equivalence between those rather meaty butchers and the slabs of meat they seem so eager to display. But savoring this "richness of surface" detail is just one half of the picturesque experience. To complete the aesthetic process, according to Gilpin, one must recombine those parts into a highly abstract visual object. Those who want to grasp the picturesque element of any scene must look for general shapes, dresses, groups, and occupations, for these constitute "the idea of *simplicity*; from which," he says, "results the picturesque."[38]

Figure 4.5 "Slum Life in Our Great Cities" (1890).

The first slide of a stereoscope series of such images declares that the primary purpose of the things and people populating the streets is that of being seen (figure 4.5). For this reason, *Slum Life in Our Great Cities* was a somewhat misleading title for the series, as David Francis suggests: "*Life in the back streets* would have been a better name for most of the scenes depicted: the slums themselves are more secret places."[39] In another image, a chimney sweep appears to have been going nowhere in particular when his sooty exterior, curious pack of implements, and impish apprentice caught photographer John Thompson's eye during the 1870s (figure 4.6). But photographs by another reformer of two decades later dramatize especially well this lack of concern for the local contexts in which people actually lived and worked. Scholars like to place Paul Martin's work alongside Thompson's in the tradition of documentary photography and read them as realistic portrayals of London labor. Rather than illustrate the need for social reform, however, these images testify to the picturesque aesthetic's capacity to subvert this intention, if not to the ultimately conservative objectives of reform itself. Apparently inspired by the treatment that he had seen given to some photographs of statues, he decided to distinguished the working man from the welter of visual information with which his body tended to merge (figure 4.7).

Figure 4.6 John Thompson, *The Temperance Sweep* (c. 1876–1877).

In so resisting the tendency of the picturesque to reduce people to the status of objects, however, Martin removed the image of labor, in the figure of the worker himself, from the situation in which that labor had been performed. Indeed, looking at their images detached altogether from the visual space that presumably defined them, we find it difficult to tell what such men were doing when Martin happened upon them with his camera. His efforts to monumentalize them ironically do to working people exactly what the picturesque tends to do, which is to detach its object from the symbolic economy in which it once had a utilitarian purpose and value. More ironic still, the individuals who most often appear within this particular framework were not members of the modern working class but the very people—artisans, independent laborers, and petty tradesmen—who were the casualties of modernization. Yet, thanks to the play of light upon the surface of their bodies, they appear solidly opaque and thus more durable than the bodies of the fashionable and well-to-do.

Before considering where photography locates the observing subject within this system of visual images, let me emphasize how various, how contradictory, and yet how seamless is the world of objects that passed before the eyes of that observer in countless photographs. We should remember that photography performed this magic at the very moment when other forces of modernization were infusing that observer's world with an amazing array of new objects, breaking up land into parcels for lease or sale, forcing city people to migrate from one section of the city to another, and altering their sense of themselves as they did so. It can be argued that the more completely the visible facts work in the service of the public meaning of a photograph, or *studium*, the more `subtle and potent is the photographic effect. By comparing the image of the butcher's stall first with the image of the chimney sweep and then with the photographic statuette (figures 4.4, 4.6, 4.7), we can observe the context receding progressively from the human figure. Scholars tend to respond to this decontextualization by putting Martin's figures back into the larger photograph from which he carved them (figure 4.8).

Figure 4.7 Paul Martin, *Loading up at Billingsgate Market: Cutout Figure* (c. 1894).

No matter how crudely it stages an object, the nineteenth-century photograph never allows us to entertain the possibility that its material is less than real. If the image is false or, as in this case, offers a fragmented image, it simply conjures up the true or complete image of the object as it was before the camera intervened. As the scholarly restoration of Martin's statuette indicates, however, photography's success in pointing outside its various frames to the thing itself actually drew observers further into the kinds of space defined by such images. When photographs began to pile up around certain sites of visibility, they also converged with one another to make an object that could in theory be visualized in its entirety. Oscar Rejlander was among those who attempted this feat when he used a method of printing that combined pieces carefully cut from different negatives in one seamless collage (figure 4.9). Because it incorporated the contradictions organizing nine-

Figure 4.8 Paul Martin, *Loading up at Billingsgate Market* (c. 1894).

teenth-century society, however, the field of vision that resulted also fractured that object into ontologically incompatible spaces. By situating Hannah Cullwick within frames that alternately idealized and degraded her, Arthur J. Munby notoriously privatized the capacity of photographic images to fracture the woman, and produced his own signature form of erotic pleasure.

THE ABODE OF THE OBSERVER

We cannot really give the observer of these images the status of an object within this visual field, since he is omnipresent there. Things presumably exist in order to be seen or remain unseen by him. As John Tagg observes, "At the level of spatial zoning, the city itself—at least, the respectable city of middle class life—was structured around the dif-

Figure 4.9 Oscar Gustav Rejlander, *The Two Ways of Life* (1857).

ferentiation of a feminized private and domestic sphere from a masculinized public domain."[40] Being seen even in the most respectable places outside the home, exposed a woman to "the predatory public gaze of the male" and put her "in consequent peril of confusion with that other, unspeakable order of womanhood, which entered the public arena only as the brazen object of an exchange and desire that were decently repressed in the closeted spaces of domesticity."[41] This is no doubt why Munby found it especially titillating to make the image of his servant-wife transgress the boundary separating the woman of the street or scullery from her respectable counterpart (figures 4.10, 4.11).[42] But the abode of the observer does require object status as well as a specific genre of photography to place it within the visual order of the city. Pastoral scenes of private life sought to reintroduce nature as the source of value in an urban milieu from which the other genres of photography conspired to banish it. In these images, nature assumes a feminine form under the protection of bourgeois masculinity, whether the male is actually figured there or not. During the 1860s, Lady Clementina Hawarden produced especially memorable scenes featuring the spacious interiors of fashionable London and the women they concealed from public view (figure 4.12). Such scenes were taken near a window or natural light source that ensured their characteristic luminosity, and usually provided some kind of membrane or barrier to separate inside from outside. Her contemporary, Julia Margaret Cameron, similarly sought, in the words of Gerhard Joseph, "to materialize in the camera what her great-niece later metaphorized as 'a room of one's own', a female space within which woman might realize her potential by making explicit the terms of her own interior discourse."[43]

It is fair, I think, to regard the kind of family portraits that became the rage during the same period as both proto-types and appropriations of these efforts to turn photography into an artistic medium (figure 4.13). Such images tend to use objects where Hawarden and Cameron relied on sheer radiance

Figure 4.10   A. J. Munby, *Hannah Cullwick*.

to indicate the value of the bodies it contained. Nature glows within an artificially illuminated interior, blossoms in the folds of rich clothing and gauzy curtains, bursts out in organic carvings on a piano front, and peers down from the chinoiserie poised near the top of the frame. Where Hawarden's naturally illuminated spaces and Cameron's fuzzy focus obscure the kind of detailing associated with the picturesque, these pictures try to capture individuals and the objects surrounding them as precisely as possible. Such photographs were originally circulated among members of the family and their acquaintances, providing a private historical record of a closed social group. Yet they give us very little sense of the "trespassing voyeurism" generated by artistically more ambitious images, according to Bryan Lukacher, where, as he explains, "the internal fiction of the tableau often implied the simultaneous negation of the camera's observing and recording presence."[44] Though destined for those who already knew and recognized the people being photographed, the image obviously displays them not as they really were, but as they wanted to be seen by the camera.

Figure 4.11   A. J. Munby, *Hannah Cullwick*.

One of a number of the official photographs of Victoria mourning the Prince Consort's death illustrates beautifully the paradox shaping such endeavors to publicize the private (figure 4.14). On the one hand, the surviving family members simply provide the raw material for an aesthetic tableau in which nature—in the form of an overinscribed domestic surface—mourns the father of the household, represented by his marble effigy.[45] On the other hand, the members of the royal household represent only themselves, arranged before the camera in a state of mourning, and captured in fully individuating detail. The contradiction between the picturesqueness of the busy room and the techniques that tell us the image is striving to be art (the ostentatious inclusion, off center, of the bust of Albert, whose power, to begin with, was never more than that Victoria symbolically bestowed on him) lends such public images of the private Victoria their almost kitsch character.

We can only speculate as to exactly what part a method of cultural reproduction that defined the observing subject as within but not of the city might have played in transforming land into property.

Those who could lay claim to a space that photography represented as impermeable to the public view did not look at all the same as those whose homes were disappearing along with the old city or those who appeared to be at home on the busy commercial streets and in the public view. The power to introduce spots of artificial nature in the urban landscape not only enhanced the value of surrounding property, but also identified the signs of pastoralism with those of value itself.

It is only when we appreciate the number of family photos, of *faux* family photos, and of other nineteenth-century versions of the city pastoral that we can begin to understand how they affected countless lives that had not been so mapped out in terms of the opposition between the streets and bourgeois interiority. We know that the popularity of this kind of image increased at such a rate that by 1900 one out of six English households had been photographed. We also know that the rise of family photography accompanied a massive reorganization of urban space itself, as various groups presumably strove to climb inside the photographic frame and live within such cultural spaces.[46]

Figure 4.12   Clementina, Lady Hawarden, Photographic Study (c. 1860).

In an essay such as this, I can only suggest how the invertible relationship between image and object unique to photography played out in terms of urban space.[47] From the 1850s on, there was evidently a steady march of the so-called "stink industries" to the East End. As new thoroughfares and railways cut through the old city, those who lived in its narrow alleyways and crowded tenements had to go where rent was cheapest, which was also where air, space, and drainage were in least supply. Those who could afford to pay the rent or buy the property migrated to the West End, where comfortable townhouses rested along tree-lined streets. At first, we can assume, life within such exclusive neighborhoods provided the material for urban pastoralism. By the time photography was little more than a decade old, photographs depicting the gratification of private life were everywhere, and seemed to offer it to everyone. These, in turn, sent still more observers in search of the thing itself, which held out the promise of wholeness to a subject that evidently felt it was being fractured and even threatened with extinction under the regime of visuality. These images of a generic family defined the inside of the house as both a metaphor and a refuge for the subject from the dehumanizing flow of commercial traffic, the darkly twisted passageways of the old city, and the degradation of the laboring body as depicted by topographic, gothic, and picturesque photography, respectively.

Figure 4.13 *The Music Lesson* (1857).

Perhaps an advertisement for a housing development in the London suburbs provides the best example of this transformation of the cultural behavior of images (figure 4.15). Rather than adhering to an original, one copy (namely, the photograph) begat another in the form of this kind of drawing. The drawing features a house that has not been built and a social space that is yet to materialize. It requires an observer who thinks of housing as the encasement for the kind of interior that had been reproduced and circulated in photographic images—a spot of artificial nature that could contain and care for a single family. At the point where topography began to recapitulate photography, the gap between image and object began to close, and it must have become rather difficult to distinguish that way of seeing the city from the city that one saw. Photography was certainly not the only cultural means of reproducing, expanding, and hierarchizing ontologically hostile kinds of urban space, but it certainly collaborated with exhibitions, museums, and all the machinery of spectacle for which the Victorian period is known. Moreover, photography alone brought the production of a visual field to an unprecedented level of efficiency, and made it suddenly and radically portable.

FOR THE LOVE OF THINGS THEMSELVES

Like the exhibition, the advent of the photograph made viewers long for the very things that photos were displacing—not only for the remnants of an earlier England that had been demolished to make way for modern thoroughfares, but also for contact with whatever the camera had identified as real. Put another way, photography instilled desire in a middle-class

Figure 4.14 *Mourning Group, Windsor Castle* (1862).

viewer—who was after all the agent of modernization—for the very sorts of people, places, and things that modernization tended to marginalize and ultimately eliminate. Out of this form of nostalgia, modern iconophobia was born. That is to say, the effect of a rampant appetite for images on those who made and consumed them was to generate much the same aversion to images that we find in Lukács, Barthes, Foucault, and a whole list of other critics. I would like to consider their aversion as a later version and necessary companion of the love for objects that nineteenth-century realism aroused and then refused to gratify.

Let us recall that Marx was writing *Capital* during the very period when photographic images were flooding the market, along with objects bearing names and containing ingredients from all over the Empire. Thanks to a sequence of innovations that made them relatively cheap to make and easy to reproduce, these images could arrive at one's home on the front of postcards. They could be found filling a variety of albums, hanging on the walls of respectable parlors, or displaying themselves in public exhibitions. We can read Marx's analysis of "The Commodity Fetish and its Secret" as a response to this situation. As these mendacious objects proliferate, he predicts, the signs of things will begin to replace things themselves. Things will no longer acknowledge the fact they are the products of human labor, and will begin to behave in the manner of a "fetish," religious "figure," or "social hieroglyphic."[48] Marx cautions that a second inversion would ensue from this behavior were it to occur on a sufficiently wide scale. When this happens, people will not even realize that the signs of things have replaced the things themselves, and once images take over the circulation of objects in this way, those things will necessarily acquire an occult power over those who produce and consume them.

Figure 4.15   Poster (1908).

In boiling down his foundational analysis of the culture of late capitalism to this tale of two inversions, I want to stress the importance Marx assigns to the visual component of objects. He bases his gothic account of the future at least in part on his sense that people were already losing contact with one another and with the things that were supposed to mediate their relationships, and he attributes this loss to a loss of visibility: there is something about the commodity that keeps us from *seeing* what is real. "In the act of seeing," he explains, "light is really transmitted from one thing, the external object, to another thing, the eye. [Seeing] is a physical relation between physical things." By way of contrast, the commodity-form has "absolutely no connection with the physical nature of the object itself."[49] When we look at a commodity, we do not really see it, according to his argument, because the traces of its production become invisible whenever the product becomes a commodity: we cannot know how, by whom, or for what purpose it was made. In the process of commodification, the human relations that arise from making and exchanging products consequently acquire "the fantastic form of a relation among things."[50] The commodity, in other words, collapses the difference between image and object, creating what might be called an image-object, something whose value—sometimes whose very existence—depends on its position within a differential system of signs. In such a world, one can hardly tell the image from the object.

According to the cultural logic implicit in the camera obscura as well as in William Gilpin's description of the picturesque experience, the individual could encounter an object directly and produce a copy that more or less accurately represented the thing itself. The advent of the photograph makes such a theory of unmediated, or natural, vision impossible. The lesson to be extracted from the world-as-exhibition is that people can see only what has already been put on display for them. Moreover, what one saw there was never the thing itself but the way in which objects of its kind are customarily seen. Whether close up and full of gritty details, distanced and sweeping, or luminously voluminous, repeated glances infused things with a whole new range of curious emotions that fed, expanded, and intensified a class-specific nostalgia for the regime of visibility. Is there any wonder that such a strong sense of loss permeates Marx's argument? He was obviously convinced that seeing is believing, and yet felt that—thanks to the production of signs that posed as things themselves—the time when one could really see things was fast coming to an end. Marx's essay on the secret of the commodity fetish can thus be read as the first theoretical articulation of the problematic of visuality.

If the difference between products and commodities boils down to a difference between objects and images for him, and if "objects themselves" are in fact nothing more than the visible traces of things, or what can be seen with the eye, then the difference he strives to maintain between object and image is not really a difference between things and images at all. It is a difference between good and bad images. To imagine a world in which social relationships could be natural, self-evident, or gratifying, Marx has to posit a world prior to mediation, a world, what is more, that is rapidly and irretrievably vanishing. Indeed, to provide an example of a legible object world, he reaches for—what else but—*Robinson Crusoe*.[51] Our understanding of the world-as-photograph suggests that this picture of the world of things as they once were, in all their pristine honesty, does not picture the real world so much as idealize the picture. What it gives us is the alluringly transparent flip side of the degraded image. Thus, in Marx's description of the secret of the commodity fetish, the commodity-form is a bad image because, as he puts it, that form has absolutely nothing to do "with the physical nature of the object itself," which can be seen directly with the human eye. From this, however, it also follows that the so-called "thing itself" is something that can be seen. The very things that Marx considers to be most real are therefore already images.

The collapse of the thing into its image and the original into its copy only makes seeing real things more desirable for Marx. His analysis of commodities perfectly articulates the paradox of nineteenth-century realism, in that it demonstrates how the desire to get beyond the image might have intensified the love of images and created a greater image-dependency. Where iconophilia inevitably fosters disappointment with things themselves, which in turn produces a market for more subtle and comprehensive forms of visual representation, disappointment with the poverty of images conversely masks an iconophilia that has made knowledge of the real depend on seeing it. Written at the moment of mass visuality, Marx built his argument around this contradiction, and we have inherited his love-hate relationship with visual objects along with his definition of materialism.

NOTES

1. Roland Barthes, *Camera Lucida: Reflections on Photography*, trans. Richard Howard (New York: Hill and Wang, 1981), p. 87; hereafter abbreviated *CL*.

2. Georg Lukács, *The Historical Novel*, trans. Hannah and Stanley Mitchell (Lincoln: University of Nebraska Press, 1983), p. 201; hereafter abbreviated *HN*.

3. Although Louis Daguerre is known to have nosed out William Henry Fox Talbot in formulating a process for chemically reproducing the light traces of objects on photosensitive material, I am associating the invention of photography with Talbot's publication of *The Pencil of Nature* in 1844. For purposes of this essay, I am less interested in the technological competition between the two men than in the fact that Talbot's project established the format, subject matter, and aesthetic debates for nineteenth-century photography. In the early 1850s, after some years of controversy, he gave up the patent that had restricted use of his process to a narrow circle of amateurs (see, for example, Grace Seiberling, *Amateurs, Photography, and the Mid-Victorian Imagination* [Chicago: University of Chicago Press, 1986]). Larry J. Schaaf observes that by the 1860s, when photographic images had begun to saturate the cultural scene,

   > Henry Talbot and Louis Daguerre had unwittingly traded places. Each eventually met his rival's goal. Daguerre was the public communicator and it would be fair to assume that his pursuit of the daguerreotype was initially motivated by a desire to bring ever more realistic images to his audiences. Ironically, what he created was the most intimate of all photographic representations, a precious and shiny little plate under glass. Henry Talbot, on the other hand, started with the goal of making an amateur sketch for his own use. He eventually achieved something far greater—one of the most powerful mass communication mediums ever devised.

   Out of the Shadows: Herschel, Talbot, & the Invention of Photography (New Haven: Yale University Press, 1992), p. 159.

4. Indeed, as Barthes confesses in the early pages of his book, "[e]ach time I would read something about Photography, I would think of some photograph I loved, and this made me furious. Myself, I saw only the referent, the desired object, the beloved body" (*CL* 7).

5. W. J. T. Mitchell claims that contemporary critical theory's concern with "grammatology," "discourse," and the like echoes "Wittengstein's iconophobia and the general anxiety of linguistic philosophy about visual representation." He regards this anxiety as "a sure sign that a pictorial turn is taking place." *Picture Theory* (Chicago: University of Chicago Press, 1994), pp. 11–13. Martin Jay's *Downcast Eyes: The Denigration of Vision in Twentieth-Century French Thought* (Berkeley: University of California Press, 1994) documents how and from what sources "an essentially ocularphobic discourse has seeped into the pores of French intellectual life" (p. 15).

6. Michel Foucault, *Discipline and Punish: The Birth of the Prison*, trans. Alan Sheridan (New York: Random House, 1979), p. 200.

7. Foucault, *Discipline and Punish*, p. 205.

8. Lefebvre still provides perhaps the most helpful encapsulation of this entire line of argument in his well-known definition of what he calls "social space":

> (Social) space is not a thing among other things, nor a product among other products: rather, it subsumes things produced, and encompass-es their interrelationships in their coexistence and simultaneity—their (relative) order and/or (relative) disorder. It is the outcome of a sequence and set of operations, and thus cannot be reduced to the rank of a simple object. At the same time, there is nothing imagined, unreal or "ideal" about it as compared, for example, with science, rep-resentations, ideas or dreams. Itself the outcome of past actions, social space is what permits fresh actions to occur, while suggesting others and prohibiting yet others.

The trick is to determine precisely how these spaces are produced and their rela-tionship to production *per se*. Having raised this question, Lefebvre turns in the next paragraph to what would become the primary site for researching answers: "Consider the case of a city—a space which is fashioned, shaped and invested by social activ-ities during a finite historical period. Is this city a *work* or a *product*?" Henri Lefebvre, *The Production of Space*, trans. Donald Nicholson-Smith (Cambridge: Blackwell, 1991), p. 73. Edward W. Soja's *Postmodern Geographies: The Reassertion of Space in Critical Social Theory* (London: Verso, 1989) provides a detailed account of the dialectical rela-tionship between the temporal linearity of orthodox Marxisms and the kind of spatial analysis resulting from collaborations among new cultural historians follow-ing Foucault, such historians as David Harvey, and social geographers, who include Soja himself.

9. In *The Urban Experience* (Baltimore: The Johns Hopkins University Press, 1989), Harvey argues:

> Urbanization, together with money rent, usurer's interest, merchants' profits, and state taxation, had to appear on the historical stage before the standard form of circulation of capital through production could begin (cf. *Capital* 1:165). The historical sequence was exactly the reverse, therefore, of the analytical and logical sequences we would now use to analyze the relations of production and distribution of long-term invest-ment in physical and social infrastructures in their urban context. A built environment potentially supportive of capitalist production, con-sumption, and exchange had to be created before capitalism won direct control over immediate production and consumption. (p. 24)

10. *Postmodern Geographies*, p. 59.

11. Soja explains the antagonism to spatial theoretical concerns in these terms: "Most

Marxists, especially at a time of rising orthodoxy, could perceive in the asserted spatial contingency of class only another attempt to impose an 'external' constraint
upon the freedoms of class consciousness and social will in the making of history"
(*Postmodern Geographies*, p. 59). My own argument links such antagonism to the production of images that aided and abetted the urbanization process and to a therefore
well entrenched middle-class assumption that in concerning ourselves with visual
or cultural surfaces, we neglect real things and people. In "Mass Culture as Woman,"
After the Great Divide: Modernism, Mass Culture, Postmodernism (Bloomington: University
of Indiana Press, 1986), p. 45, I find it significant that Andreas Huyssen describes the
figure of woman that shapes the way in which a wide range of authors and theorists regard mass culture in much the same terms as Laura Mulvey describes the role
of woman's image in Hollywood Cinema: as the debased object of the gaze ["Visual
Pleasure and Narrative Cinema," *Screen* 16, 3 (1975): 6–18]. What Huyssen reads in
this figure is a fear of the seductive power of mass culture, while what Mulvey sees
is only its passivity before the spectator's active desire. As a representation of critical
theory's relationship to mass visuality, then, the figure could be said to embody a
complex constellation of fears and desires that prompt us to resist images for the
love of real things.

12. Jonathan Crary, *Techniques of the Observer: On Vision and Modernity in the Nineteenth
    Century* (Cambridge: MIT Press, 1990), p. 129.

13. Norman Bryson has distinguished the glance from the gaze in terms that lay the
    ground for a new historical reading of the Western tradition of painting. I find it
    significant that the opening paragraph of his chapter entitled "The Gaze and the
    Glance" accounts for his project in these terms: "theoretical interest in the image,
    over the past few decades, has been largely preoccupied with the new order of the
    image represented by Photographs," leaving the spectator of painting conspicu-
    ously untheorized. *Vision and Painting: The Logic of the Gaze* (New Haven: Yale
    University Press, 1983), p. 87. Bryson implies that this new work in film and espe-
    cially photography is what allows him to go back and refigure Western painting as
    a dialectic of the Glance (the production and consumption of visual information
    bound by the limits of embodiment in space and time) and the Gaze (which arrests
    and displaces the motion and productivity of the Glance). Because photography
    appears to be the principle of motion-productivity incarnate, we might be tempt-
    ed to equate our relation to such images with what Bryson calls the Glance. But if
    the Glance is what photography objectifies, without any traces of the displacement
    of human eye by camera lens, then it is more accurate to say that the Photograph
    collapses Glance and Gaze in a way that significantly changes the nature and social
    effect of both.

14. Pierre Bourdieu uses the habit of taking photos on the most intimate of all expe-
    riences, the honeymoon, to make this point:

    > The truly complete honeymoon is revealed by the couple [known as
    > J.B. and his wife] photographed in front of the Eiffel Tower, because

Paris is the Eiffel Tower, and because the true honeymoon is the honeymoon in Paris. One of the pictures in J.B.'s collection is bisected by
the Eiffel Tower; at the bottom is J.B.'s wife. What seems to us an act
of barbarism or barbarity is actually the perfect fulfillment of an intention: the two objects designed to solemnize one another are placed
right in the centre of the photograph, as centering and frontality are
the most decisive ways of stressing the value of the object captured in
this way. As a result, the photograph becomes a sort of ideogram or
allegory, as individual and circumstantial traits take second place.

Photography: A Middle-brow Art, trans. Shaun Whiteside (Stanford: Stanford University
Press, 1990), p. 36.

15. Edward Said, *Orientalism* (New York: Random House, 1979); Sander Gilman,
Difference and Pathology: Stereotypes of Sexuality, Race, and Madness (Ithaca: Cornell
University Press, 1985); Malek Alloula, *The Colonial Harem*, trans. Myrna Godzich
and Wlad Godzich (Minneapolis: University of Minnesota Press, 1986); Allan
Sekula, "The Body and the Archive," *October* 59 (Winter, 1986): 3–64; V.Y.
Mudimbe, *The Invention of Africa* (Bloomington: Indiana University Press, 1988);
Thomas Richards, *The Commodity Culture of Victorian England: Advertising and Spectacle
1851–1914* (Stanford: Stanford University Press, 1990); Rey Chow, *Woman and
Chinese Modernity: The Politics of Reading Between West and East* (Minneapolis:
University of Minnesota Press, 1991); Sara Suleri, *The Rhetoric of English India*
(Chicago: University of Chicago Press, 1992).

16. John Tagg, for example, argues "that the meaning and value of photographic practice could not be adjudicated outside specific, histocial language games. Photography
is neither a unique technology nor an autonomous semiotic system." "The
Discontinuous City: Picturing and the Discursive Field," *Strategies* 3 (1990): 147.

17. In *Writing Diaspora: Tactics of Intervention in Contemporary Cultural Studies* (Bloomington:
Indiana University Press, 1993), Rey Chow raises the question that is so rarely asked
about the complicated affect motivating contemporary critiques of Orientalism,
much less about our nineteenth-century predecessors and what attractions exotic
cultures had for them:

> What are we doing talking about modern Chinese literature and Chinese
> women in the North American academy in the 1990s? As such activi-
> ties of speaking and writing are tied less to the oppressed women in
> Chinese communities "back home" than to our own intellectual careers
> in the West, we need to unmask ourselves through a scrupulous decla-
> ration of self-interest. Such declaration does not clean our hands, but it
> prevents the continuance of a tendency, rather strong among "third
> world" intellectuals in diaspora as well as researchers of non-Western
> cultures in 'first world' nations, to sentimentalize precisely those day-to-
> day realities from which they are distanced." (p. 117)

See also Renato Rosaldo, "Imperialist Nostalgia," in *Culture and Truth: The Remaking of Social Analysis* (Boston: Beacon Press, 1989), pp. 68–87.

18. Bourdieu, *Photography*, p. 15.

19. Timothy Mitchell, "Orientalism and the Exhibitionary Order," in *Colonialism and Culture*, ed. Nicholas B. Dirks (Ann Arbor: University of Michigan Press, 1992), p. 295.

20. Gérard de Nerval, *Oeuvres*, 1: 883, quoted in Mitchell, "The Exhibitionary Order," p. 311.

21. Mitchell, "The Exhibitionary Order," p. 304.

22. Bourdieu explains the relationship between the hegemony of middle-class family life and the sheer amount of domestic photography, almost from the beginning of its public availability, but especially after successive inventions brought technology for making faster, simpler, and cheaper images:

    > As the need to take photographs is usually only a need for photographs, it is understandable that all the factors which determine an intensification of domestic life and a reinforcement of family ties should encourage the appearance and intensification of photographic practice: the practice decreases with age because of a decline in involvement in social life and particularly in the life of the scattered family, which does away with the reasons for taking photographs. (*Photography*, p. 25)

23. Lennard Davis argues that novelistic descriptions of place had a similar impact on readers. People did not consider the slums an integral part of their reality, much less find them interesting, prior to the detailed description of such places in the fiction of Balzac and Dickens, which subsequently, according to Davis, "took on a relative life of its own." *Resisting Novels: Ideology and Fiction* (New York: Methuen, 1987), pp. 89–91.

24. Bourdieu, *Photography*, p. 9.

25. Lefebvre, *The Production of Space*, p. 73.

26. Harvey, *The Urban Experience*, p. 33.

27. The *carte de visite*, a photograph mounted on a card two-and-one-half by four inches, could portray any number of things, including celebrities, native peoples, landscapes, artifacts, buildings, important events, and animals. The rage for these images offers just one example of the degree to which photographs saturated the lives of ordinary people. Of "'Cartomania' or 'photomania,'" as it was called, the author of a history of the phenomenon has this to say: "In England alone 300 to 400 million cartes were sold every year from 1861 to 1867." How does he explain its enormous popularity? *Cartes de visite* were small, sturdy, cheap, novel, and diverse, "but the most significant features was their purpose or function, to provide visual information. Despite the name, they were seldom used as visiting cards." William C. Darrah, *Cartes de Visite: In Nineteenth Century Photography* (Gettysburg, Pennsylvania: W.C. Darrah, 1981), p. 4.

28. Bourdieu makes much the same point in rather different terms:

> Although the field of the photographable may broaden, photograph-
> ic practice does not become any more free, since one may only
> photograph what one must photograph, and since there are photographs
> which one must "take" just as there are sites and monuments which
> one must "do." Under the terms of its traditional functions, this prac-
> tice therefore remains traditional in the choice of its objects, its moments
> and its intention. (*Photography*, p. 37)

29. Shelley Rice links the impulse to individuate and aestheticize photographic images directly with the reigning tradition of art history that privileges modernism: "Twentieth century histories of photography are almost invariably Stieglitz-centered, an emphasis that spotlights not only [P. H.] Emerson's ideas but also a certain type of artistic development that, in actual fact, never really excluded alternative forms," especially the forms of pictorialism that offered what can only be called stereotypical images of Victorian life. "Parallel Universes," in *Pictorial Effect/Naturalistic Vision: The Photographs and Theories of Henry Peach Robinson and Peter Henry Emerson*, ed. Ellen Handy (Norfolk, Virginia: The Chrysler Museum, 1994), p. 66.

30. In *Mythologies*, trans. Annette Lavers (New York: Farrar, Strauss & Giroux, 1991), Barthes offers his sharpest critique of the subsumptive function of photography in his analysis of *The Family of Man*. The essay begins: "A big exhibition of photographs has been held in Paris, the aim of which was to show the universality of human actions in the daily life of all the countries of the world: birth, death, work, knowledge, play, always impose the same types of behavior; there is the family of man" (p. 100).

31. Eve Blau, "Patterns of Fact: Photography and the Transformation of the Early Industrial City," in *Architecture and its Image: Four Centuries of Architectural Representation*, eds. Eve Blau and Edward Kaufman (Montreal: Centre Canadien d'Architecture, 1989), p. 44.

32. In her analysis of Manila's new metropolitan form, Neferti Xina M. Tadier argues that in undergoing modernization, "[t]he state understands traffic as it understands the economy—as a system of practices upon the efficiency of which the nation's development depends." It is true that "the liberalized flow or 'drive' [of traffic] allows one who is afforded the privilege of overseeing the city to occupy a self removed from face-to face confrontations with its social contradictions, which are heightened in congested moments." But, Tadier observes, the "desire articulated by this new metropolitan form, . . . does not emanate from a subject outside that articulation; rather, the articulation itself helps to produce the effect of subjectivity," which she describes as "a self that can transcend the human mass." "Manila's New Metropolitan Form," *differences* 5, 3 (1993): 162–164.

33. Mitchell, "The Exhibitionary Order," p. 305.

34. In contrast with the work of such early reformers as John Thomson and Paul

Martin and the later work of Jacob Riis, Blau observes that "Annan's shows no direct engagement with the inhabitants he is documenting. The reformers and photographers of street life went into the slums in search of their inhabitants—to discover and record how and where they lived. For Annan the subject was the *place* itself, not its denizens, except insofar as they were a visible part of the reality of that place" (Blau, p. 49).

35. Given the bluntly documentary purpose of his 1868 volume of thirteen images entitled simply *Photographs of Glasgow,* it is rather ironic that Annan's photographs were recast in a nostalgic format in 1878, when public demand following an exhibition led the Glasgow City Improvement Trust to publish forty carbon prints under the title of *Photographs of Old Closes, Streets, etc. of Glasgow taken 1868–1877.* In the photogravure edition of Annan's Glasgow photos, published in 1900, thirteen years after his death, Blau tells us, "the subversion of the sense of the original set was carried further. . . . Only twenty-eight of these had been in the original set, and some of them had been retouched to remove blurs and other imperfections, so that it had little left of the original survey" by the time certain images were excerpted from the collection and valued for their intrinsic aesthetic qualities (pp. 49–50).

36. See my discussion of spirit photography in "Emily's Ghost: The Cultural Politics of Victorian Fiction, Folklore, and Photography," *Novel* 25, 3 (1992): 245. Also see Gerhard Joseph's discussion of blurring and transparency in "The sharp and the blurred," *Tennyson and the Text: The Weaver's Shuttle* (Cambridge: Cambridge University Press, 1992), pp. 75–87.

37. *Three Essays: On Picturesque Beauty; On Picturesque Travel; and on Sketching Landscape: To Which is Added a Poem on Landscape Painting* (London: R. Blamire, 1972), p. 20.

38. Gilpin, *Three Essays,* p. 28.

39. G. H. Martin and David Francis, "The Camera's Eye," in *The Victorian City: Images and Realities,* eds. H. J. Dyos and Michael Wolff (London: Routledge & Kegan Paul, 1978), illustration No. 91.

40. Tagg, "The Discontinuous City," p. 140.

41. Tagg, "The Discontinuous City," p. 140.

42. See Leonore Davidoff, "Class and Gender in Victorian England," in *Sex and Class in Women's History,* eds. Judith L. Newton, Mary P. Ryan, and Judith R. Walkowitz (London: Routledge and Kegan Paul, 1983), pp. 17–71.

43. Joseph, *Tennyson,* p. 78.

44. Bryan Lukacher, "Powers of Sight: Robinson, Emerson, and the Polemics of Pictorial Photography," *Pictorial Effect/Naturalistic Vision,* p. 39.

45. In "'To the Queen's Private Apartments': Royal Family Portraiture and the Construction of Victoria's Sovereign Obedience," *Victorian Studies* 37, 2 (1993), Margaret Homans explains how "Victoria's performance as a middle-class Queen depended upon the maintenance of a considerable distance between private and

public meanings" and why "[m]ourning brought these public and private meanings of her wifehood into direct conflict" (p. 38).

46. "Of the photographs showing [middle-class) people," observes Bourdieu, "almost three-quarters show groups and more than half show children, either on their own or with adults." He contends that the photography of the family gathering does not preserve a structure of feeling that already exists, so much as it provides the basis for that feeling. Indeed, as the only group to prove capable of preserving its identity in a modern urban society, the bourgeois family could be said to exist by virtue of verbal and visual images that produce the feelings necessary for its survival (*Photography*, pp. 26, 28).

47. See, for example, *Metropolis London: Histories and Representations since 1800*, eds. David Feldman and Gareth Stedman Jones (London: Routledge, 1989); Gavin Weightman and Steve Humphries, *The Making of Modern London 1815–1914* (London: Sidgwick & Jackson, 1983); *The Victorian City: Images and Realities*, eds. H. J. Dyos and Michael Wolff (London: Routledge & Kegan Paul, 1978); Anthony S. Wohl, *The Eternal Slum: Housing and Social Policy in Victorian London* (Montreal: McGill-Queen's University Press, 1977).

48. Karl Marx, *Capital*, vol. 1, trans. Ben Fowkes (New York: Random House, 1977), pp. 165, 167.

49. *Capital*, p. 165.

50. *Capital*, p. 165.

51. Of Crusoe's island, he has this to say: "All the relations between Robinson and these objects that form his self-created wealth are here so simple and transparent that even Mr Sedley Taylor could understand them. And yet those relations contain all the essential determinants of value." *Capital*, p. 170.

BARBARA JOHNSON

I N ONE OF the best known poems
in the English language, John Keats proclaims the superiority of silence over
poetry by addressing a Grecian urn in
the following terms:

> Thou still unravished bride of quietness,
>
>   Thou foster child of silence and slow time,
>
> Sylvan historian, who canst thus express
>
>   A flowery tale more sweetly than our rhyme . . .
>
> Heard melodies are sweet, but those unheard
>
>   Are sweeter . . .

MUTENESS

ENVY

> A slumber did my spirit seal;
> I had no *human* fears:
> She seemed a *thing* . . .
>
> —William Wordsworth
> (emphasis added)

The ego ideal of the poetic voice would
seem, then, to reside in the muteness of
things.

Why does Keats choose to write
about an urn? Why not, for example, a
Grecian frieze? Is an urn somehow
overdetermined as an example of a
thing? When Martin Heidegger had to
choose something as an example of a
thing in his essay "The Thing," he chose a jug. And when Wallace
Stevens placed an exemplary object in Tennessee, it was a jar. What is
it that might make an urn impose itself? Why does Cleanth Brooks
entitle his New Critical treatise on poetry *The Well-Wrought Urn*?

Urns are containers. They can contain the ashes of the dead. They
can also contain water, wine, nourishment. As containers or vehicles,
they lend themselves as metaphors for form itself, or language itself, as
in Francis Ponge's poem about a jug, which ends, "Couldn't everything

I have just said about the jug be said equally well of *words*?" Urns can be metaphors for the relation between form and content, but also between body and soul, expression and intention. Like the most general description of a human being, they have an inside and an outside. Whether we speak of eating or of thinking, we see the human being as a thing with interiority, an outside with something happening inside. Thus, urns are not so much anthropomorphic as humans are urnomorphic. The thing, the human, the poem, and indeed language itself all become metaphors for each other through the urn.

But Keats's urn wears its contents on its *outside*. Does this have anything to do with its idealization of muteness?

Of course, Keats is not the only poet to have made muteness into a poetic ideal. Mallarmé oriented his theory of poetic language toward *"le poème tu, aux blancs."* And in what is perhaps the most explicit expression of the idealization of muteness as a prerogative of things, Archibald MacLeish proclaims in his "Ars Poetica":

A poem should be palpable and mute
As a globed fruit,

Dumb
As old medallions to the thumb,

Silent as the sleeve-worn stone
of casement ledges where the moss has grown—

A poem should be wordless
As the flight of birds.

Yet these poems do not seem to be able to maintain the privilege of muteness to the end. No sooner does Keats convince us of the superiority of the Grecian urn's aphonia, than it speaks. "Beauty is truth, truth beauty," it says; "That is all ye know on earth and all ye need to know." MacLeish's poem, too, is unable to leave well enough alone. It concludes, "A poem should not mean / But be," a sentence that disobeys its own prescription, since, in saying what a poem *should* do, it is "meaning" rather than "being." "Ars Poetica" can be read as a more explicit version of the Grecian urn's final violation of its own apparent rules. Is muteness not really a value, then, or is it simply that language cannot, by definition, say so? Or is it that the utterance "Beauty is truth, truth beauty" *is* a form of silence? What is behind the poem's incomplete commitment to its own muteness envy?

In choosing the expression "muteness envy" to name a recurrent poetic condition, I am consciously echoing Freud's expression "penis envy," which for him marked the nature of sexual difference from the woman's point of view. Since muteness envy seems to be a feature of canonical poetry written by men, could it somehow play into the question of sexual difference? Does the muteness that men envy tend to be feminine? Certainly Keats's urn is feminized, a "still unravished bride of quietness." Doubly feminized, indeed, if the containerlike shape of the urn is denied as anthropomorphic and affirmed instead as gynomorphic. In an essay published in 1954, Charles Patterson offers a "comprehensive and virile interpretation" of the ode, comparing the urn's shape to "the outlines of the feminine body": "the urn is a receptacle, just as is the body of woman—the receptacle from which life springs."[1]

For Mallarmé, too, the blanks and the "white page" that are the material inscription of silence are also the analogues of the female body. And numerous are the Parnassian poems addressed to silent female statues, marble Venuses and granite sphinxes whose unresponsiveness stands as the mark of their aesthetic value, and whose whiteness underscores the normative whiteness of canonical representations of women. Baudelaire parodies this conceit by making Beauty speak her own unresponsiveness and gloat over the muteness of the poets' love for her, while Stevens parodies it by refusing either to feminize or to idealize his jar as it takes deadpan control over the slovenly wilderness. The parodic edge to these poems seems only to confirm the normative image of a beautiful, silent woman addressed by the idealizing rhetoric of a male poet for whom she "seems a thing." There is, of course, nothing new in saying that in Western poetry, women are often idealized, objectified, and silent. Feminist criticism has been pointing this out for at least thirty years. But why is female muteness a repository of aesthetic value? And what does that muteness signify?

Interestingly enough, the silence of women seems to be a *sine qua non* of sexual difference for Jacques Lacan, too, in his translation of Freud's story of anatomical destiny into a story of discursive destiny:

> There is woman only as excluded by the nature of things which is the nature of
> words, and it has to be said that if there is one thing they themselves are com-
> plaining about enough at the moment, it is well and truly that—only they don't
> know what they are saying, which is all the difference between them and me.
>
> It none the less remains that if she is excluded by the nature of things, it is
> precisely that in being not all, she has, in relation to what the phallic function des-
> ignates of *jouissance*, a supplementary *jouissance*.
>
> Note that I said supplementary. Had I said complementary, where would we be!
> We'd fall right back into the all.[2]

In contrast to Freud, whose geometry of castration implies a complementarity between presence (penis) and absence (vagina), Lacan theorizes
feminine *jouissance* as something other than what would fit into that
schema of complementarity. In sexual complementarity, everything is
a function of only one of the terms: the phallus. In sexual supplementarity, woman is that which exceeds or escapes. Which does not
mean that she speaks.

> There is a *jouissance* which is proper to her, to this "her" which does not exist and
> which signifies nothing. There is a *jouissance* proper to her and of which she her-
> self may know nothing, except that she experiences it—that much she does know.
> She knows it of course when it happens. It does not happen to all of them. . . .
> What gives some likelihood to what I am arguing, that is, that the woman knows
> nothing of this *jouissance*, is that ever since we've been begging them . . . —beg-
> ging them on our knees to tell us about it, well, not a word! (pp. 145–146)

In his efforts to collect reliable testimony from women about their pleasure, Lacan finally turns, astonishingly, to a statue, thus writing his own
Parnassian poem:

> You have only to go and look at Bernini's statue [of Saint Theresa] in Rome to
> understand immediately that she's coming, there is no doubt about it. (p. 147)

As Stephen Heath, Luce Irigaray, and Barbara Freeman have remarked,[3]
this is a very odd way to listen to women. But it fits in perfectly
with the idealization of female muteness already in place in the aesthetic tradition.

Returning now to Keats's urn, we find that the question of feminine *jouissance* (or lack of it) is very much at issue. By calling the urn a
"still unravished bride," Keats implies that the urn's destiny is to become
a *ravished* bride. The word "ravished" can mean either "raped" or "sent
into ecstasy." Both possibilities are readable in the scenes depicted
on the urn:

> What men or gods are these? What maidens loth?
>
> What mad pursuit? What struggle to escape?
>
> What pipes and timbrels? What wild ecstasy?

The privileged aesthetic moment is a freeze-frame just prior to rav-
ishment.[4] But how does pressing the pause button here make us sublate
the scene of male sexual violence into a scene of general ecstasy? How
does the maidens' struggle to escape congeal into an aesthetic triumph?

If we turn now to one of the primal scenes of Western literature,
Apollo's pursuit of the nymph Daphne and her transformation into a laurel tree, we will find that the same questions apply. Whether because of
Cupid's mischief or out of her own resistance, Daphne struggles to escape
the god's embrace, becoming a tree—a thing—in a last desperate attempt
to avoid rape. But Apollo not only does not lose; he enters a whole new
dimension of symbolization, plucking off a laurel branch and using it as
a sign of artistic achievement. "Instead of becoming the object of a sexual conquest," writes Peter Sacks in his book on *The English Elegy*,

> Daphne is thus eventually transformed into something very much like a consola-
> tion prize—a prize that becomes the prize and sign of poethood. What Apollo or
> the poet pursues turns into a sign not only of his lost love but also of his very
> pursuit—a consoling sign that carries in itself the reminder of the loss on which
> it has been founded .... If there is a necessary distance between the wreath and
> what it signifies, that distance is the measure of Apollo's loss. Daphne's "turning"
> into a tree matches Apollos "turning" from the object of his love to a sign of her.
> It is this substitutive turn or act of troping that any mourner must perform.[5]

Thus, "any mourner" must identify with Apollo, not Daphne, and the
fact that Apollo does not carry out the intended rape is coded as "loss"—
a loss that becomes a model for the aesthetic as such. The rapist is

bought off with the aesthetic. And the aesthetic is inextricably tied to a silence in the place of rape.

As Christine Froula and Patricia Joplin have argued, that silence has been so inextricably tied to the aesthetics of the literary canon that even the most subtle and insightful of readers have, as we have just seen, tended to perpetuate it. Joplin analyzes the "elision of gender" and the "mystification of violence" in Geoffrey Hartman's celebration of the phrase "the voice of the shuttle" as a beautifully condensed trope for Philomela's tapestry (which testifies to her rape and mutilation after her tongue has been cut out).

> When Geoffrey Hartman asks of Sophocles' metaphor "the voice of the shuttle": "what gives these words the power to speak to us even without the play", he celebrates Language and not the violated woman's emergence from silence. . . . When Hartman ends his essay by noting that "There is always *something* that violates us, deprives our voice, and compels art toward an aesthetics of silence,' the specific nature of the woman's double violation disappears behind the apparently genderless (but actually male) language of "us," the "I" and the "you" who agree to attest to that which violates, deprives, silences only as a mysterious, unnamed "something."[6]

Once again, an "aesthetics of silence" turns out to involve a male appropriation of female muteness as aesthetic trophy accompanied by an elision of sexual violence.

There seems, then, to be two things women are silent about: their pleasure and their violation. The work performed by the idealization of this silence is that *it helps culture not to be able to tell the difference between the two.*

What happens when women attempt to break that silence? Sometimes their speech is simply discounted, as when Lacan claims that feminists get it right about silence but do not know what they are saying, "which is all the difference between them and me." Even in the case of the Grecian urn, penalties apply. Summarizing a history of reservations critics have expressed about the wisdom of allowing the urn to speak at the end of Keats's poem (T. S. Eliot called the final lines "a serious blemish on a beautiful poem"), Cleanth Brooks notes that "[s]ome critics have felt that the unravished bride of quietness protests too much."[7] His reference to Hamlet's mother's reading of women's guilty speech implies that, to many readers, the urn would have been better off observing the silence that, in Milton's words, "gives the proper grace to women." Overdetermined by the aesthetic tradition of women's silence, any speech at all appears as guilty speech. It is as though women were constantly subject to the Miranda warning: "You have the right to remain silent. If you waive that right anything you say can and will be used against you." No wonder Shakespeare's Miranda can only exclaim as she notes the completion of the patriarchal set, "Oh brave new world, that has such people in it!"

Two recent feminist approaches to the speech of girls corroborates these functions of silence. Carol Gilligan's study of adolescent girls' development suggests that when culture teaches girls that their sexual feelings are unseemly, or irrelevant, or secondary to the needs and initiatives of men, they learn to say "I don't know" about their desire.[8] (Interestingly, this is Maria Torok's interpretation of the nature of penis envy: girls who have learned to repress knowledge of their own sexuality project their sexual feelings as the experience of the other sex.[9]) And recent work on child abuse and father-daughter incest, reinforced by Jeffrey Masson's *The Assault on Truth*, his account of Freud's abandonment of the "seduction" theory of hysteria,[10] suggests that girls learn silence not only about sexual pleasure but also about sexual abuse.

Christine Froula, in an essay entitled "The Daughter's Seduction: Sexual Violence and Literary History," makes an analogy between Homer's silencing of Helen and Freud's discrediting of his hysterical patients:

> As the *Iliad* tells the story of a woman's abduction as a male war story, so Freud turned the hysterics' stories of sexual abuse into a tale to soothe a father's ear.... Freud undertook not to believe the hysterics not because the weight of scientific evidence was on the father's side but because so much was at stake in maintaining the father's credit: the "innocence" not only of particular fathers— Freud's, Freud himself, the hysterics'—but also of the cultural structure that credits male authority at the expensive of female authority.[11]

In switching from an alliance with the daughters to an alliance with the fathers, Freud had to translate the "truth" of abuse into the "beauty" of psychoanalysis. At this point we might conclude after Molière, "*Et voilà pourquoi votre fille est muette.*"

Now I would like to explore all these issues as they play themselves out in a recent film and in a series of responses to it. The film, written and directed by Jane Campion, is called *The Piano*. The heroine, Ada McGrath, played by Holly Hunter, is mute. Her "voice" is a piano. It could be said that the piano in the film plays, with respect to Ada, the role traditionally assigned to the Muse with respect to the poet: it is her significant other, herself, and her missing piece. Ada has a daughter, Flora, played by Anna Paquin. Ada has been sent by her father from Scotland to New Zealand to be married to a man she has never met. When she is deposited by sailors on a deserted beach with her daughter, her piano, and a large number of other boxes, she is met by two European men—her husband-to-be, Alisdair Stewart, played by Sam Neill, and another man named George Baines, played by Harvey Keitel—and fourteen Maori men and women. Stewart decides that there are too few people to carry all the boxes plus the piano, and the piano is left on the beach while the party, with Baines translating Stewart's orders to the Maori, makes its way through the dense, muddy New Zealand bush. Ada communicates by writing on a pad hanging around her neck and by signing to her daughter, who translates. She is enraged at the abandonment of her piano.

Shortly after a marriage that seems to take place as a photographic sitting, Stewart leaves to buy some Maori land, and Ada and Flora attempt to persuade a reluctant Baines to retrieve the piano. The three of them visit the piano on the beach, where Baines is fascinated by the emotional abandon of Ada's playing, so different from her normal resistant demeanor. Soon Baines has brought the piano to his own hut and has traded some of his land to Stewart for ownership of the piano, claiming a desire to learn to play. When Stewart tells Ada of the deal, and indicates that she is to give Baines lessons, she is outraged, writing, "No, NO, THE PIANO IS MINE!" on her note pad. Stewart disregards her, saying everyone in the family must make sacrifices. Baines then persuades Ada that she can win back her piano, key by key, in exchange for sexual contact, which begins while she plays, but eventually, for a larger number of keys, takes place in his bedroom. His approach is gradual; her response is resistant, then hesitant. Flora is generally left resentfully outside Baines's hut during these sessions. Then Baines abruptly abandons the bargain, saying, "I am giving the piano back to you. I've had enough. The arrangement is making

you a whore and me wretched. I want you to care for me, but you can't."
Once the piano is installed in Stewart's hut, Ada is confused about her
relation to it, and runs back into Baines's arms. Stewart follows her and
peers at their lovemaking through the cracks in the hut walls. That night
Stewart seems to make no response to what he has seen, but the following day he intercepts Ada as she tries to return to Baines. Stewart
wrestles her to the ground and tries to kiss and touch her. Then he locks
her into his hut. She play the piano furiously, then, at night, enters Stewart's
room and begins to stroke his body, not allowing him to touch hers. This
is the first sexual contact of the marriage. When later Ada learns that
Baines is leaving the area, she removes a key from the piano, writes on
it "Dear George, you have my heart, Ada McGrath," and asks Flora to
take it to him. Instead, Flora takes it to Stewart, who is working with his
axe on his boundary fence. In a paroxysm of rage, Stewart returns to Ada
and chops off one of her fingers, telling Flora to take *it* to Baines. That
night Stewart hovers over Ada's feverish sleep, apologizing, and is then
on the point of taking sexual advantage of the seemingly unconscious
woman when he notices her full attention on him and stops. He then
goes to Baines and tells Baines he has heard Ada's voice saying, "Let Baines
take me away." Soon Ada, Flora, Baines, and the piano are loaded by Maori
oarsmen onto a canoe. As the canoe leaves the shore, Ada asks that the
piano be tossed overboard. When the others obey, she puts her foot in
a loop of the piano rope and is pulled into the sea after the piano. Yet
she does not drown but kicks herself free and returns to the canoe, to
Baines, and ultimately to life in Nelson, New Zealand, as a wife and piano
teacher. While Ada escapes us into banal colonial wifehood, the film ends
by seeming to want to display its allegiance to the English poetic tradition of aestheticizing silence: the last lines uttered are a quotation from
a sonnet by Thomas Hood called "Silence."

How are we to read Ada's muteness in the movie? First of all, like
the urn's, Ada's muteness is not absolute. Not only does she both sign
and write, but at the beginning and end of the film there is a voice-
over that purports to be the voice of Ada's mind. Similarly, Keats's
apostrophe to the urn ensures that it never exists outside the realm of
the anthropomorphic, and even then, it has to talk back in the end.
Like the urn, Ada reassures the spectator that she is not really other,
never absolutely beyond the reach of communication. But also like the

urn, she does not directly answer the questions the spectator might ask. The speaker in Keats's poem asks the urn for names, narratives, legends; the urn answers with chiasmus, tautology, abstraction. The speaker asks for history; the urn resists with theory. Inversely, the men in the film attempt to establish an I–Thou relation with Ada, but her voice-over only links the events of the movie to the past and to the future, and does not offer interpretive guidance through the period—the time actually dramatized in the film—between the initial landing and the final departure from the deserted beach.

The voice opens the movie by saying: "I have not spoken since I was six years old. No one knows why, not even me. My father says it is a dark talent and the day I take it into my head to stop breathing will be my last." First interpretation, then: Ada's muteness is a talent, a talent as strong as life itself.

Stewart, the husband-to-be, is said not to mind the muteness before he sees her, considering that it makes her like a dumb animal, but when he meets her, he begins to wonder whether it is a sign of mental deficiency. This is not because he wants to listen to her—he disregards every explicit expression of her wishes concerning the piano—but because he worries that the merchandise he has bought might be defective. Yet it is he who ends up recognizing Ada's muteness as voice, as will, as resistance. As he reports it to Baines, Ada has in the end said to him, "I have to go, let me go, let Baines take me away, let him try and save me. I am frightened of my will, of what it might do, it is so strange and strong." Of course, Stewart, having just chopped off his wife's finger, may well be frightened of what his *own* will might do. But at least he recognizes Ada as a center of will and desire.

That Ada's muteness is a manifestation of will is confirmed when the voice-over returns at the moment Ada frees herself from the piano rope that is dragging her under the sea: "What a death! What a chance! What a surprise! My will has chosen life!?"

But the final voice-over of the movie suggests that Ada, now married to Baines and fitted with a prosthetic finger, is beginning to pronounce syllables aloud. While the voice-over, like the urn's voice, may be read as a projection, a narrative fiction, perhaps even a prosopopoeia, Ada, at the end of the movie, is beginning to fade into the sound of common voice.

Thus, although Ada is passed from father to husband as a piece of merchandise, her muteness is not a form of passivity or objecthood. It is a form of resistance and subjecthood. But does the resistance and subjecthood of Ada's *character* outweigh the objecthood thrust upon her by the male bargains and decisions that structure the *framework* of her life? What is the movie saying about the muteness that articulates and confuses women's oppression and women's desire?

Reaction to this movie have been remarkably varied. "Jane Campion Stirs Romance with Mystery," wrote Vincent Canby when the film won the Palme d'Or at the Cannes Film Festival. "Wuthering Heights, Move over," wrote Jay Carr in one of two long pieces he published in *The Boston Globe*. Yet some viewers of my acquaintance found its pace intolerably slow and its characters and setting repulsive. Some found it fascinatingly romantic and emotionally gripping. Some consider it pretentious; others marvel at its subtlety. Before I saw it, I was told by one friend that it was a hauntingly beautiful love story, and by another that she experienced it as a narrative of rape. How can we determine whether it is about sexual awakening or sexual violence?

Here I am going to quote two representative readings of the film, both written by women. The first is a quotation from the filmmaker, Jane Campion, herself:

> I have enjoyed writing characters who don't have a twentieth-century sensibility about sex. They have nothing to prepare themselves for its strength and power. . . . The husband Stewart had probably never had sex at all. So for him to experience sex or feelings of sexual jealousy would have been personality-transforming. . . . Ada actually uses her husband Stewart as a sexual object—this is the outrageous morality of the film—which seems very innocent but in fact has its power to be very surprising. I think many women have had the experience of feeling like a sexual object, and that's exactly what happens to Stewart.[12]

For Campion, then, the film is about sex and power and sexual power reversals. It is also, quite explicitly in the published stage directions, about the appeal of fetishistic displacement as sexual surprise: Baines is surprised into excitement while watching Ada play the piano; Ada is surprised into excitement while watching Baines fondle her clothing; Stewart is surprised into sexual jealousy while watching Ada make love to Baines.

In these scenarios, there are only displacements and substitutions—*all* sexuality, not just female sexuality, is supplementarity and excess rather than complementarity. It is interesting, however, that Campion describes the film's depiction of sexual awakening in terms of Stewart rather than Ada. It is he, not Ada, who is the virgin in the story.

Now I would like to quote from another reading of the film, this one a long essay by Margaret Morganroth Gullette, published in *The Boston Globe*. Gullette writes:

> I felt sullied by *The Piano*, muted, mutilated, threatened by rape, pulled underwater and shrouded. Yes, I identified with the heroine. . . . I knew I was supposed to identify as a woman with her Victorian fragility and silencing and her redirected expressiveness. . . . Holly Hunter, one of the tiniest stars in American movies, is used for her anorexic vulnerability. . . . She has the female body type that can be brutalized by men. . . . Serious movies can still get away with torturing women in the audience by portraying them as vulnerable heroines and forcing them through a soft porn experience. . . . What is staggering is how we're asked to relinquish instantly the resentment and obstinacy we've felt on [Ada's] behalf. She may fall in love right on time, by [Baines's] emotional time table, but why should we? At this point my vicarious anger turned into disbelief.[13]

Gullette's review continues in a more autobiographical vein, narrating the feeling she had that the movie, which she saw with her husband of twenty-five years, had gendered and sundered its male and female spectators, that while she was seeing women's entrapment in men's bargains and men's timetables, her husband was seeing the revelation of men's vulnerability and awakening.

The response to Gullette's review from *The Boston Globe*'s readers was astonishing. The *Globe* printed two long rebuttals and seven letters to the editor. One rebuttal protested the projection of twentieth-century feminist ideals upon a nineteenth-century woman (even though it is, of course, a twentieth-century film). Written by someone who calls herself "a feminist and a diminutive woman," the first rebuttal also protested Gullette's use of the phrase "anorexic vulnerability." The writer argues that Ada is strong, bold, vital, and in control every moment. The rebuttal ends:

> *The Piano*'s subject is the empowerment of women despite difficult circumstances, and, as an extension of that, the voices women developed when silenced by a history of

submission. I am curious about the time and space [the *Globe*] devoted to condemn-
ing a film like *The Piano*. . . . Gullette's article would rather make Ada a victim, and
it took a lot of words and, at times, 20th century clichés, to do an inadequate job.[14]

The second rebuttal, also written by a woman, also takes the *Globe*
to task for giving so much space to Gullette's review. The writer rejects
Gullette's reading of the body-for-piano-key bargain as rape, writing,
"Rape is out-of-control violence: Here, in contrast, is a lover's painstaking delight in the sight, touch, texture of the beloved."[15] And the writer
concludes with a portrait of Baines as sensitive and empathic, able to
communicate well not only with Ada but also with the Maoris. The
seven letters published in the *Globe* expressed, in less nuanced terms,
their contempt for Gullette's feminism, their sympathy for her husband,
and their outrage that the *Globe* had given so much space to her review.

I think these reactions are highly significant. The genius of the
movie lies in the fact that it can provoke such diametrically opposed
readings. Like the aesthetic tradition on which it implicitly comments,
The Piano would seem to be about telling, or not telling, the difference
between women's violation and women's pleasure. Yet the readings are
not *simply* symmetrical. Those who view it as a love story and as a reversal of sexual power roles concentrate on the *characters*: Ada is strong,
willful, and in control; Baines is sensitive, restrained, and in love; Stewart
is surprised by emotion and made physically vulnerable. But Gullette's
reading was not based on the individual characters but on their alle-
gorical resonance, the framework within which they operated, and on
the way the *movie*, not the characters, spoke. What message does it convey? she asked. It says that women can find the way of their desire within
a structure in which they are traded between men like land, ebony, and
ivory. It also says that "no" means "yes." Women may be angry, but as
soon as men show any restraint, sensitivity, or need, women will abandon their anger, fall in love, and adapt happily to society as it is. Nothing,
therefore, needs to be changed in the social *structure*. But in that *structure*, Ada does *not* have power. Stewart and Baines may both be responding
to a *sexual* power that Ada does have over them (and there is nothing
new in seeing women's power as sexual), but Baines, not Ada, can decide
to go away, and Stewart has the power to either mutilate her body or
give her to another man. By focusing on the contrast between Stewart

and Baines, rather than on the relation of domination between both men and Ada, or, for that matter, between the Europeans and the Maori, the film encourages us to value the better of the two men rather than to question the whole structure. As bell hooks has noted,[16] the film reveals an analogy among sexual violence, patriarchal power, colonialism, capitalism, and violence against the earth. By romanticizing the borderline between coercion and pleasure in the sexual domain, the film implicitly romanticizes the rest of the chain as well.

While readers of the *Boston Globe* are eager to idealize Ada's muteness—to prove that Ada is not a victim, that her muteness is *not* silence—they are intent on producing a silenced woman elsewhere: Margaret Gullette. Calling her "hysterical" and "strident," they castigate the *Globe* for allowing her so much space. It is as though the taboo on women's speech has simply moved to a new place. Now it is possible for Ada to say both her anger and her pleasure, but not for another woman to object to the message Ada's story might convey. The *Boston Globe* has become the new, respectable father who ought to have known how to keep his daughter mute. This recourse to *institutional* power to keep a woman from speaking is precisely what Margaret Gullette was protesting against.

Interestingly, following a period of otherwise almost unanimous critical enchantment with the film, a different kind of disgruntlement began to surface after its nine Oscar nominations. *Newsweek* quoted one "well-known producer" as saying about the pre-Oscar hype, "I think it's pretentious. . . . 'Aren't we artsy? We're the fancy movie.'"[17] In the same week, *New York* magazine published "Seven Reasons Not to Like *The Piano*":

> Little Girl Vomits on Beach, Too Much Mud, Too Much Ironic Symbolism, Too Much Harvey, Cruelty to Pianos, Revoke that Poetic License! and Impending Appendage Trend (Hunter receives a très chic replacement for her severed finger. If *The Piano* wins Best Picture, won't Tiffany's want to sell authorized movie-tie-in versions? And won't they be too expensive for the people who really need them?)[18]

Somehow, Steven Spielberg's multiple nominations can translate into greatness, but Jane Campion's make her look like just another spoiled woman with expensive and artsy tastes.

Women with expensive and artsy tastes *can*, of course, be idealized, but probably only if they project an image of graceful muteness. One has only to think of the outpouring of feeling around the death of Jacqueline Kennedy Onassis to realize the genius of her adoption of the role of silent image from the moment of the assassination onward. Prior to that time, the woman with a taste for French cooking, redecoration, and Oscar Wilde was a far less idealized figure in the American press. And the contrast between Jackie O's muteness and Hillary Clinton's outspokenness only served to give cultural reinforcement to the notion that grace, dignity, and class could only be embodied by a woman who remained silent.

But the claiming of silence around the film *The Piano* turns out not to be confined to women. The *International Herald Tribune*, reporting on what it called "the backlash" against the film, speculated:

> One theory holds that the initial critical blast that launched the film into the stratosphere simply stunned any doubters into silence.
>
> Slowly, timidly, the naysayers are gathering courage to speak. Most of them appear to be men. "I defy you to tell me what that film is about," said one hyper-male Hollywood producer. . . . Kurt Anderson, the editor of *New York* magazine, said, "I have discovered, to my happiness, that there are significant numbers of people like me who think it has been highly overpraised." The reluctance to carp, he speculated, may have been political: "It arrives with this feminist baggage, or presumed feminist message, that probably shuts people up."[19]

So the whole thing becomes a political game of "muteness, muteness, who's got the muteness," and feminism, having been accused of privileging silence and victimhood, now becomes so powerful that it is a cause of silencing in others.

One of the political successes of feminism, indeed, seems to reside in its understanding of the power of reclaimed silence, a power that is not unrelated to the idealization of muteness found in the aesthetic tradition. It is no accident that every actress who has been nominated for playing the part of a mute woman—Jane Wyman, Patty Duke, Marlee Matlin, and Holly Hunter—has won an Oscar. Indeed, it might be said that the current hysteria about protecting free speech against political correctness, in implicitly claiming that white heterosexual men are being silenced, is enacting its own form of muteness envy.

Feminism seems to have become reduced, in the public mind, to complaints about sexual victimization. Recent publications exemplifying this trend, many of them written by women, include Katie Roiphe's *The Morning After: Sex, Fear, and Feminism on Campus*. I would like to look for a moment at the ways in which this book intersects with what I have been saying about culture's investment in not being able to tell the difference between female victimization and female pleasure. By calling her book "the morning after," Roiphe implicitly ties that undecidability not to a silence that does cultural work but to the question of retrospective individual interpretation ("one person's rape is another person's bad night"). Much of her irritation is directed at the rituals that have grown up around "Take Back the Night" marches on college campuses, in which women who have been raped or abused testify to their experience. What particularly disturbs her is the way in which the speeches on those occasions have tended to constitute a literary genre:

> As I listen to the refrains, "I have been silent," "I was silenced," "I am finally breaking the silence," the speakers begin to blur together in my mind. . . . As the vocabulary shared across campuses reveals, there is an archetype, a model, for the victim's tale. Take Back the Night speak-outs follow conventions as strict as any sonnet sequence or villanelle. As intimate details are squeezed into formulaic standards, they seem to be wrought with an emotion more generic than heartfelt.[20]

Perhaps inevitably, the complaint about genre leads to a complaint about false rape accusations. The power of the literary form to engender fictions becomes the danger of feminism out of control.

Yet, as we have seen, control over the undecidability between female pleasure and female violation has always already been at the heart of the literary canon. Is the "Ode on a Grecian Urn," then, a meditation on date rape? Roiphe claims that contemporary campus feminism resurrects from the Victorian era an image of women as passive sexual victims, an image that her mother's generation of feminists worked so hard to overturn. "Proclaiming victimhood," she writes, "doesn't help project strength."[21] But doesn't it? Why are so may First Amendment defenders so eager to claim a share in the victimhood sweepstakes? Why did Petrarch, the father of the love sonnet, insist that it was he, not Laura, who was wounded, burned, enslaved, and penetrated by love? Even if this is "just rhetoric," why has it achieved such authority? Is it just the sexual equivalent of Christianity?

To speak about female victimization is to imply that there is such a thing as a model of male power and authority that is other than victimization. But what *The Piano* so convincingly demonstrates is that that is only partly true. Yes, for every sensitive man there is a man who chops off women's fingers. But both men are actually depicted in the movie as in some sense powerless. Jane Campion and actor Sam Neill both describe the husband Stewart as "vulnerable."[22] And the movie pivots on George Baines's wretchedness. "I am unhappy because I want you," he tells Ada in true Petrarchan style. "My mind has seized on you and thinks of nothing else. This is how I suffer. I am sick with longing. I don't eat, I don't sleep. If you do not want me, if you have come with no feeling for me, then go!" It is in this male two-step—the axe wielder and the manipulative sufferer, *both* of whom see themselves as powerless—that patriarchal power lies.

Far from being the opposite of authority, victimhood would seem to be the most effective *model* for authority, particularly literary and cultural authority. It is not that the victim always gets to speak—far from it—but that the most highly valued speaker gets to claim victimhood. This is what leads readers of Apollo and Daphne to see Apollo's failed rape as "loss," or readers of "the voice of the shuttle" to say that there is always *something* that violates "us." If feminism is so hotly resisted, it is perhaps less because it substitutes women's speech for women's silence than because, in doing so, it interferes with the official structures of self-pity that keep patriarchal power in place, and, in the process, tells the truth behind the beauty of muteness envy.

NOTES

1. Charles I. Patterson, "Passion and Permanence in Keats's *Ode on a Grecian Urn*" reprinted in *Twentieth Century Interpretations of Keats's Odes*, ed. Jack Stillinger (Englewood Cliffs, NJ: Prentice-Hall, Inc., 1968), p.50.

2. J. Lacan, *Feminine Sexuality*, ed. J. Mitchell and J. Rose (New York: Norton, 1982), p. 144.

3. Stephen Heath, "Difference," *Screen*, Vol. 19 No. 3 (1978); Luce Irigaray, "Cosi Fan Tutti," *This Sex Which Is Not One*, trans. Catherine Porter (Ithaca: Cornell University

Press, 1985); Barbara Claire Freeman, "A Union Forever Deferred: Sexual Politics After Lacan," *qui parle* 4:2 (Spring, 1991).

4. For a brilliant analysis of the relation between aesthetics and sexual violence in Keats's urn, see Froma I. Zeitlin, "On Ravishing Urns: Keats in His Tradition," in *Rape and Representation*, eds. Lynn A. Higgins and Brenda R. Silver (New York: Columbia University Press, 1991). The aesthetic displacement has also been analyzed by Deborah Pope in "The Dark Side of the Urn: A Re-evaluation of the Speaker in "Ode on a Grecian Urn," *Essays in Literature* X, 1 (Spring, 1983). Pope reads the poem as the speaker's increasingly egocentric response to the *urn's* maidenly refusal to answer his questions, nevertheless culminating in his self-effacement before her oracular, perfectly balanced, final pronouncement.

5. Peter Sacks, *The English Elegy* (Baltimore: The Johns Hopkins University Press, 1985), p. 5.

6. P. Joplin, "The Voice of the Shuttle is Ours," *Stanford Literature Review*, 1 (1984), 1, pp. 26, 30.

7. C. Brooks, *The Well-Wrought Urn* (New York: Harcourt Brace, 1947), p. 152.

8. See C. Gilligan, A. Rogers, and D. Tolman, *Women, Girls, and Psychotherapy* (New York: Harrington Park Press, 1991).

9. Maria Torok, "The Meaning of 'Penis Envy' in Women," *differences*, 4 (1992), p. 1.

10. See J. Herman, *Father-Daughter Incest* (Cambridge, MA: Harvard University Press, 1981); and J. Masson, *The Assault on Truth*, (New York: Penguin, 1984).

11. C. Froula, "The Daughter's Seduction: Sexual Violence and Literary History," *Signs* 11:4 (1986), pp. 626, 631.

12. Jane Campion, *The Piano* (New York: Miramax Books, 1993), pp. 135, 138, 139.

13. M. M. Gullette, "'The Piano': Imperfect Pitch," *The Boston Globe*, December 3, 1993, pp. 51, 59.

14. Jane Savoca, *The Boston Globe*, December 17, 1993, pp. 93, 102.

15. Ellie Mamber, *The Boston Globe*, December 17, 1993, p. 93.

16. bell hooks, "Sexism and Misogyny: Who Takes the Rap?", *Z magazine*, vol. 7, no. 2 (February, 1994).

17. *Newsweek*, March 14, 1994, p. 8.

18. *New York*, March 14, 1994, p. 28.

19. *International Herald Tribune*, March 12–13, 1994.

20. Katie Roiphe, *The Morning After* (Boston: Little, Brown, 1993), p. 36.

21. Katie Roiphe, *The Morning After*, p. 44.

22. *The Piano*, p. 139, 147.

DAVID WILLS

1 5 5 3 :

PUTTING A

FIRST FOOT

FORWARD

(RAMUS, WILSON,

PARÉ)[1]

ABOUT THE MIDDLE of the sixteenth century there is a parting of the ways. The medieval trivium of grammar, logic, and rhetoric is breaking up and its parts are being reassigned. But before being a meeting of three ways, the tri*vium* formed the lesser "half" of a dyad existing between it and the quadrivium of arithmetic, geometry, astronomy, and music: knowledge was first divided into a quadrivium of "sciences" and a trivium of discursive arts. Roland Barthes used to suggest that the sense of the commonplace or trifling conveyed by our word "trivial" came not just from the inferior position of the trivium within the medieval model but also from the idea that the intersection of three ways was a place of frequentation, a common place that was also a beat, the locus of prostitution.[2] It would be at that point or by those means that commerce and usury were introduced into human intercourse; it would be therefore the place of corruption in general. One can imagine, from the rhetorical point of view, the space of the prostitute being shared by that of some generic sophist, with the expected attendant degeneracy of discourse. The rhetorical art of "setting forth" one's ideas or discourse would thus be indistinguishable from the "putting oneself forth" that constitutes, etymologically at least, the solicitation of a prostitute.

Through the breakup of the trivium, another "putting forth" emerges, one that is more precisely an "attaching to," namely prosthesis:

to prosthetize is literally to proposition, to prostitute. With the sense
that prosthesis has now obtained, it connotes as much an unholy alliance
as a corrupted rhetoric or prostitution, for by means of it the human
is subjected to an intimate relation with the inanimate. The first recorded use of the word "prosthesis" in the English language occurred in
1553. At that time, against a background of the rise of Protestantism,
the ideas of Aristotle and many other classical forms of knowledge that
had either survived the Middle Ages or even heralded the arrival of
humanism were in retreat. Not least among those were the rhetorics
of Cicero and Quintilian. In 1549, Petrus Ramus (Pierre de la Ramée)
published his *Rhetoricae distinctiones in Quintilianum*.[3] Where Cicero had
installed a five-part rhetoric of *inventio, dispositio, elocutio, memoria*, and
pronuntiatio, Ramus was asking that it be reduced to delivery (*pronuntiatio*) and style (*elocutio*), in effect to the matter of ornamentation that
it represents for us today.

What was true of the philological disciplines was also true in respect
of medicine, particularly anatomy. Andreas Vesalius's *De humani corporis
fabrica* dates from 1543, when he was teaching at Padua. In it, he challenged the classical teachings of Galen, and he is said, as a result, to have
founded modern anatomy. 1543, it should be remembered, was also the
year of Copernicus's *De revolutionibus orbium celestium*. Vesalius
(1514–1564) is almost exactly contemporaneous with Ramus
(1515–1572). So also is another important figure for prosthesis.

In 1552 Ambroise Paré (1510?–1590), a barber who would later
become the king's surgeon, is making his living putting back together the soldiers who are now being more effectively blown apart as a
result of the introduction of handheld artillery and mobile cannon.
He is there at the siege of Metz, where Henri II, taking advantage of
a deal he has made with the Protestant German princes fighting Charles
Quint, is seeking to occupy the town. At a village called Damvillers
near Verdun, in the killing fields of a particularly persistent European
predilection, he tends to the injuries of a *gentilhomme* who is wounded in the leg by a shell that hits the tent of his employer, M. de Rohan,
who is also paying Paré's salary. In order to treat his patient, Paré has
recourse to a practice perhaps formerly used by the Alexandrian school,
but which he will now rediscover and, by so doing, inaugurate modern surgical technique, namely ligature rather than cauterization of

the arteries following amputation. It won't do anymore to amputate a leg with an ax on the field of battle, apply hot oil or sulphur, and watch in puzzlement as the victim bleeds to death, or spends the rest of his life with a constantly reopening wound. I shall spare you the details of Paré's description of how to identify a gangrenous member by its color, by the fact that if you press the flesh it doesn't regain its shape, by its stench such that "standers-by cannot endure it," and so on. Likewise his instructions for amputation of a member: how to nourish the patient with meats, egg yolks, and bread dipped in wine, how to carefully slice away the muscle and ligament around the bone before sawing through it so as to reduce the pain, and so on.[4]

This medical renaissance of the sixteenth century runs parallel with the development, and the immediate dissolution, of humanist rhetoric. There is nothing surprising about that. Classical and medieval forms of knowledge, in various disciplines, were being reappraised and modified; in fact the disciplines themselves were being reconfigured to take their modern forms. Nor is it surprising that a common language and savoir are to be found in fields we now consider to be far apart: rhetoric, medicine, geometry. The scientists of the classical ages could be practitioners or theoreticians as easily of one as of another. But it is within such a context of the rearrangement of fields of knowledge that there occurs, in 1553, the first appearance in English of a word borrowed directly from the Greek, the word "prosthesis," in its rhetorical sense of the addition of a syllable to the beginning of a word. Only in 1704 will Kersey's revision of Phillip's *Dictionary* give to it the contemporary meaning of the "replacement of a missing part of the body with an artificial one."[5] But in 1553, the word is already edging its way into the language in a precise form, as I shall discuss shortly.

I would suggest already, if only for rhetorical effect—the precise figure of which remains to be determined, especially if its effect be the ruination of rhetorical precision—that prosthesis first edges its way into the English language in a period when knowledge in general and the disciplines of rhetoric and medicine in particular are being not just rearranged, but prosthetized, broken apart, and artificially reconstructed. This form of the epistemological break, if that is what it is, is to be read, then, as a prosthetic reattachment. From the perspective of this particular juncture of the sixteenth century, the principles governing knowledge look to have something of the contrived about them; it is as though they have been newly invented, artificially constructed.

But there is, of course, something else that serves as a background to the renaissances of the sixteenth century, something that, although belonging to the previous century, is highly relevant to questions of discourse and rhetoric, as well as to questions of prosthesis; namely the invention of the printing press. The resultant dissemination of texts allowed for debate on the basis of authenticity—questions of correctness of transcription and translation—and at the same time installed the whole problematics of reading and interpretation, the dialectic of commentary versus text. In what might be called this first cybernetic moment, no different of course from the first "moment" of the *techne* in general—memory, the wheel, the pen, what you will—the human hand is superseded by the machine in the service of truth.

This is never in clearer focus than in the case of Ramus. In 1555 he republished his 1543 critique of Aristotle in the French vernacular, a work entitled *Dialectique.* As Antoine Compagnon recounts, the argument with Aristotle aside, the originality of Ramus's text resides in the material form of its typeface:

> In the *Dialecticae Partitiones* of 1543 only a single typeface, namely Roman, is used, except for the preface, which is entirely in italics. Quotation marks are not used, they do not exist. On the other hand, starting with the first French edition of his *Dialectique*, all citations inserted in the text are distinguished by typography: when they are in verse they are printed in italics ... when they are in prose, exclusively that of Cicero, a back-to-front comma appears in the margin at the level of the lines where the citation begins and ends, two such commas appearing in the margin of the intervening lines. These indications, pointing to the quotation marks of the future ... represent an extraordinary innovation.[6]

Thus the written word comes to be marked by its diacritical other, confined first to the margins but already invading the context of writing. What had been uninterrupted discourse, *flumen orationis*, comes to be a text marked with its contrived differences, the artificial enfoldings and articulations that we now take for granted as the markers of accuracy and authenticity. As Compagnon notes, it is this modification of textual forms that characterizes the first printed documents much more than the idea of multiple reproductions, for to begin with, the press did not produce any more copies than could be produced by the largest guilds of scribes (p. 245). But once words attain this materially independent form, their structure can be more explicitly called prosthetic. Writing is based on the explicit cutting up of the printed text, on the manufactured character of the word, on the contrivance of its visual form, on the technologization of knowledge, its removal from human control. It is not for nothing that the press was at first called *ars artificialiter scribendi*, literally the art of writing artificially. "In the sixteenth century," Compagnon writes, "the quality proper to the sign is artifice" (p. 258).

But Peter Ramus is an ocean ahead, or at least away from Thomas Wilson, who publishes his *Arte of Rhetorique* in 1553 and introduces "prosthesis" to the English language. Wilson seemingly offers no radical challenge to rhetorical norms, none, that is, outside of the humanism of his age. He simply sets out to represent the Ciceronian model. 1553 was a good year for words. Probably no better than any other year, but one with some telling introductions. "Cannibal" and "cardamom," "dollar" and "enjoyment," "hyacinth" and "nemesis" are all supposed to have found their way into English that year, as well as both the nouns "prosthesis" and "prostitution."[7] The two forms of unnatural or unholy alliance are named in the language in the same year. The first names a degenerate relation between one integral body and another, an illicit coupling with an outsider; the second names a supplementary relation interior to the body of a word.

"Prosthesis" appears in the third book of Wilson's *Arte of Rhetorique*, "Of apte chusyng and framyng of wordes and sentences together, called Elocucion," in the section entitled "Figures of a worde":

> Those be called figures of a word, when we chaunge a worde, and speake it contrarie to our vulgare and daily speache. Of the whiche sorte, there are sixe in nomber.
>
> i.   Addition at the first.
> ii.   Abstraction from the first.
> iii. Interlacyng in the middest.
> iv.   Cuttyng from the middest.
> v.   Addyng at the ende.
> vi.   Cuttyng from the end.

Examples follow. First:

Of Addition. As thus: He did all to berattle hym.   Prosthesis
Wherein appereth that a sillable is added to this worde (rattle.)

Then examples of apheresis, epenthesis, syncope, proparalepsis, and apocope.[8]

What must be noted about this list of Greek words ornamenting the margins of a section of Wilson's *Rhetorique* is precisely their marginality. Wilson does not yet follow Ramus's lead in using quotation marks (first used in an English text in 1579),[9] but the rubric headings are clearly separated from the text. And, by a strange quirk that we could well make much of, the single word "prosthesis," in contradistinction to the other terms and the text proper, appears in Roman type rather than black-letter gothic. It is also in a larger pitch than the other terms in the margin. "Prosthesis" thus more clearly marks its foreignness, the fact of its being a translation, and for us of course, the fact of its effecting a translation. For being the first known printed use of the word, it is doubtful, therefore, to what extent this event signals the entry of "prosthesis" into English. Or rather, then as now, it can never simply enter the language, never be simply assimilated, for it is the sign and index of nonassimilation, the originary dehiscence that ruptures the integrity of language and meaning itself. This nonentry signifies precisely a form of foreignness that is revealed to be always already attached to the body lexical and philological. As the continuous stream of medieval discourse is being broken by spatial articulations that appear on the printed page, one of the words performing that task is a word whose sense is hereunto restricted to a minor orthographical variation, but on the basis of which the integrity of any body will come to be dismantled and reconstructed.

The question of foreignness returns in Wilson's disparaging of what he calls "ynkehorne terms," borrowed linguistic mannerisms that those who have just come back from abroad like to pepper their plain, "native" English with (p. 326). But as he explicitly acknowledges in another context, the exercise of translation or linguistic importation is fundamental to rhetoric itself: it is a bending of discursive norms, a digression towards difference (pp. 341–343). More difficult still is the need to distinguish between bending and breaking, a difficulty that can be read through a complicated configuration of questions of the rhetorical commonplace as image, of the church as paradigm for the commonplace, and the problem of idolatry. I do not have space to discuss that in detail, but briefly, Wilson's argument can be analyzed as the difficulty of advocating the iconoclastic fervor of the Protestant impulse while at the same time preserving the integrity of the holy commonplace. Idols, and by extension images, should be banished from the kingdom, he says, without realizing that Aristotelian rhetoric, to the extent that it assigns an image to some sort of sanctuary, is by definition idolatrous.

But nowe, because I have halfe weried the reader with a tedious matter, I will harten him agayne with a merye tale.

Four hundred years later, about the middle of the twentieth century, in 1953 to be precise, another Wills' son is born, born to a man who, some fourteen years earlier, had his left leg amputated. Some nineteen years after that date, they part ways. They ride in the car to a point on the edge of the town where the son will get out to hitchhike his way to the city where he now lives and studies. It is early one winter morning with the frost on the ground and the light shining in eerie refractions through the shroud of fog as my father sets me down at an intersection that gives birth to a straight stretch of road leading into the countryside. There he bids me farewell. It is a meeting of four ways, this place of separation, a well-frequented nexus of common automobile comings and goings and perfect for the particular solicitation I am about to embark upon. Someone will pick me up, provided I am walking rather than appearing to loiter, and for the price of some company and humdrum if inquisitive conversation, I will be given a ride at least part way to my destination. And so we part ways, my father and I, but only in a manner of speaking. There is nothing momentous about the incident, just an unidentifiable sentiment of emptiness coupled with an uneasiness about what to say more exaggerated than the normal taciturnity of our relations. Even sitting side by side in the car, with its automatic gearbox that no longer requires the use of two legs, we both know we are already traveling in different directions. But gone is the tug of fierce resistance or open revolt on my side, gone the ultimatums and threat of rejection on his. This is not yet an acceptance of a new relationship on renegotiated terms, but something a little more reassuring than an uneasy peace. We come to the same spot where he has deposited me before, and he lets me go with a friendly handshake, and presses a five-dollar note into my palm. Suddenly there is a place and an image for my memory. This point, halfway alighting from a car, between two places rather than safely positioned within one, on the mobile threshold of a separation, becomes the locus for my recollection of the scant extent of my medical experience. For whereas he at my age had suffered through the pain of the scalpel, the loss of a limb, the fear of a recurring disease and likely death, or at least the anticipation of a crippled adulthood, I had felt nothing more than the prick of an occasional inoculation.

There is one in particular that comes back to me at that precise moment. The inoculations were dispensed with bureaucratic regularity—a special form of irregularity that is dependable in its repetitions but less so in its punctuality—by the health authorities through the public school system. It seems we were vaccinated against polio, measles, tetanus, and the like, mostly by injection, but later more and more by oral ingestion. It was an event that disrupted the tedium of classes but brought with it its own dose of adrenaline and nervousness, the more so the younger we were. But I have to say I was used to the idea of inoculations. I no longer remember why I missed the one in question, but the reason was no doubt one of the minor illnesses that children fall prey to, which had kept me at home on the appointed day. As a result, I had to go to another school to catch up on an injection. I recount this only because the prospect was as terrifying to me as the threat of the scalpel or the rack. Not the injection itself, but having to go to a foreign place to subject myself to it.

It seems likely that I was seven or eight years old, but I may have been nine or ten. The memory is of an inordinate fear completely out of proportion with both the gravity of the occasion and my supposed maturity and ability to cope with it. I came home at lunchtime, walking the block and a half, across the pedestrian crossing to the tiny "dairy" as we called it, the corner store that survived my final departure by only a couple of years, and by then it was no longer the place where one could purchase fresh bread baked daily or where the delegated class representative would take the orders for those fortunate enough to get to buy lunches rather than having to eat the boring sandwiches we got up early each morning to make once we were old and able enough, before that it was my sister or my mother, and only once a year on our birthdays were we allowed to add our order to the list carried that morning across the road to the dairy, an event that required days of forethought, but however difficult the task it was not one that concerned me that day as I walked home past the dairy, crossing the road on my own, looking left, then right, then left again, I could never shake that routine nor manage to reverse it correctly once I came to countries where they do roads and cars back to front, but that wasn't concerning me either that day, I was simply looking forward to the half hour or so of sanctuary I would have once I was home and eating whatever my mother had prepared for lunch before leaving with my father to go to that other school. I turned left at the end of the long driveway that led to our house, at the point where the garbage bins were placed on Sunday nights, the point at which I would wave to my cohorts in the first year of school when those of us they called "tiny tots" were escorted home in pairs holding hands and I was always first to fall out until someone else had the temerity to live even closer to school than me, and the others would continue on their way I never understood exactly how far, for surely their destinations would begin to diverge exponentially after a few blocks, but be that as it may, I turned left where I had a couple of years previous been used to parting ways from my classmates and headed up the driveway just as my father turned his car in off the road, which became the pretext for a feigned race up to the house, where sure enough lunch was waiting, and where the time passed altogether too fast, even including the ten minutes my father stretched out on his back on the bare floor for his catnap, and we were soon in the car together again heading in the same direction down the driveway and across the narrow bridge spanning the river called the Waikato, it means "swiftly flowing water" in Maori, across to the other side of town where my father worked at a job that was far from a calling, but whatever calling may have come his way had been preempted both by his parents' reluctance—informed by their religious beliefs—to let him embark upon an intellectual career, and the fact of an amputation coming soon after the end of his secondary studies, and then later by the fact of an increasing number of mouths to feed, four in reasonably quick succession and then two more after me, but he went to the job every day and came home nearly every day for lunch and he took me back with him to a school that was far from mine and let me go in the care of someone I didn't recognize and don't remember, I don't remember much about it at all, just sitting waiting on a bench with a group of children who were all complete strangers and who saw no reason to speak to me, I don't even remember the injection, and there may or may not have been an increase or diminution of a personal touch accorded me once they were informed I was a special case with a file sent from another district, I couldn't tell and wouldn't remember, only that the supervising teacher was kind and when it was all over I walked the short distance from the school back to my father's place of work and he drove me home again, and it was then, at about two o'clock in the afternoon, with an hour or so of schooltime remaining, that I balked at the idea of returning to school, it seemed such a monstrous thing to do, not because I didn't enjoy class-es, on the contrary, and not because I couldn't have caught up on what I had missed, or wouldn't have been accepted back into the swing of things, or wouldn't even have had a tale or two to tell my friends about the school on the other side of town, but there was no getting away from it, I just didn't want to do it, I even broke down and cried in the bitter dejection that has me astonished even now from which perspec-tive I still cannot fathom the reason of it, some rubicon had been crossed, in some way I had gone over, I had left, I had parted ways with my own sense of direction and found myself drowning in the uncertainty of my eight year old position in the world all over the matter of a vaccination, my overwhelmingly minor skirmish with the fringes of the medical establishment outside of the experienced boundaries of my own school, or the doctor's surgery, or the sickbed at home, I was floundering in a rhetorical void without so much as a commonplace to set my bearings on, I just cried from the confusion and my parents explained that my absence for the whole afternoon had not been envisaged and that I would have to return to school, and I could only be induced by having my father put me back in the car once more and drive me the block and a half to the school gate, the only time in memory that he ever did so, and though my tears were dried by that point he tousled my hair before I alighted and pressed a coin into my hand, it was a sixpence and my prize for being grown up enough to do what had to be done, but

I felt an inexplicable combination of gratitude and resentment, gratitude for his staying with me through the whole thing, going the extra seventy-five yards, and resentment because I didn't think I deserved the sixpence, and besides those two a third sentiment, that which comes with being party to a collusion, for the sixpence fitting neatly in the centre of my palm was like a talisman that betokened a pact, the secret of that experience that was shared only by my father and myself, the sign that an amputee buffeted by the rigors of pains real and phantom understood a child's fear of a needle administered by a strange hand in a foreign place, it was a coin the size of a nickel but the thickness of a dime, with the impression of a queen on one side and a bird called a fantail on the other, and it would not survive the changeover to decimal currency, once the dollar had entered the language and the mechanics of exchange, the sixpence disappeared taking with it all it betokened, the details of a moment between father and son, the mystique of a prize given by one to the other, it had long disappeared by the time prize-giving came around some years later, when I had doubled my age, and was close to the point of departure of this recounting, there were two prizes that came my way in my last year in high school, one for English and one for Latin, endorsable for books only, I had never possessed many of those, the occasional birthday present, the annual prize, and the texts we used in classes were provided by the school and had to be returned to the common pool, and through most of my childhood the only books at home were a small number of reference volumes and a shelf full of tomes of biblical exegesis and the like, so it was with a delight approaching kleptomania that still loosens my bowels among the library stacks that I looked forward to choosing my two volumes, and not from the selection that was set aside for that purpose on a table in one of the study rooms, for in recognition of my status as a final year student I was given a token for a certain sum and accorded utter liberty in procuring the books of my choice from a local bookstore, and I knew what I wanted already, and I knew that I wanted it as much out of provocation as anything else so I walked straight up to the attendant and asked for a copy of *Ulysses* to be placed aside and inscribed with the insert for presentation at the prize-giving ceremony, after which I took it home to show my father and his father who happened to be visiting at the time, and it was a long time before I read the book but I had handed it as a challenge back to my father, as if it were bought with the sixpence of my discomfort all those years earlier, not so much as an act of revenge, conscious or unconscious, for all this is a contrived association in any case, a rhetorical convergence more than anything else, but rather as if to declare that I had assumed that type of discomfort as a way of life, to acknowledge that to some extent I had learned it from him and from his infirmity, and in response to nothing more threatening than an occasional inoculation this son of his prosthesis had opted for such a form of masochistic pleasure that I now chose to enter the foreign world of unease that a *Ulysses* opened up, to become a purveyor of translation and the byways of discursive transfer, whichever way one looked at it, and although the word was never uttered, never to my knowledge entered the language of our familial intercourse, not from 1953 till 1972, no such word uttered by these Willssons and daughters in spite of the striking example of it that was permanently attached to the margins of all their dealings, although I never remember hearing the word he quietly passed me his prosthesis across the generational divide, like a new word coined, or a coin pressed into the hand at the point we parted, when I was to set out on my own from the intersection of ill-formed desires and indistinct ambitions he surreptitiously handed over a quandary, slipped me a clunker or a pickle I could only smile and be grateful for, an aptitude for the discomfort of strange relations, a contrived convergence between patent differences that appears to have been shadowing the discursive vagrancy for four centuries until this particular triage, this intersection of argument and digression, this double commentary of the scholarly and the dilettantish that meets only to part ways again.

As early as 1525 the prosthetic was involved in complicated networks of exchange. Referring to a teenage experience Ambroise Paré recounts the following:

> Anno Dom. 1525. when I was at Anjou, there stood a crafty beggar begging at the Church dore, who tying and hiding his owne arme behind his backe, shewed in steed thereof, one cut from the body of one that was hanged, and this he propped up and bound to his breast, and so laid it open to view, as if it had been all enflamed, so to move such as passed by unto greater commiseration of his. The cozenage lay hid, every one giving him mony, untill at length his counterfeit arm not being surely fastened, fell upon the ground, many seeing and observing it: hee being apprehended

and layed in prison, by the appointment of the Magistrate, was whipped through the
towne, with his false arme hanging before him, and so banished. (p. 993)

About that time the discipline of medicine was breaking up and
its parts being reassigned. At first only lowly barbers had interfered with
the integrity of the living body, but they gradually gained the right to
their own academic training and the discipline came to be divided
among barbers, barber-surgeons, surgeons, and doctors. Paré was a mar-
ginalized medical practitioner until his experiences in the field hospital
led to a meteoric upgrading of his status. It is thus as a new man of
science who is also an iconoclastic reformer that he publishes his very
comprehensive works, defending himself against the attacks of doctors
and writing in French so that his knowledge might be shared with a
wider audience.

But the surgeon who speaks of certain areas of knowledge with a
rationalism we would more readily recognize as belonging to later centuries is the same writer who lapses into descriptions of monsters as
well as a lengthy digression on the unicorn, never doubting its existence
both terrestrial and subterranean, but seriously questioning the use of
its horn for remedies against the plague. He is surprised at the reactions
to opinions he had published on the subject, and even more surprised
by the "linguistic excesses" of his detractors. He becomes for a moment
a rhetorician, claiming that by publishing his opinions he was only seeking to provoke a debate, and presuming that anyone who disagreed
would still respect the norms of such debate. But we should read this
concern over the fragility of academic civility as concern about the
integrity of his own discipline, an anxiety that arises precisely from the
fact that he is rewriting its norms and reconfiguring it (his anxiety is
thus parallel to that of Wilson over the image). For Paré, surgery is quite
simply the discipline of the prosthetic: from the very beginning its operations are five in number, "namely: taking away what is superfluous;
putting back what has been displaced; separating the continuous; join-
ing the separate; helping nature by adding what is lacking" (p. 4). But
the structure of the prosthetic is also the structure of monstrosity.

The matter comes into clear focus in Books 21 to 25 (respectively on smallpox, measles, worms and leprosy; the plague; prostheses;
human reproduction; monsters and marvels). Such a juxtaposition of

a rich teratology and a detailed treatise on prosthetics is particularly telling. The monsters appear everywhere: Paré cannot advance his discussion of the parts of the body that need to be protected from smallpox without digressing for a number of pages to write "Of certain monstrous animals that inhabit the bodies of men, women and children," including the little red living creature he draws for us that M. Durer expelled from his penis after a long illness, and the mass of formless flesh that moved and lived like a sponge that he believed to have come out of the womb of a woman, shortly to be followed by a monster with a hook nose, a long neck, a pointed tail, and agile feet, a cross between a dragon and a lizard with a slightly human head, which is also drawn for our edification (pp. 762–764). Many more such monsters are described in Book 25, where Paré goes into their causes at some length. Within the same discussion, there occurs the account of the charlatan beggar cited above, and that of a forty year-old Parisian man with no arms who could perform "all those things which are normally done with the hands . . . lash[ing] a coach-mans whip, that he would make it give a great crack. . . . He ate, drunke, plaid at cardes, and such like, with his feet. But at last he was taken for a thiefe and a murderer, was hanged and fastened to a wheele" (p. 976).

In Paré's schema, the monster, the mutant, the criminal, and the amputee share the same discursive space, a space that is also that of prosthesis. Book 23, "Of the Meanes and Manner to repaire or supply the Naturall or accidentall defects or wants in mans body," is extensive in its explanation of the use of prosthetic devices, all of them accompanied by diagrams, taking into account aesthetic as well as orthopedic concerns: artificial eyes, either round objects inserted into the sockets or flat fronts made of painted leather and held in place by a taffeta- or velvet-covered wire around the head; a mask to correct squinting in children; gold, silver or papier-mâché noses; teeth, obturators of the palate fit for a cancerous psychoanalyst; tongues; ears attached in the same way as an eye; corsets to correct a stoop; portable bedpans for incontinence, a canula for lopped-off penises; artificial hands, including one with a pen permanently held between its fingers. When it comes to legs there is the ordinary wooden leg, a peg leg consisting of a leg, an open socket, straps to hold the stump in the socket, and—the problem of articulation of animate and inanimate a constant concern—

a cushion for the stump to rest on. And then there is the full-fledged artificial leg, with fifteen movable parts and armorlike coverings. Paré reads here like nothing so much as the extraordinarily familiar calling across the divide of four centuries; or the extraordinarily foreign looking as familiar as something my father discarded nightly in the corner of his bedroom, or propped against the wall of a changing shed at the edge of dozens of childhood beaches.

The prostheses of Book 23 keep such close company with monstrosity, contagion, and natural generation precisely because, in allowing for the artificial so close to what is natural, prosthesis opens the structure of mutancy. The monsters "exist" because the surgical interventions that made possible the wearing of modern prosthetic devices, for which the paradigm remains the artificial limb, brought into particular focus the competing discourses of the organicist and mechanicist conceptions of the human body, putting the machine into a close and uneasy relation with the organic. History will claim that it is William Harvey's discovery of the circulation of the blood in 1628 that represents the Copernican revolution in medicine that is absent from the sixteenth century, but such a discovery remains within the organicist continuum.[10] Paré's amputations and prostheses, on the other hand, make explicit the very break that constitutes the human body; the mechanicist rupture that is its relation to and dependence upon the inanimate, the artificial. Such a break is readily identifiable as belonging to the middle of the fifteenth century, in Paré's amputations and prostheses, and before that in Vesalius's *De humani corporis fabrica*, whose title alone is suggestive of the mechanical.

Prosthesis does not simply give rise to the monstrous, or revive a fear of the same: monstrosity, and by extension criminality, is a function of the mechanical or technological itself. That is evident everywhere, from Paré's beggar waving a hanged man's arm, to Hoffmann's automaton analyzed—insufficiently I would hold—in Freud's "The Uncanny." Prosthesis occurs on the border between the living and the lifeless; it represents the monstrosity of interfering with the integrity of the human body, the act of unveiling the unnatural within the natural. But as Paré makes clear from the outset, prosthesis also defines the very act of surgical intervention, and, as my associating him with Ramus and Wilson suggests, it also defines the contrivance that is rhetoric and indeed all discourse.

Let me conclude with this reflection. The history of European languages provides for two categories of rhetorical relation. The first consists in terms borrowed directly from the quadrivium, in particular geometry, namely trope, parable, hyperbole, and ellipsis, spatial configurations referring to the curving departures from a presumed flat or straight, zero-degree line of discourse. The second type, exemplified by the term "prosthesis," consists in a lexicon shared with medicine, where the terms describe a range of medical or surgical conditions or procedures. Now, apart from the already-stated, obvious explanation for that—namely the fact of shared disciplinary space within either or both of the classical and medieval configurations of knowledge—one might be able to speculate a little more on differences between the two rhetorical terminologies, the geometrical and the medical. An obvious contrast between the two sets of figures is that the first refers to variations in the flow of discourse, whereas the second signifies interventions with respect to the morphology of the word. In the case of the tropes, the specific departures from normal usage are charted against static axes; there is, as it were, an elliptical distortion of what is called standard usage. In the case of interventions within the word, it is as if the line of discourse has been broken rather than stretched. It might be argued that, in the case of these "medical" figures, it is not so much a spatial relation that is set in play, that which fits within the topos, as the actual articulation of linguistic elements: operations of removal or addition waiting in the limbo of a foreign language, on the edges of a treatise on rhetoric and on the edge of an institutionalized admission to English. But waiting not so much for the door to open, as for the whole adjacent ground to shift enough to include them.

The gamble undertaken here is to produce a text whose writing becomes an exemplar of the rhetoric of that taxonomy and that history: something of the lost rhetoric of the divergence between philology and medicine, and something of a rhetoric of shifts or divergences in general, the always possible and necessary future divergences of discursive and disciplinary cohesion. Thus prosthesis will be a figure for which the term "figure" is no longer appropriate, for it betokens a writing that obeys a whole other dynamism, that of constantly shifting relations—or at least a figure for which neither Euclidean geometry nor modern surgery can provide the models, requiring us to look towards some cybernetic or bioengineered future. With respect to such a future, a prosthetic rhetoric has a vague ambivalence. It can only be told in a combination of declaration and instantiation, and then in the analogies, hyperboles, and ellipses against whose background it emerges. But its mutation is such that all of those figures are denied any consistency, being prey to the dynamic of the shift. This prosthesis cannot tell a straight analogy from an inconsistent one, for it is the figure of an inconsistency that it cannot adequately describe, the inconsistency that has it limping outside its own limits, hobbling uneasily towards some unknown that it knows it will never reach, across a parting of ways or at least some token of it, like a sixpence handed across a space too cluttered for either plainness or figure to tell, where I go to take a step and can't find forward, for the leg I am using is borrowed, and I am using it for the first time.

NOTES

1. Reprinted by permission of the publisher, Stanford University Press, from David Wills, *Prosthesis*, copyright 1995 The Board of Trustees of the Leland Stanford Junior University. No portion of this text may be reproduced without the express permission of the publisher.

2. "A writer . . . must have the persistence of the watcher who stands at the crossroads of all other discourses, in a position that is *trivial* in relation to purity of doctrine (*trivialis* is the etymological attribute of the prostitute who waits at the intersection of three roads)." Roland Barthes, "Inaugural Lecture, Collège de France," in Susan Sontag, ed., *A Barthes Reader* (New York: Hill and Wang, 1982), p. 467.

3. Petrus Ramus, *Rhetoricae distinctiones in Quintilianum (Arguments in Rhetoric Against Quintilian*, trans. Carole Newlands (Dekalb: Northern Illinois University Press, 1986).

4. See Ambroise Paré, *The Collected Works of Ambroise Paré, Translated out of the Latin by Thomas Johnson, from the First English Edition, London, 1634* (Pound Ridge, NY: Milford House, 1968), pp. 457–463.

5. *The Barnhart Dictionary of Etymology* (New York: H. H. Wilson, 1988), p. 852.

6. Antoine Compagnon, *La seconde main ou le travail de la citation* (Paris: Seuil, 1979), pp. 246–247, my translation. According to a recent study, the 1529 edition of Geoffroy Tory's *Champfleury* is the first French text to use quotation marks. See M. B. Parkes, *Pause and Effect: An Introduction to the History of Punctuation in the West* (London: Scolar Press, 1992), p. 58.

7. Thomas Finkenstaedt, Ernst Leisi, and Dieter Wolff, *A Chronological English Dictionary* (Heidelberg: Carl Winter Universitätverlag, 1970), pp. 487–489.

8. *Cf. Arte of Rhetorique by Thomas Wilson*, ed. Thomas J. Derrick (New York: Garland, 1982), pp. 353–354.

9. "During the sixteenth century the *diple* was employed as a nota in the margins of printed books. . . . In type the *diple* was represented by a pair of semi-circular comma-marks. . . . At first the *nota* was printed in the margins outside the regular type measure, and, as in manuscripts, opposite each line of text containing part of a quotation. . . . Towards the end of the sixteenth century the comma-marks representing the *diple* were removed from the margins and set within the page measure. They were employed in this position alongside quotations within the gloss to 'Maye' in the first edition of Spenser's *The shepheardes calender* (London: H. Singleton, 1579)." Parkes, p. 58.

10. "Although the Renaissance doctor, man of all the sciences, is indeed implicated in the intellectual ferment that marks his epoch, it still remains that as far as his own field of knowledge is concerned he does not call into question Galen's system. . . . Contrary to the other sciences there is no Copernican revolution in medicine." Marie-José Imbault-Huart, "La Renaissance, la médecine et la chirurgie." in B. Crenn, ed., *Actes du colloque international "Ambroise Paré et son temps"* (Laval: Association pour la Commémoration du quadricentenaire de la mort d'Ambroise Paré, 1991), p. 109, my translation.

CHILD

CORA KAPLAN

TWO WHITE and spectral, little, little girls, hybrids of the human and faery, haunted the childhood passages of women's fiction in the late 1840s, sign and symptom of a historical rewriting of the nature of identity that was much more, yet not much less, than personal.

The first child, reflected in the "visionary hollow" of the Red Room's "looking-glass" (p. 11) is still familiar to us as Jane Eyre alienated to herself—become briefly, through abuse, rage, incarceration, and terror, "the strange little figure there gazing at me, with a white face and arms specking the gloom, and glittering eyes of fear moving where all else was still . . . like one of the tiny phantoms, half fairy, half imp, Bessie's evening stories represented as coming out of lone, ferny dells in moors. . . ." (p. 11).

The second child, a revision and intensification of the first, is more elaborate: the tiny crippled heroine of Dinah Mulock Craik's 1850 novel *Olive*, as first presented to her horrified father, Captain Angus Rothesay:

"A HETEROGENEOUS THING":

FEMALE CHILDHOOD AND THE RISE OF RACIAL THINKING IN VICTORIAN BRITAIN

Thus from a Mixture of all Kinds began,
That Het'rogeneous Thing, An Englishman. . . .
—Daniel Defoe, *The True-Born Englishman*[1]

They were not bound to regard with affection a thing that could not sympathize with one amongst them; a heterogeneous thing, opposed to them in temperament, in capacity, in propensities. . . .
—Charlotte Brontë, *Jane Eyre*[2]

The door opened and Elspie led in a little girl. By her stature she might have been two years old, but her face was like that of a child of ten or twelve—so thoughtful, so grave. Her limbs were small and wasted, but exquisitely delicate. The same might be said of her features; which, though thin, and wearing a look of premature age, together with that quiet, earnest, melancholy cast peculiar to deformity, were yet regular, almost pretty. Her head was well-shaped, and from it fell a quantity of amber-coloured hair—pale "lint-white locks," which, with the almost colourless transparency of her complexion, gave a spectral air to her whole appearance. She looked less like a child than a woman dwarfed into childhood; the sort of being renowned in elfin legends, as springing up from a lonely moor, or appearing by a cradle-side; supernatural yet fraught with a nameless beauty. She was dressed with utmost care, in white, with blue ribands; and her lovely hair was arranged so as to hide, as much as possible, the defect, which, alas! was even then only too perceptible. It was not a humpback, nor yet a twisted spine; it was an elevation of the shoulders, shortening her neck, and giving the appearance of a perpetual stoop. There was nothing disgusting or painful in it, but still it was an imperfection, causing an instinctive compassion—an involuntary "Poor little creature, what a pity!"[3]

The girls in these scenes of faery ethnography represented in one aspect the vanishing point or the question of mark of their gender, race, and species, their spectral whiteness, minimal embodiment, and elfin or dwarfed inheritance placing them at the borders of the European, the female, the human. From another perspective—and there are more than two—they were an exaggeration, an idealized diminutive of all these categories: their pallor a denial of a treacherously racializing pigmentation, their smallness encoding an infantile presexual femininity, their folklore genealogy, so firmly British and rural—antimetropolitan as well as anticolonial—retranslating them into a national superhuman.

In this essay I intend to pursue the larger questions that these fictional children pose through a mini-inquiry into a fragment of the historical development of modern childhood. I am interested in analyzing a pattern of small changes that took place during a few critical years in the late 1840s, mutations in the protofeminist narratives by women that featured small female persons and that incorporated both wide-ranging contemporary discussions about human origins and difference and debates about national belonging. I have chosen Brontë's *Jane Eyre* (1847) and Craik's *Olive* first of all because both books brought these debates overtly within their covers, appropriating, critiquing, and feminizing their theory, their domestic and imperial politics, their Africanist discourse and their cast of characters. This they each did quite independently, but there was also, one may conjecture, an indirect critical engagement between the later and earlier texts, for *Olive* followed close upon the heels of *Jane Eyre*'s success, and its precocious author, still in her mid-twenties, paid a backhanded tribute to *Jane Eyre* by reproducing some of the contours of Brontë's plot. From this partly shared narrative ground, Craik mounted her own literary claims by contesting, through her revisions of *Jane Eyre*, several of its central arguments.[4]

Little girls, of course, figured prominently in fiction by men in the 1840s and 50s; we have only to remember Dickens's Florence Dombey, Esther Sommerson, and Little Dorrit, imagined children who also condensed and provoked anxieties about the categories of the human. We might begin therefore by asking what position these diminished and/or deformed female children held in the structure and content of protofeminist fantasies in these years. It may help our inquiries if we provisionally ascribe such fantasies to an imagined entity, let us call her a Subject of Feminism, a figure of speech who represents not a person, an author, or a character, or even an established discourse, but rather a developing stance, a set of ideas in process which question the logic of women's subordination in culture and nature. This Subject of Feminism has been described variously as aspiring to the status of a desiring subject, as taking desire for her subject, even as displacing history with a narrative of desire.[5] However, if we can agree to shift our focus a little from the supposed desires of our putative subject—bracketing but not forgetting them—we can pay more attention to other elements of her constitution, emphasizing instead identification, desire's symbiotic structuring event, specifically the multiple identifications by which these authors presented what we may now read as the birth—or infancy—of the Subject of Feminism. Identification, even as it begins to be imagined by these nineteenth-century women writers, can be usefully understood through Judith Butler's recent definition, not as part of "the world of events" but as "a phantasmatic staging of the event . . . phantasmatic efforts of alignment, loyalty, ambiguous and cross-corporeal cohabitation . . . the structuring presence of alterity in the very formulation of the 'I'."[6] We must understand, however, that "phantasmatic staging" is always historically specific, not least because the stage and the dramas performed upon it keep changing. And although the Subject of Feminism, even at this particular historical conjuncture, has no single textual persona any more than it has a lived psychic life (and will therefore be summarily demoted to the lower case from now on) it can still be useful to see the dynamic of its political rhetorics not only analogically with those of subjectivity as understood both by psychoanalysis and by cultural theory, but as a trying out of ideas about psychic life and the creation of culture.

The Victorian authors who constructed the subject of feminism often articulated identifications with other races, other genders, other species, and other women in the childhood sections of their written narratives, for the period's emerging ideas of childhood gave novelists a kind of permission to pursue within fiction's discursive frame what Butler calls "the volatile logic of iterability," which marks identification as "that which is constantly marshalled, consolidated, retrenched, contested, and, on occasion, compelled to give way."[7] Representing these acts in terms of symbolic economies must not, however, implicate them too heavily in a system of agreed or positivized values. Whether we are discussing the author's identificatory moves or those she ascribed to her characters, these imaginary transactions are made in the register of fantasy, and remain half-known fictions, which is only to say how much—as well as how little—identity there is to acquire or offload. The "heterogeneous thing" that the adult Jane Eyre half-ironically labels her phantasmatic and fantasizing younger self may partly recognize and partly disavow the hybrid lability to these shape-shifting "Is." For the subject of feminism in mid-century Britain, an expressive narration of an identificatory process could help to forge a textual politics of resistance to dominant femininity, yet at the same time its instrumental location in the narrative space of Victorian childhood generated its own terrors. Like Slavoj Žižek's "sublime object of ideology," the excess of meaning attached to the female child at mid-century may point to gendered childhood as a trouble/troubled spot at this historical moment in the represented categories and temporalities of the human, signifying the inassimilable, unspeakable status of such mixed and mutable things.[8]

In the deployment by mid-nineteenth-century women writers of identifications that are narratively located in childhood as a strategy with which to resist feminine abjection from the human, we can see how fully psychic processes were embedded in and given meaning through the social, and conversely, how the social constituted the political geographies of the psychic. For Brontë's and Craik's little girls—not only their eponymous protagonists, but the many other female children in their fiction—were, to a large extent, conjured by and captive to the ethnographic and ethnological discourses these writers so knowingly appropriated, discourses whose popularity and explanatory scope were at an unprecedented high in the mid- to late 1840's. The Ethnological Society of London, founded in 1843, aimed to give the study of the natural history of man a firmer scientific platform and imprimatur, something it did not immediately achieve within the scientific world. Nevertheless, a more informal legitimation was occurring across the discursive terrain, where ethnological and ethnographic topics and objects of study were becoming a staple feature of general periodicals and helped to sell lavishly illustrated books.[9]

If, however, we want to find the most resonant site for understanding how the expansion of ethnology and ethnography implicated the child and childhood in these years, we need to raise our glance from print to the world of entertainment, to the spectacular displays of humanity in the London shows and exhibitions at mid-century. In so doing, we are still following the traditional gaze of British science, for what might seem to modern sensibilities the most vulgar and retrograde cultural expression of interest in human and animal variety was for the Victorians, as it had been for several centuries of their antecedents, the object and subject of scientific enquiry. The London Exhibition halls from the mid-forties through the mid-fifties mounted one tribal or racial performance after another. Groups of Bushmen, Ojibways, Kaffirs, Hottentots, and Pygmies—including several pairs of indigenous children—drew records crowds from all classes, before touring the provinces. These racial *tableaux vivants* were both cross-referenced and in competition for stage space and audiences with the individual freaks on show—midgets and dwarves were the period's specialty. The casts of these entertainments were often interrogated and analyzed at scientific meetings, and frequently presented to the Royal Family. The use of performers as scientific specimens conferred on the shows an aura of intellectual and moral seriousness, while their audiences with bourgeois royalty enhanced their respectability. Most important, the shows became significant occasions for discursively linking science with politics, since intellectuals of all kinds joined jobbing journalists in interpreting the performative displays of "native" life as an accurate representation of the dismal *mis-en-scène* of other cultures and races, placing them in apposition both to the often foreign human curiosities and to the "normal" white population of England, and using them as set pieces from which to draw harsh lessons about the shaping of domestic and colonial policies.[10] Everywhere in public culture from the mid-forties onwards there was an acknowledgment that a profound destabilization of an earlier period's enlightened—though of course never egalitarian—common sense around human differences was taking place. And these tremors, which were not yet the seismic shift that would create the new ground for the rationales of imperial hegemony, were accompanied by a radical ambivalence about the effects and implications of a reorganization of Christian sympathy, scientific truth, and political agendas.

Real children, including several little girls, appeared in the sequence of tribal exhibitions in this period, and the pint-sized children of smaller races had a durable fascination for audiences. Among the human anomalies, midget men and boys, especially Barnum's American General Tom Thumb—represented as being in his "thirteenth year" when exhibited in 1844—and Thumb's rainbow spectrum of imitators, proved to be particular favorites. Child midgets and dwarves heightened what a Punch cartoon called the "Deformito-mania" of showmen and audiences, but though deformity was frequently elided with ugliness, Tom Thumb effectively represented foreign masculinity in a properly reduced scale, his appearance neither disgusting nor painful, with nothing, presumably, missing.[11] For the *Athenaeum*'s reporter, he provided an example of "this dapper 'epitome of all that is pleasant to man'," and was used to contrast and disparage the humanity of "those fierce gentry the Ojibbeway Indians, who are to be seen and heard on the other side of the staircase!"[12] Indeed, embodied children, especially the super-small, created a sympathetic curiosity about exotic types rarely extended in these years to adults in the "savage" shows, whose managers, Richard Altick argues, began increasingly to go out of their way "to deny . . . exhibits any connection with the human race" (p. 281), a shift in production values that both responded and contributed to the more general change of mood within Britain about the meaning of difference.[13] More specifically, one can see these corporeal kids on exhibit as *exemplary texts* for the ethnological debates about the interaction between the races, debates which paid particular attention to the instinctive reaction of Europeans in interethnic encounters. For example, where responses were sympathetic, they were frequently seen as gendered, driven by a feminine sentimentality tinged with national and racial disloyalty. By 1853, in the wake of the divisive debate over *Uncle Tom's Cabin*, *Punch* pilloried in doggerel the "*penchant* for niggers" exemplified by the "Belles of Belgravia" in their preference for the "little dark" babies in the Kaffir exhibition over the more deserving "young savages" in the "back courts of St. Giles."[14] It was therefore not just the show on stage but the whole spectatorial event of the London Exhibitions and its discursive representations in the daily and periodical press which provide the dramatic scenario that produced, as one of its symptoms, morbidly white little girls.

These shifts in theory and sympathies within the ranks of British ethnology by the mid-forties were the work of many hands, but their significance for both science and politics was highlighted by the interventions of one of its most colorful public figures, the Scottish anatomist Robert Knox. Knox's controversial lectures across metropolitan and provincial England in these years were addressed as a challenge to the long-held Christian monogenist theories of England's leading ethnologist, the Christian physician James Cowles Prichard.[15] Prichard's argument for a single origin for mankind, for a theory of diffusion and of social development, went through several stagings in a long career that ended with his death in 1848. His 1813 paradigms were the most radical, for they proposed an innate mechanism through which humans recognize species sameness when faced with shocking difference, immediately acknowledging exotic, unknown others as "fellow creatures" in spite of the "differences of voice and gesture and manners of life" or "those of the peculiarities of natural structure."[16] By the forties, in tune with a general breakup of the fragile humanitarian coalition that had effected the abolition of colonial slavery, Prichard had retreated, not from his general theory of a single origin, but from its dependence on an innate psychology of human affinity. Now it was the scientist who must explain to a bemused "stranger from another planet" the invisible substratum of likeness that makes the European "monarch" and the "hungry savage" two of a kind.[17] In both Prichard and Knox we can trace the rise of what Knox was to call so presciently the "new sense" of race: master of the memorable slogan, Knox's self-aggrandizing claim that "race is everything" predicted what it affirmed—its revisionist power in political discourse.[18]

Knox set up Prichard's theories and the residue of his humanism as the adversarial ground from which to launch his own politicized polemic, which he cleverly keyed in to sequential public anxieties over current events, including the Kaffir Wars, the racial components of the violent class antagonisms in Britain, the 1848 revolutions, and the general withdrawal of public sympathy from the newly freed slaves in the West Indies.[19] While Knox's "transcendental anatomy" had, as its bottom line, the "philosophic view" that mankind "is of one family, one origin" because in "every embryo is the type of all the races of men," his theory emphasized the prehistoric development of races—which he sometimes confusingly called separate species—into fixed, unalterable, unequal, and antagonistic types. Insisting that no new races can be created because nature "produces no mules; no hybrids, neither in man nor animals" Knox argued that the mulatto "becomes non-productive after a time, if he intermarries only with the mulatto." This counterfactual claim, however, was shored up by the "horror," "abhorrence," and repugnance that Knox insisted characterized not only the attitude of "saxon" to "negro" but of celt to saxon, a horror that he intermittently extended to the refusal of races to interbreed as well as their more common propensity to fight.[20]

Indeed a theory that focused on instinctual aggressivity and revulsion formed the core of the interactive model Knox advanced as the normative, "natural" way in which human group identity was maintained, a theory which drastically curtailed the possibilities and pleasures of both identification and desire. Although Knox's texts were fissured with eruptions of moral and intellectual contempt for the common prejudices of race against race, a reminder to the reader of his (and Knox's) superior understanding of a more egalitarian and pluralist notion of difference, these asides act only as a kind of conceptual chiasmus, reversing but not actually derailing the thrust of his main argument that the most ethnocentric and hostile collective psychic responses follow remorselessly from fixed and unalterable physiological and psychological differences between races. It was, in fact, through his contradictory self-construction as a democratic and anti-imperialist subject almost schizophrenically at odds with his other half, the scientist who understands the inexorable political effects of the logics of race, that Knox may have most effectively wooed the mobile loyalties of his audiences and readers. His particular brand of racial determinism may have fed into the Darwinian paradigm, as Evelleen Richards argues, but his equivocal political stance played out rhetorically a kind of unequal dialogue between the older rights-of-man radicalism of his parents' allegiances, whose moral ground he intermittently claimed, and a new, scientifically discovered *realpolitik*. This latter supported and was ideologically associated with the more unambiguously reactionary polygynist theories of the multiple and unequal creation of human races adopted by Knox's contemporaries and followers. A knock-em-dead speaker from the days of his respectable medical career, Knox was the P. T. Barnum of the ethnological circuit. In proselytizing for his "new sense" that "race is everything," Knox's showman–scientist acted as a kind of *agent provocateur*, at once inciting and rationalizing a supposedly innate revulsion against difference.

In a period when, as Nancy Stepan has shown, the scientific theories of race and of sexual difference were being reciprocally constituted, the Knoxian model, taken to the extremes of its logics, especially in its disavowal of exogamy, could produce as one of is by-products a phobic account of sexual difference and sexual relations. The analogic thinking common from the eighteenth century onward, especially in theology and economics, was deeply at work in the nineteenth-century development of theories of difference; its contradictory effects surfaced when writers like Knox foregrounded issues of miscegenation and hybridity in the animal and the human. Knox appeared to have recognized and even attempted to head off this dangerous but logical spin-off of his argument when, early in *The Races of Men*, he hurriedly elevated the European woman to a transcendental ideal of the white races, "the highest manifestation of abstract life, clothed in a physical form," thus removing her from the inexorably hostile systems of differences and relations within the human.[21] But interestingly, he refused this idealizing strategy with childhood, that other disturbing difference that intraracial human relations had to accommodate. While the generic human embryo as a concept contained the form of higher and lower races, the "Negro" and the "European" as well as nonhuman animal elements, Knox argued that its typical development into human varieties involved a shedding rather than an addition of characteristics, a movement away "from one grand

type" so that "variety is deformity."[22] The young as a category were closer to but also contaminated by this heterogeneous unity, for "the young
of every species, and of all, bear the closest resemblance to each other;
and it is chiefly by laying aside some of the characters present in all the
young that the adult comes afterwards to be recognized."[23] Adults of any
species or race therefore, manifested the most extreme forms of deformed
difference form an extraordinarily broad category that includes "the
young of every species, and of all."

Children, however, emphatically did not represent an ideal form
of the human. Knox argued that in spite of the "beauty" of their miniature hands and feet, the child's body with its "shapeless" torso displayed
aesthetic deformity, for if compared to the classic contours of adult
humanity, it was "deficient in proportions and forms." Youth "never
attains the perfect and the beautiful, whilst disease, or penury, or vice
can transform the child into an object of pity or disgust. . . ." The attraction of children for adults, Knox explained, was in their embodiment
not of actual physical perfection, but of an impossible fantasy of species
immortality, "the hopes that nature will never die."[24] Knox described
this hope as at once universal and vain, unless translated into a "theory" of the unity of nature which included all the stages of life. Yet we
might read his own hope of using theory to fix human racial difference and genealogy as an equally fantastic disavowal of the terrors of
human mutation and entropy.

Too great a focus on Knox's brief references to children would mis-
represent the curiously marginal place of childhood in the ethnological
and anthropological debates, where it was often obliquely addressed,
even when the ethnographic specimens whose humanity was at stake
were children. This marginality in turn points up just how unevenly
developed were the concepts of childhood in the 1840s and 1850s.
However the issues of origins, development, transformation, and difference, of idealization and degeneration adumbrated in Knox's association of generic form with the category of the young in its typical stages
of embryo, fetus, and child point towards the knot of meanings in which
childhood was entangled. When childhood was finally carved out of
bourgeois temporality, and elaborated as a separate category of being
within the family, part of the child's security from abuse, and the normative rhetoric of normal family affection, came to depend on the

acceptance by adults of the child's temporary difference from, but underlying likeness to, its parents or whatever broad or narrow classification of adults culturally designated to stand in for them. Both a developmental schema and a reciprocally affective paradigm of feeling began to underwrite progressive concepts of child-rearing and childhood in Victorian Britain, and these became increasingly an emblematic focus for ethical adult humanity in both sexes. A minimal understanding of and toleration for the mutability of the child's body, imaginative life, and passions became, if we are to believe Victorian fiction at mid-century, was becoming a condition of adequate bourgeois parenting. Such parenting, in turn, was beginning to be constituted as an ideal but elusive form of subjectivity.[25]

However, bourgeois Victorian childhood had its own civic responsibilities. It was enjoined to transcend its negative association with earlier stages of human and animal development, controlling its atavistic "savagery," just as women were expected to cast off their regressive association with both inferior types of humans and children so that they might become good-enough wives and mothers. Here the interweaving of the definitions and dynamics of species, race, and subject makes the child peculiarly vulnerable as the least differentiated, most monstrously syncretic form of humanity. The child was a being whose only safety lay in becoming, so that it might mature, to pick up Knox's figure, into the pure deformity of variety. Knox's dramatic way of posing these paradoxes was deliberately meant to shock and disturb what he perceived as the wrongheaded ethnological common sense of Prichardian monogeny, and he did, in fact, succeed in highlighting his rival's contradictions. Although the monogenist paradigms of human origin had emphasized development, and had also framed the negative association of childhood with women and inferior racial others, its cultural rationales specifically allowed for, and often demanded, progressive transformations. Racial theory of the Knoxian kind, on the other hand, suffered from another brand of paradox; by aiming to fix interracial difference, its denial of change and its emphasis on the hostile psychodynamics of difference potentially constructed childhood as a monstrous anomaly.

We might speculate that the abused male and female children who littered the fiction of the late forties produced by those authors—Charles Dickens, Charles Kingsley, Charlotte Brontë—who most

obviously had absorbed and articulated the import and the spirit—if
by no means always the letter—of these revisions of thinking about
both children and race, are partly the expressible texts of seemingly
incompatible theories of the human, the national, the sexual. The
bourgeois child became the imaginary site of a cultural accident: the
crossroads where incommensurable narratives, inassimilable political
histories, collided head on. At the same time, the violence so explicit
in the child's embodiment as the stake, the future, the atavistic past,
and the failure of these categories ought to lead us towards, not away
from, a theory of their possible interdependence. For the particular
apparitions of childhood that concern me in this essay, representing
as they do both a deformation and idealization of the origins and differences of the human, affirmed with peculiar poignancy Etienne
Balibar's argument that racism often acts as "*a supplement internal to
nationalism,*" and performs its daily, ideological work "in the name of
and by means of a humanist discourse," by its reference both to uni-
versalism and "*supranationalism*" for which the definition of the "human
species is the key notion."[26] These representations in the period I am
describing came not in the form of a seamless logic, but precisely as
"paradoxical." It may be a later moment in the nineteenth century
that confirms Balibar's suggestion that "it is in the 'race of its children'
that the nation could contemplate its own identity in the pure state,"
yet this realization, taking shape from the 1840s, pointed to "the profound ambivalence of the signifier of 'race' . . . from the point of view
of national unity and identity."[27]

These paradoxes could be heard as a kind of discursive discord in the
narrative and poetry of the mid-century (but also in other genres of
writing), an untuning that manifested itself through the recurrence of
oddly unsecured moral and rhetorical registers—blank irony, indirect
address. What Freud terms negation, something that must be spoken but
is simultaneously disavowed by the speaker, was a characteristic strategy
in the discourses about race in the 1840s, and suggests one way in which
the contradictory statements in Knox might be read. However, these
effects found some of their most intense and disturbing expressions in

the protofeminist writing that initially emphasized the female child's like-ness to and/or identifications with racial, hybrid, or deformed others en route to presenting her adult self as the ethical model of national sub-jectivity. Every stage of this imagined trajectory was fraught with ideological difficulty, not least the problem of national identity itself if it was meant to be more than that of a single "race" in dominance.[28] It is to the implications of these representations that I now want to turn in the second half of this essay.

The adult Jane Eyre in the historical present of Brontë's novel con-cludes her account of the child's raging incomprehension that she "could never please" anyone in the Reed family, though she "dared commit no fault" and "strove to fulfil every duty," with "at the distance of—I will not say how many years, I see it clearly" (p. 12).

> I was a discord in Gateshead Hall; I was like nobody there; I had nothing in har-mony with Mrs. Reed or her children, or her chosen vassalage. If they did not love me, in fact, as little did I love them. They were not bound to regard with affection a thing that could not sympathize with one amongst them; a heterogeneous thing, opposed to them in temperament, in capacity, in propensities; a useless thing, inca-pable of serving their interest, or adding to their pleasure; a noxious thing, cherishing the germs of indignation at their treatment, of contempt of their judgment. I know that had I been a sanguine, brilliant, careless, exacting, handsome, romping child—though equally dependent and friendless—Mrs. Reed would have endured my presence more complacently; her children would have entertained for me more of the cor-diality of fellow-feeling; the servants would have been less prone to make me the scapegoat of the nursery. (pp. 12–13)

Brontë had several philosophical axes to grind in this passage, but one of the ways in which we might understand its peculiarly unstable moral key is to think of it as Knox's negative social compact writ small, but with all its cruelty exposed. As Jane recounts the mutual hostilities of difference, they become essentialized, rooted in the accidents of tem-perament and, as we will see, of complexion. Yet with the very phrases in which they are so secured, Jane's tone and language ruthlessly reveal the wilfully selfish, antisocial instrumentalism of their dynamic. The irony, both crude and gnomic, provides, above all, a history lesson that contrasts the "ignorant" innocence of the child's plea for social justice and parity of treatment with an adult's bitter but settled knowledge about the unyielding psychic and physical economies of difference. Read in one way, with the adult voice heard as sincerely conveying unpleasant but true ethical and historical wisdom, the passage situates the passionate humanitarian questions of an earlier antislavery conjuncture as an infantile, personal rebellion. However, this literal reading is cut across, but not, significantly, entirely delegitimated, by the indirect address which draws back from valorizing either the bitterly tight-lipped rationalizing of the adult or the angry child's recurrent "Why was I . . .?" as she highlights the color-coded color consciousness of the British bourgeois household, with its racist son who "reviled" his mother for her "dark skin, similar to his own" and its daughter, the "beauty" full of "acrid spite" whose "pink cheeks and golden curls . . . purchase indemnity for every fault" (p. 12).

In the child's account, as ventriloquized by her adult self, noxious heterogeneity was as much the property of the "white," middle-class, British family, represented here as an always already hybrid group, as of the alien female child of possibly base origin.[29] This perspective reproduced the message of its referent, Defoe's wickedly lubricious defense of the English as a bastardized, "mongrel" mixture against the fictive claims of early-eighteenth-century ethnic purists, but did not, I think, share its spirit.[30] Instead, Jane's "adult" voice responds to the question posed by differences by bleakly naming them as an unanswerable set of fixed antipathies, articulating only too clearly what Raymond Williams called the "structure of feeling" in Britain in the forties as one which believed that there were no solutions to social antagonisms.[31] At this point in Brontë's story, the text seems precariously balanced on the pivot of its own radical ambivalence, unwilling either to approve or wholly to disavow a positive principle of heterogeneous identity.

In the passages I have been considering, there are several generic orders of female childhood: the debased reality of the Reed sisters, the ideal, ideological child nowhere represented in this novel or in Brontë's oeuvre, and the child as the trace, the residue of history, remembered in the narrating present. This last evocation of the child is the richest but also the most elusive. If narration had a psyche, this child would be a screen memory, a memory of childhood whose events and affect have been composed in terms of the present, a nostalgic but also punitive redrawing of a prelapsarian politics in which the mutability of the female child's gender and ethnicity and humanity—as she is figured by hostile others but most significantly as she imagines herself—is followed quickly and surely by her physical incarceration. Even as little Jane's identification with "any other rebel slave" (p. 9) is narrated as an identification with racial others as resisters, aggressively redressing the violence done to them, the psychological move that permits her resistance is posed as an analogic subjectivity of doubly foreign origin— "I was a trifle beside myself, or *out* of myself, as the French would say" (p. 9)—from which she will be able to disengage. Identification and disavowal are almost simultaneous, for the text immediately moralizes against the identification it invokes as one which produces uncontrolled and perhaps irreversible effects. Jane's angry thoughts are described in terms of a psychically saturated and sedimented blackness: "a dark deposit in a turgid well" (p. 12). It is this imagined blackness that incites, if only as manic defense, a compensatory identification with the faery white figure, a white princess, in a red marriage chamber with a white bed, who has a white "ample, cushioned easy chair ... with a footstool" for a "pale throne" (p. 11). This phantasmatic affiliation in turn precipitates in Jane a crisis about identifications—perhaps about having to choose between these equally frightening "fictive ethnicities"; its immediate effect is to make the child Jane really ill.[32]

Why should this crisis be so extreme, and what are its narrative effects? If we read the passage in relation to the contemporary shift in racial thinking for which Knoxian and Prichardian racial politics provided related rather than simply competing rationales, we might want to emphasize the pressure of something like the Knoxian paradigm on the ideologies it critiqued.[33] From this perspective, Jane's empathy with racial others would be a sign of her developmental immaturity which, biologically as well as psychologically, indicates her closeness to them, a sign, that is, of her childishness. Such an identification sets up, as well, a problem for her maturing self in its dangerous perversion of human beings' supposed innate attraction to racial likeness. It also constitutes a radical denial of dominant femininity, for an alignment with *rebel* slaves transgressively appropriates the aggression repeatedly associated—within the novel as in the culture at large—with both masculinity and the uncivilized. Yet, for reasons the novel as a whole makes clear,

Jane's flight, in the Red Room scene, to an enforced purity of whiteness in which the subject is at once imperious and wholly abject, proves just as scary.

   Jane Eyre's tropes of pure whiteness attach themselves to vexed and unresolved problems of gender, geography, and scale, as these coalesce as sites of anxiety about national, colonial, and imperial imaginaries. The ambiguities of whiteness in the novel become more visible, however, if we first play out with Brontë the implications of geography and scale in the historical parable told through little Jane's victimization, rebellion, incarceration, breakdown, and recovery, noting how both the humanoid small and the oversized are equally pathologized by the traumatic rite of passage, at once cultural and subjective, that this sequence depicts. During her convalescence, Jane asks for her favorite *Gulliver's Travels*, a book she had considered "a narrative of facts" with "a vein of interest deeper than . . . fairy tales" and had "again and again perused with delight" (p. 17).

> Lilliput and Brobdingnag being, in my creed, solid parts of the earth's surface, I doubted not that I might one day, by taking a long voyage, see with my own eyes the little fields, houses, and trees, the diminutive people, the tiny cows, sheep, and birds of the one realm; and the cornfields forest-high, the mighty mastiffs, the monster cats, the tower-like men and women, of the other. Yet when this cherished volume was now placed in my hand—when I turned over its leaves, and sought in its marvellous pictures the charm I had, till now, never failed to find—all was eerie and dreary; the giants were gaunt goblins, the pigmies malevolent and fearful imps, Gulliver a most desolate wanderer in most dread and dangerous regions. I closed the book, which I dared no longer peruse. . . ." (p. 17)

Here, in thumbnail sketch, is rendered the paranoid transformation of the child's prelapsarian ethnographic imagination. Her innocent imperial eye, once safe not only in its tourist's gaze, but in its assumption of the human and civilized continuum across the differences of scale, is now actively threatened by what it once so desired to behold. This gothicized revision actively conflates the racialized and the nonhuman large and little—goblin, pigmy, imp—with alien landscapes of terror. No textual commentary draws out the lessons of this fearful, disrupted, literary encounter which brutally marks little Jane's loss of her taxonomic utopia and her entry into a distinctly post-Edenic culture. The scene's replacement of scopic desire with fear and aversion constitutes a severe and permanent punishment for this child's (any child's) curiosity and her dangerous identifications. It remains a moot textual point whether it is little Jane who actually deserves to be so punished, for the state of mind that governs the new meanings she now finds in Swift is the aftereffect of an ensemble of perverse actions and identifications endemic to the whole Reed household, including Jane. These episodes, I have suggested, condense and reprise a narrative version of the history of colonial slavery and its overthrow, memorializing it, literally and figuratively, as an English child's story. The melodramatic reversal of affect in Jane's reader-response to *Gulliver's Travels* draws the most obvious parallel for the novel's contemporary readers to the shift in collective attitudes towards human difference, perfectibility and relation taking place in the 1840s.[34]

This historicized scene of reading, in which the child-reader's identificatory pleasure with Swift's travelogue turns into a fear that seems to have the hallucinatory power of transforming the text itself, is later replayed as the real of Jane's adult narrative of romance and betrayal. Here the focal figure is Bertha Mason, Rochester's white creole wife—metamorphosed by marriage, madness, and incarceration into a fully racialized figure—whose "savage face" with its "fearful blackened inflation of the lineaments" and "lips swelled and dark" is reflected in the mirror of another bedroom, this time Jane's own (p. 249).[35] In the alternating descriptions of Bertha Mason by Jane and Rochester, the grotesque juxtaposition of the large and the small, adumbrated in Jane's encounter with Swift, are brought together. Jane describes Bertha as "tall and large" with a "gaunt head" (p. 250); Rochester calls here a "goblin" (p. 251) with a "pigmy intellect" and "giant propensities" (p. 269). When encountered by Rochester and Jane and the wedding party in her "goblin's cell" (p. 272), Bertha's performance combines elements of the displays in the London exhibitions, the uncertainty of species and gendered identity exploited by the freak shows—"beast or human being, one could not at first sight tell" (p. 257)—resolving itself into the spectacle of a corpulent, violent, "virile" madwoman of indeterminate race who, when restrained by husband and keeper, emits the "fiercest yells and the most convulsive plunges" (p. 258). The bleak conclusion of Jane's revision of Swift is also repeated in the adults' story as a doubled identification with Gulliver. Rochester's Jamaican *mesalliance* has already made him a "desolate wanderer"; as Jane leaves Thornfield, warned in a vision by a maternal moon in "white human form" to "flee temptation" (p. 281), she too becomes a miserable sojourner in "dread and dangerous regions."

In this scene, whiteness is a protective presence, but elsewhere in the novel it has a distinctly fatal aspect, representing the antithesis of the ideal humanity that the narrative develops. *Jane Eyre* opens with the discontents of whiteness as little Jane encounters them in Thomas Bewick's *History of British Birds*:

> the vast sweep of the Arctic Zone, and those forlorn regions of dreary space—that reservoir of frost and snow, where firm fields of ice, the accumulation of centuries of winters, glazed in Alpine heights above heights, surround the pole, and concentrate the multiple rigors of extreme cold.[36]

Jane's "shadowy . . . half-comprehended child's association of the "death-white realms" and "bleak shores" of this fixed and frozen sublime were with the "cold and ghastly moon," "churchyard," and "headstone" of Bewick's illustrations (p. 6). These related images of whiteness as stasis and death reappear much later in adult human form, as the novel's ideological imperialist and its least affectionate male, Jane's cousin and suitor, the Reverend St. John Rivers. The constant evocation of Rivers's whiteness becomes increasingly ambivalent, then fully critical, as his "austere and despotic" (p. 360) character is revealed in his interactions with Jane. His skin, in Jane's first description of him, is "colourless as ivory" (p. 303); later his "chiselled marble" visage tops his "tall figure all white as a glacier" (p. 332). The exterior whiteness of bone, stone, and ice is syntagmatically related to his "chilling" "frozen" "frigidity" of temperament (p. 348), until they crystallize as subjectivity. In confrontation with Jane, Rivers becomes one of the "cold people" with the "fall of the avalanche in their anger" and the breaking up of the frozen sea in their displeasure" (p. 363). Whiteness as frigid adult phallicism represents an aberrant extremity of the human; Rivers calls his own "cold, hard" ambition a "human deformity" (p. 330), and the text represents his ability to terrorize, his incapacity for warm familial affection or deep love, and his repudiation of heterosexual desire as at least a frightening as Bertha's racialized animality; two aversive varieties of grown-up deformation. Four years later, in *Moby Dick* (1851), Herman Melville would write of whiteness more memorably, but in the same vein, as a sublime antihuman quality: "this thing of whiteness" that exaggerated "the terror of things otherwise terrible," a "dumb blankness, full of meaning, in a wide landscape of snows—a colorless, all-color of atheism from which we shrink. . . ."[37]

Hysterical or terrible sublime, faery femininity or frozen masculinity, absolute whiteness in *Jane Eyre* is less the attribute of a viable raced human subject than an apparition, a specter called forth by contemporary prohibitions against those affective ties, whether of desire or identification which must inevitably cross or blur the lines of difference.[38] In a period where Knox's proposition that "race is everything" resonated for many people, its invidious material distinctions seemed suddenly to be dematerialized and everywhere; its favorite disembodied haunt by far was the sphere of the emotions. Each of the figures in *Jane Eyre* touched or suffused by such deadly whiteness suffers a kind of arrested development. Unsurprisingly the productive couple of Jane and Edward Fairfax Rochester, whose marriage and parenthood end the novel, are both distinguished by their difference from English norms of beauty, marked not by dark skins, but by another kind of internal heterogeneity, the "irregular features" that act as a displacement of skin color so otherwise important to the novel, as well as condensation of Brontë's acceptable, eccentric type of English hybridity (p. 351).

Anger is the emotion most visibly at stake in the supernatural whiteness of little Jane and St. John Rivers and the supernatural blackness of Jane's imagined "rebel slave" and Bertha Mason. Anger is represented throughout *Jane Eyre* as the most raced and gendered of human feelings, permissible in white males and black people, but perverse and shocking in white females. Yet the rebel female child and woman of this text—the subject of feminism—survives through her angry resistance to familial, institutional, sexual, and ideological oppressions, her anger acquired, as Jane's Christian friends and critics—her saintly schoolmate, Helen Burns, the vicious school governor, the Reverend Brocklehurst, and Rivers himself—are only too eager to tell her, through her transgressive identification with "heathens and savage tribes" (p. 50). To an "untaught girl" (p. 50), these identifications are offered a limited but crucial—even lifesaving—indulgence; perhaps that is why the adult woman who continues her "heathen" behavior must remain physically "a little small thing . . . almost like a child" (p. 375). The vulnerability, permissions, and prohibitions of childhood and the feminine are deeply entwined in this novel. The presence of convoluted racial thinking marks the historical specificity of this conjuncture, linking the subjectivity of little girls with that of heathens and savages in ways the text itself cannot control, entangling rather than separating their fates. We might hazard however, that the brief appearance and speedy disappearance of the white disembodied female child in the Red Room was a moment when the subject of feminism recognized the impossibility of the racialized psychic strategies it had imagined for the survival of bourgeois English girls.

Olive's reworking of *Jane Eyre* responded to the same contemporary versions of racial thinking, now preeminently including Brontë's thematization of anger, childhood and race, with a different social and psychic narrative. Perhaps aiming to disarm those critics who labeled *Jane Eyre* and its author coarse, unchristian, and revolutionary, Craik attempted to write a protofeminist narrative in which the anger of the European female child is disavowed. The result is a story in which anger was more simply—and vulgarly—raced and gendered than in *Jane Eyre*; in *Olive*, only white men and mixed-race women may feel or express it. The result was a one-sided attempt to contest the psychopolitics of aversion, to protect some human subjects—the future subject of feminism, an idealized British subject—from their taint. Little Olive is created as an exercise in Christian patience and abjection; her energetic passivity, together with her capacity to offer love in the face of rejection, is seen as a winning tactic that eventually rewards her with her parents' affection and contrition, a career as a successful painter, the virtual disappearance of her deformity, and a partner of her own. Yet this characterization undermines its own aim, for while it asks the reader to emulate Olive's saintly ways, it irresistibly invites her to feel anger on the girl's behalf.

Such failed attempts to fend off certain kinds of identifications may be an unintended effect of Craik's narrative strategy, but they are also, at crucial points, self-consciously sewn into the story itself. In the scene cited at the beginning of this essay, the child Olive is presented to her father as shades of white, a pathetically inept metaphorical and metonymic device to deflect attention from her physical flaw. Instead of evoking childhood, innocence, and racial unity with her parents, her masquerade in white only emphasizes her physical difference, which in turn highlights the dysfunctions of British (rather than English) family life. The adults who reject and are repulsed by the girl-child in Craik's story are her ill-matched English mother Sybilla and Scottish father Angus, whose incompatibility, at once cultural and temperamental, is also accentuated by the exaggerated gender types they represent: the hyperfemininity of Sybilla—her childishness, smallness, and selfish love of pleasure—and the hypermasculinity of Captain Angus Rothesay, who turns out to be an unpleasant mixture of prudish patriarch and regency rake.

As in so many novels of the forties which relied on—even as they may have contested—aspects of the "new sense" and prominence of racial determination, Craik's novel depended on narrative and rhetorical ambiguity to open up the paradoxes it could in no way resolve. Olive, whose birth begins the novel, is at first anychild—and anything but white or elfin—"a small nameless concretion of humanity, in colour and consistency strongly resembling the 'red earth,' whence was taken the father of all nations" (p. 1). In fact, she is everyperson at both ends of human temporality, for her "purple, pinched-up, withered face ... as in all newborn children, bore ... a ridiculous likeness to extreme old age...." (p. 1). Craik could get away with her very frank and—for the times and the writer's sex —coarsely physical description of the newborn partly because contemporary ethnography gave body language a wider currency and respectability. The grotesque, material body of female infancy is, Craik daringly suggests, the common origin we must all acknowledge, for:

> if we, every one, were thus to look back, half in compassion, half in humiliation, at our infantile likeness—may it not be in the world to come some who in this world bore an outward image, poor, mean, and degraded, will cast a glance of equal pity on their well-remembered olden selves, now transfigured into beautiful immortality. (p. 1)

The earnest, sentimental, Christian piety of this plea masks its boldness: this opening passage proselytizes for a humanist, feminized, monogenist ethnology that the novel, in the end, will not quite be able to sustain. Initially Craik sets up her challenge to the doctrine of natural antipathy very well. Before Sybilla knows her child suffers from "hopeless deformity" (p. 11), she defiantly calls her "brown"-haired and -skinned baby "Olive." Olive's abject "whiteness" is in one sense created by her parent's repugnance to her, invented as it were for the dramatic occasion when the paternal must, but cannot, claim her for its own. Angus's and Sybilla's own lack of understanding of each other as well as of their child is presented as a deformity of spirit, an unthinking though perhaps not "innate" attachment to likeness and to the supposed human normal. But this parental failure of sympathy across difference does not affect the reality of Olive's imperfection, nor its social stigma; in spite of Craik's promising opening, the normal remains the physical ideal for children and women. As long as it does so, the ethics and effects of exogamy, of marriage across ethnic boundaries, and the extreme alterities of gender remain in question. The novel therefore evokes another questions that is steadfastly refuses to pose: Is Olive's physical flaw the punitive result of Sybilla's and Angus's overdetermined differences? Does her albino coloring mask the miscegenation of her parents?

Part of the pathos and sadism of Olive's presentation to her father lay in its generic closeness to and its deliberate distance from the public exhibitions' spectacles of other people's, other nations' deformed children. Performed in the home between bourgeois father and daughter, what may have been innocent entertainment in another sphere was here a sign of familial pathology and abuse. A later scene, more traditionally part of the genre of domestic melodrama, suggests how the interplay between gender, deformity, childhood, and aberrant whiteness become multiple and related liabilities for Olive. As the adolescent Olive coaxes her drunken father to bed, Angus first challenges her authority by calling her "a mere chit of girl—a very child" and then, when she meekly reminds him of her daughterdom, he adds "My daughter! How dare you call yourself so, you white-faced, mean-looking hunchback—" (p. 65).

Angus's abuse is not merely a family affair, but was in tune with the affective economies coming into play in the 1840s and 1850s, which, in arguing that Britain had abandoned and neglected its poor, hierarchically its "children," blamed this failure of empathy on a perverse, humanitarian identification with the West Indian ex-slaves and with the "darker races" generally. In the late forties through the mid-fifties, Carlyle and Dickens in particular, through their rhetorical dehumanization of Africans, turned this argument into a virtual campaign to persuade the English to realign their humanitarian loyalties, to withdraw their identification with African peoples and with the politics that supported them.

In *Olive* and in *Jane Eyre*, that issue returns as a question about the racial identity of other female children in Britain, and the proper role of the novels' protagonists towards them In *Olive*, the spoken question about deformity and the silent question about cross-cultural marriage are resolved by engaging the issue of realignment and identification through the issue of miscegenation. Angus Rothesay has another daughter, the illegitimate offspring of his West Indian mixed-race mistress Celia Manners, who has, like Madame de Stael's *Corinne*, followed him back to England. The reader and the now-grown Olive meet this daughter born in England, "a little thin-lipped, cunning eyed girl of eight or ten" with "black eyes and fair hair" called, ironically, Christal, who believes she is really the daughter of "a rich lady, and . . . a noble gentleman" (pp. 112, 113). This family romance has been invented by her bitter and despairing dying mother, and Christal accepts it unquestioningly. Educated abroad on Rothesay's money, she appears to all who know her as a beautiful English girl. When the truth of her bastardy and her racial origin are revealed many years later, they result in a scene of terrifying infantile rage, in which she tries to kill her half sister, Olive. Female anger in Craik's novel is entirely the property of these outcast women. In a neat move, the revelation of Christal's parentage and her retributive, violent response to it shift "the curse of hopeless deformity" from Olive's shoulders to Christal's psyche. Olive's imperfection virtually disappears; she is allowed to marry, and Christal remains by her own wish in a religious order. Nothing shakes the Christian humanitarianism of Olive towards her violent and distracted sister. Instead it is the reader, in a now-familiar role, whose less perfect character supplies the revulsion the text refuses to acknowledge. This, we might say, is monogeny under extreme stress, so hierarchically ordered in terms of gendered racial virtue that it undermines its own lopsided assertion of intrafamilial affinity and cross-racial sympathy. It is nevertheless a response to the handling of some of the same issues in *Jane Eyre*. For there the problem of self-identifications, set up in the childhood section of the novel, persists as a questions about Jane's status and authority almost to the book's close. Its resolution depends, as in *Olive*, on the appearance in the text of other, racialized little girls. It is this narrative move that simultaneously aligns Brontë more fully with the "new sense" of race, yet offers her a significant role in the making of an harmonious English nationality. The adult Jane confesses to the reader her involuntary disgust at her first contact with the daughters of the English peasantry in her village school at Morton. Her scholars:

> speak with the broadest accent of the district. At present they and I have a difficulty in understanding each other's language. Some of them are unmannered, rough, intractable, as well as ignorant; but others are docile, have a wish to learn, and evince a disposition that pleases me. I must not forget that these coarsely clad little peasants are of flesh and blood as good as the scions of gentlest genealogy; and the germs of native excellence, refinement, intelligence and kind feeling are as likely to exist in their hearts as in those of the best born. (pp. 315, 316)

Yet Jane feels

> desolate to a degree. I feel—yes, idiot that I am—I feel degraded . . . dismayed at the ignorance, the poverty, the coarseness of all I heard and saw round me. But let me not hate and despise myself too much for these feelings. I know them to be wrong . . . and a change for the better in my scholars, may substitute gratification for disgust. (p. 316)

Jane's convoluted response—not quite negation—is meant to show her to be superficially cured of involuntary identifications with degraded others, cured, one might say, of female childhood and its dangers. Though she has refused a role in what Gayatri Spivak evocatively calls the "soul-making" of the imperial project abroad by refusing St. John Rivers's offer of missionary marriage and service in India, with difficulty but determination she overcomes her natural disgust at her English pupils and proudly educates them into a civilized, "docile," female peasantry.[39] Her success in so doing both conforms to the injunction to women to make benevolence and sympathy a domestic

concern, a project in which English "savages" are turned into laborers and servants, at the same time as it emphasizes and forgives the
natural antipathy to difference that exposes class as a fully raced and
therefore problematic typology for those who would make racial likeness the precondition of sympathy and affiliation. These little peasant
girls, though they may be "of flesh and blood as good as the scions of
gentlest genealogy," are nevertheless part of the Africanist discourse
of the novel which determines, through the concatenation of race
and female childhood, just which classed and raced little girls may
become, if ever at their peril, at once the subject of feminism and the
bearers of a new sense of national belonging, one which still harks
back to a rural England of little people. If Morton is the "healthy heart
of England" (p. 316), Ferndean, where Jane settles with Rochester, is
its lusher, damper site of regeneration. Each setting turns the reader
back to Bessie's regional folktales and Jane's fantasies about them, rein-
voking the faery ethnography through which the little girl first entered
what Eric Lott, writing of the same moment in American history, has
called "the haunted realm of racial fantasy."[40]

Two final vignettes from the 1850s feature female children and conclude my argument. When Harriet Beecher Stowe's *Uncle Tom's Cabin*
was published in Britain in 1852 and Stowe herself made a triumphant
visit to England in 1853, a new upsurge of humanitarian sympathy, a
kind of backlash against the crude recrudescent racism of the previous
years, was created in the popular imagination. In *Uncle Tom's Cabin* the
impossibly virtuous little white girl Eva is transgressively identified with
a feminized Christian black man. Dickens and many of the London
periodicals targeted the positive reaction to *Uncle Tom* as itself a sign of
the perverse, misplaced, feminized sentimentality articulated in the
"maudlin" response to the exhibition of native others.[41]

In 1854, at Reime's Anatomical and Ethnological Museum at Saville
House, Leicester Square, Gentlemen Only (the phrase included working-class men, on whose behalf the general price admission had been
reduced to sixpence) Eighteen or Over could satisfy their curiosity
about human anatomy by inspecting the "Florentine Venus . . . dis-
sectable in all its parts" or the "Greek Venus . . . Displaying the Muscular
System." Also on display were models of "Obstetrical Operations"
including a Caesarian section, "A Complete Series of Models, Illustrative

of the Sciences of Embryology, or the Origin of Mankind, From the smallest particle of vitality, the perfectly formed foetus." With the questions of origins visually resolved, the gentlemen could move on to the questions of difference, exploring Reimer's "Gallery of All Nations" which exhibited at "one glance the varied types of the Great Human Family."[42] A special attraction in 1854 were wax models of the "Aztec Lilliputians," whose living fleshly counterparts, "a male three feet four inches tall and said to be fourteen years old and a girl two inches shorter" had been exhibited to men, women, and children across the class spectrum in London and the provinces from mid-1853 as representatives of "an entirely new type—a kind of human being . . . never before seen—with physiognomies formed by descent through ages of thought and association of which we had no knowledge."[43] Graced by the imprimatur of the Ethnographic Society and the Royal Family, the children drew enormous crowds, and became the occasion of a lively controversy in the daily and periodical press, where a gathering number of skeptical scientists challenged their provenance, on both anatomical and linguistic grounds, opinion hardening that these were no new race or human type, but simply retarded and dwarfed children of some already known Indian tribes of Central America. The Aztec Lilliputians were soon in competition for mass audiences with two children from a South African pygmy tribe, dubbed Earthmen. The Aztec and Earthmen children were almost the last in this wave of popular exhibits which featured little persons and peoples.

As Jacqueline Rose, borrowing from Žižek, says of *Peter Pan*, the difficulty forming around these children, and those others, fictional and real, that I have been discussing, "instead of veiling a hidden reality . . . captures and serves to keep in social circulation what is most difficult and potentially unmanageable."[44] The contested receptions of *Uncle Tom's Cabin* and the Aztec Lilliputians were part of that rebus of signification which contributed to the developing constructs of childhood, race and sexual difference in mid-nineteenth century Britain. Fantasies of—and about—identification played a dynamic role in the ways in which the categories of identity from the individual through the species were being theorized in those constructions, which proliferated across the genres of public discourse, appearing both in individually authored work and more composite social texts like the London

Exhibitions. I have suggested that in this period the imagined bodies and psyches of racially marked little girls became a captivating fantasmatic site for the rich elaboration of speculative ideas about race, gender, and childhood. More broadly I have argued that between 1845–55 the status of the human and the national subject was debated through the image of the humanoid small, a figure that, as spectacle and as specimen, as ideal and degraded national and colonial other, was also central to the historical development of an emergent feminism.[45]

NOTES

1. Daniel Defoe, *The True-Born Englishman* (1700; rpt. Plan de la Tour: Editions d'Aujourd'hui, 1980), p. 20.

2. Charlotte Brontë, *Jane Eyre* (1847), Norton Critical Edition, 2nd edition, ed. Richard J. Dunn (New York. W.W. Norton & Company, Inc., 1987), p. 12. All future citations are to this edition and will appear in the text.

3. Dinah Mulock Craik, *Olive*, 8th edition (London: Chapman and Hall, 1865), p. 19. Future citations of this edition will appear in the text. I am preparing a modern edition of *Olive* for the forthcoming Oxford Popular Classics series, under the general editorship of David Trotter.

4. Sally Mitchell's *Dinah Mulock Craik* (Boston: Twayne, 1983) emphasizes *Olive's* imitation of *Jane Eyre*, as does Elaine Showalter in *A Literature of Their Own: British Women Novelists from Brontë to Lessing* (Princeton University Press, 1977), p. 139.

5. We might see this first formulation as a *leitmotif*, sometimes overt, sometimes implied, that runs unevenly through many studies of anglophone women's writing. As it is applied to the nineteenth century, it is certainly present in those groundbreaking books, Elaine Showalter in *A Literature of Their Own: British Women Novelists from Brontë to Lessing* (Princeton University Press, 1977) and Sandra Gilbert and Susan Gubar's *A Madwoman in the Attic: The Woman Writer and the Nineteenth-Century Literary Imagination* (New Haven: Yale University Press, 1979). The second formulation — how women write about desire—becomes an explicit and favored topic in the eighties, for example in Mary Poovey's *The Proper Lady and the Woman Writer: Ideology as Style in the Works of Mary Wollstonecraft, Mary Shelley, and Jane Austen* (Chicago: University of Chicago Press, 1984), and in my own *Sea Changes: Essays on Culture and Feminism* (London: Verso Press, 1986). The third proposition, part of the provocative Foucauldian thesis of Nancy Armstrong's *Desire and Domestic Fiction: A Political History of the Novel* (New York and Oxford: Oxford University Press, 1987), which argues more generally that "a modern gendered form of subjectivity developed first as a feminine discourse in certain literature for women" (p. 14), isolates the Brontë sisters as particularly adept at displacing history with the narrative of desire; see especially pp. 186–205.

6. Judith Butler, *Bodies That Matter: On the Discursive Limits of "Sex"* (New York: Routledge, 1993), p. 105. In "Figuring Identification," the introduction to *Identification Papers* (New York: Routledge, 1995), Diana Fuss provides a cognitive map and a critical stance for reading recent psychoanalytically-informed cultural theory that focuses on identificatory processes and their political possibilities.

7. Butler, *Bodies That Matter*, p. 105.

8. Žižek, in *The Sublime Object of Ideology* (London: Verso, 1989), suggests that there is room in every culture for certain traumatic events to take on an overdetermined symbolization, but that the very proliferation of meaning around such events—his example is the sinking of the Titanic—obscures the "terrifying impossible *jouissance*" evoked by their "inert presence": "By looking at the wreck we gain an insight into the forbidden domain, into a space that should be left unseen. . . ." (p. 71). I want to argue that something of this dynamic—in which a proliferation of meanings and affect act as a kind of white noise, screening out the terrible, unrepresentable fascination of trauma—adhered to childhood in mid-nineteenth century England. For another suggestive reading of the psychoanalytic and historical implications of childhood, see Carolyn Steedman, "New Time: Mignon and Her Meanings" in John Stokes, ed., *Fin de Siècle / Fin du Globe: Fears and Fantasies of the Late Nineteenth Century* (New York: St. Martin's Press, 1992), pp. 102–116.

9. Chapters 2, 3, 4, 6, and 7 in George W. Stocking, Jr., *Victorian Anthropology* (New York: The Free Press, 1987) contextualize and interpret different elements of this phenomenon. Michael Banton's *The Idea of Race* (London: Tavistock Publications, 1977) and Nancy Stepan's *The Idea of Race in Science: Great Britain, 1800–1960* (London: Macmillan, 1982), are, in rather different ways, helpful in framing the convergence of political, cultural, and scientific discourses on the varieties and origins of mankind at mid-century.

10. My discussion of the London Exhibitions is drawn from Richard D. Altick, *The Shows of London* (Cambridge: The Belknap Press of Harvard University Press, 1978), especially Chapters 19 and 20, "Freaks in the Age of Improvement" and "The Noble Savage Reconsidered," pp. 253–287. Future citations of these chapters appear in the text.

11. The handbill advertising Tom Thumb in 1844 includes a picture of him as a "little man" with normal men and women standing behind him, although he was actually aged seven rather than twelve. See Altick, p. 258. For the *Punch* cartoon, see Altick, p. 254. Susan Stewart, in *On Longing: Narratives of the Miniature, the Gigantic, the Souvenir, the Collection* (Durham: Duke University Press, 1993), contrasts the dwarf and the miniature in terms of "the reception of these two varieties of anomaly. The dwarf is assigned to the domain of the grotesque and the underworld, the midget to the world of the fairy—a world of the natural . . . in its attention to the perfection of detail (p. 111). Her discussions of Charlotte Yonge's *The History of Sir Thomas Thumb* (1856) and the "Tom Thumb Wedding" in North America are particularly pertinent to the questions about childhood, deformity, and subjectivity raised in this essay

(Stewart, pp. 43–47 and 117–125).

12. *Athenaeum*, April 20, 1844, p. 360, quoted in Altick, p. 278. Smallness could, however, be sinister. Tom Thumb provides the occasion for a more extended political commentary in a Cruikshank cartoon (in the *Comic Almanack* of 1847) entitled "John Bull among the Lilliputians," which shows a fettered but happily entertained Gulliver, lulled and gulled by his own complacent sense of superiority, being robbed of his gold by the American midget and a rainbow collection of miniature imitators divided into ethnic raiding parties: adult little men in kilts, loincloths, and feathered Spanish hats. A single, empty-handed young lad represents the English working class. His balloon says, "I bee the English Tom Thumb—and I'se bee loikly to come off worse nor ony o em." The xenophobia and racism in this cartoon spoke to a gathering sense that it was England's suffering social and economic body that was being exploited by false sympathy and tolerance for freedmen and "foreigners" of all kinds (including other Britons), thus creating the dire poverty of England's deserving poor. Reproduced in Altick, p. 259.

13. See Altick's excellent discussion of the contribution of the shows, and of ethnology, to the rise of overt popular racism, pp. 279–283.

14. *Punch*, July 23, 1853, cited in Altick, pp. 282–283.

15. Knox is a fascinating and ambiguous figure whose modern reputation as "the real founder of British racism" was cemented in Philip Curtin's *The Image of Africa: British Ideas and Action, 1780–1850* (London: Macmillan, 1965), and is now undergoing complex elaboration and revision by historians of science. Knox, once a popular and distinguished lecturer on anatomy in Edinburgh, lost much of his status and his employment after his implication in the Burke and Hare body-snatching scandal in 1828; his second-phase career as a roving lecturer and writer on race began in the 1840s. Nancy Stephan's *The Idea of Race in Science* gives an excellent account of Knox's challenge to Prichard. In a thorough and thoughtful recent review of Knox's scientific and political career, Evelleen Richards, in "The 'Moral Anatomy' of Robert Knox: The Interplay between Biological and Social Thought in Victorian Scientific Naturalism," *Journal of the History of Biology* 22:3 (1989), pp. 373–435, attempts to rationalize the relationship between Knox's protoevolutionism, his radical materialism, and his racism. On the question of Knox's politics and its effects, however, both Richards and Michael D. Biddiss, in "The Politics of Anatomy: Dr. Robert Knox and Victorian Racism," *Proceedings of the Royal Society of Medicine*, 69 (1976), pp. 245–250, on whom Richards draws, fail to understand how racial thinking centrally revised both radical and conservative agendas in this period. Knox is a central figure in Robert J.C. Young's *Colonial Desire: Hybridity in Theory, Culture and Race* (London, New York: Routledge, 1995), which appeared too late for discussion in this paper. For Prichard, see George W. Stocking's introductory essay, "From Chronology to Ethnology: James Cowles Prichard and British Anthropology 1800–1850," in his edition of Prichard's *Researches into the Physical History of Man* (1813: Chicago: University of Chicago Press, 1973), pp. ix–cx.

16. Prichard, *Researches into the Physical History of Man*, pp. 1–2.

17. Prichard, *The Natural History of Man*, 2nd edition (London: Hippolyte Bailliere, 1845), p. 487.

18. Robert Knox, *The Races of Men: A Fragment* (Philadelphia: Lea & Blanchard, 1850; rpt. Miami: Mnemosyne, 1969), pp. 7, 14. This American edition of Knox's most important work on race came out in the same year as the London edition published by Henry Renshaw, and indicates the transatlantic interest in his ideas. Knox's public lectures, on which *The Races of Men* was based, were published earlier in the *Medical Times* of June and July, 1848.

19. Knox, *The Races of Men*, pp. 23–24; 192–194. An advertisement in the Athenaeum, May 15, 1847, for a lecture by Knox on the Bushmen exhibited at the Egyptian Hall in 1847 was "particularly addressed to those interested in the exciting events now going on in South-Eastern Africa, in the Kaffir War, in the great question of race, and the probable extinction of the Aboriginal races, the progress of the Anglo-African Empire, and the all-important questions of Christian mission and human civilization in that quarter of the globe." Cited in Altick, *The Shows of London*, p. 280; n. p. 529.

20. Knox's assertion of the unity of mankind, which he endowed with the authority of his teachers and mentors George Cuvier and Geoffroy St. Hilaire, is made most strongly in the final pages of *The Races of Men*, p. 297. But his arguments for the present state of fixed and immutable differences and their biological, social, and political meaning take up most of his text and are adumbrated in his introduction, where he insists that as "far back as history goes . . . the races of men have been absolutely the same." (p. 34). For Knox's initial account of hybridity see pp. 52 and 53. A whole chapter of the 2nd edition of *The Races of Men* (1862) develops and modifies his earlier arguments.

21. Nancy Leys Stepan, "Race and Gender: The Role of Analogy in Science," *Isis* 77 (1986), pp. 216–277, reprinted in *Anatomy of Racism*, ed. David Theo Goldberg (Minneapolis: University of Minnesota Press, 1990), pp. 38–57. Knox, *The Races of Men*, p. 35.

22. Knox, *The Races of Men*, pp. 289 and 298.

23. Robert Knox, "Some Remarks on the Aztecque and Bosjieman Children, Now Being Exhibited in London, and on the Races to Which They Are Presumed to Belong," *Lancet* (January–June, 1855), p. 358. See Evelleen Richards, "The 'Moral Anatomy' of Robert Knox," p. 397, n. 78, for the relationship between Knox's "embryogenesis" and other versions of preformationism.

24. Knox, *The Races of Men*, p. 279.

25. Dickens's *Dombey and Son*, published in monthly installments between 1846 and 1848, sets up its critique of capitalist masculinities in terms of the affective subjectivity of ideal parenting.

26. Etienne Balibar, "Racism and Nationalism," in Etienne Balibar and Immanuel

Wallerstein, *Race, Nation, Class: Ambiguous Identities* (New York: Verso, 1991), pp. 54, 61, 56. The last citation is a quote by Balibar from Colette Guillaumin, *L'Ideologie raciste. Genese et language actuel* (Paris/The Hague: Mouton, 1972), p. 6. Knox saw his theory of race in opposition to contemporary ideologies of nationality, but he noted a central contradiction that in England "a kingdom composed of disunited races . . . the English people, strong in their *nationality*" despised "alike all other nations and races; some for their race, others for those very qualities of race which they most prize in themselves." *Races of Men*, p. 24.

27. Balibar, "Racism and Nationalism," p. 59.

28. Linda Colley, in *Britons: Forging the Nation 1707–1837* (New Haven: Yale University Press, 1992), argues that the "invention of Britishness" did not crowd out but was a supplement to other local loyalties and identities, not a "blending" of them. "The sense of a common identity here did not come into being, then, because of an integration and homogenisation of disparate cultures. Instead, Britishness was superimposed over an array of internal differences in response to contact with the Other, and above all in response to conflict with the Other." Colley, p. 6. By the mid-forties, however, the distinction between internal and external Others is less than obvious, a fear that Knox exploited and exacerbated in his insistence on the priority of racial over national feeling. See Knox, *The Races of Men*, n. 1, p. 315.

29. Two kinds of heterogeneity are figured in this passage. One, the grotesque contrast of dark and fair within the Reed family, which is evidence of its moral dysfunction and cultural degradation, and the other, Jane's self-styled difference. For a remarkable reading of the trope of slavery in *Jane Eyre* that sets up a rather different argument about its textualization of the history of slavery, see Susan Meyer, "Colonialism and the Figurative Strategy of Jane Eyre," *Victorian Studies* 33:2 (1990), pp. 247–268.

30. Two major editions of Defoe's works were published between 1840 and 1843, bringing "The True-Born Englishman" to the fresh attention of the reading public, who might also remember the lines following the reference to "That Het'rogeneous Thing, *An Englishman*:"

> In eager Rapes, and furious Lust begot,
> Betwixt a Painted *Britton* and a *Scot*:
> Whose gend'ring Offspring quickly learnt to bow,
> And yoke their Heirs to the *Roman* Plough
> From whence a Mongrel half-bred Race there came,
> With neither Name or Nation, Speech or Fame.
> In whose hot Veins new Mixtures quickly ran,
> Infused betwixt a *Saxon* and a *Dane*.
> While their Rank Daughters, to their Parents just,

> Receiv'd all Nations with Promiscuous Lust.
> This Nauseous Brood directly did contain
> The well-extracted Blood of *Englishmen*.

Defoe, "The True-Born Englishman," p. 20. In Defoe these interethnic mixtures are wildly generative in their cross-fertilizations, producing each time a new lineage ("race" in its older sense), however "Mongrel" or "half-bred" the resulting "Nauseous Brood." In Brontë, heterogeneity is more Knoxian, represented by the visible and hostile differences among family members, whose distinct racial origins appear in the dark-skinned and fair Reed children, and in cousin Jane's physical and temperamental deviation from their degraded norm.

31. Raymond Williams, *The Long Revolution* (Harmondsworth: Pelican, 1975), p. 84.

32. I borrow the term "fictive ethnicity" from Etienne Balibar, "The Nation Form," *Race, Nation Class: Ambiguous Identities*, who applies it to the "community instituted by the nation-state," arguing that no "nation possesses an ethnic base naturally, but as social formations are nationalized, the populations included within them, divided up among them or dominated by them are ethnicized—that is, represented in the past or in the future *as if* they formed a natural community, possessing of itself an identity of origins, culture and interests which transcends individuals and social conditions" p. 96. One important strand of Brontë's novel is precisely to discriminate between the different versions of such fictive ethnicity being offered in the 1840s *en route* to creating her own.

33. Charlotte Brontë probably did not encounter Knox in print until the publication of *The Races of Men*. Her publisher, W. S. Williams, sent her the book in the autumn of 1850, a fact recorded in a letter to him dated October 25, cited in Elizabeth Gaskell's *Life of Charlotte Brontë* (Edinburgh: John Grant, 1907), p. 422. In reading *Jane Eyre* and *Olive* through the ethnological debates of the forties, I am indicating both their appropriation of and contribution to the wider currents of racial thinking in this period.

34. While the story of the changing politics of race in Victorian England has been analyzed by many writers, Catherine Hall's ongoing exploration of the "shifting and contingent relations of gender, class, race and ethnicity between the 1830s and the 1860s" not only brings together these categories, but writes a whole new historical narrative and analysis of their deployment. I am grateful to her also for bringing Craik's *Olive* to my attention. See "Feminism and Feminist History," in *White Male and Middle Class: Explorations in Feminism History* (Cambridge: Polity Press, 1992), p. 25. See two more essays from that collection, "Missionary Stories: Gender and Ethnicity in England in the 1830s and 1840s," pp. 205–254, and "Competing Masculinities: Thomas Carlyle, John Stuart Mill and the Case of Governor Eyre," pp. 255–295. See also "From Greenland's Icy Mountains to Afric's Golden Sand: Ethnicity, Race and Nation in Mid-Nineteenth Century England," *Gender and History*, Vol. 5, No. 2 (Summer 1993); "White Visions, Black Lives: the Free Villages of

Jamaica," *History Workshop Journal*, No. 36 (Autumn 1993), pp. 100–132; and "Rethinking Imperial Histories: The Reform Act of 1867," *New Left Review*, No. 208 (November/December 1994), pp. 3–29.

35. The threat of the metamorphosis of race in a single subject appears as both phantasmatic and literal in texts by men and women in this period, and may be read as a kind of hysterical symptom within representation that flows from the taboo on miscegenation, the disavowal of productive hybridity, the deligitimation of identification across racial lines, and the fear that environment swiftly transforms racial identity. In Bertha's case, her racialization begins with her marriage, and is intensified by her forced transportation to England in the hold of a ship.

36. Thomas Bewick, *History of British Birds*, 2 vols., (1797 and 1804), cited in *Jane Eyre*, p. 6.

37. Herman Melville, *Moby Dick* (Oxford: Oxford University Press, 1988), p. 199. For the most powerfully suggestive modern essay on the creation of "literary whiteness" through an American Africanist discourse, see Toni Morrison, *Playing in the Dark: Whiteness and the Literary Imagination* (New York: Vintage, 1992).

38. Morrison comments on the "fields of desire and need" that the fantastic Africanist discourse speaks to and enables. Morrison, p. 90. Eric Lott explores the needy, criminal, and erotic component of Africanist borrowings and identifications by whites in *Love and Theft: Blackface Minstrelsy and the American Working Class* (Oxford: Oxford University Press, 1994), which also deals with the 1840s and 1850s. Both these ways of thinking inform my understanding of British or English Africanism.

39. Gayatri Chakravorty Spivak, "Three Women's Texts and a Critique of Imperialism," in Henry Louis Gates, Jr., ed., *"Race," Writing and Difference* (Chicago: Chicago University Press, 1986), pp. 262–280.

40. Lott, *Love and Theft*, p. 4.

41. See Altick on the multiple motives for Dickens's relentless attack on the "idea of the noble savage," not least the coincident appearance of *Bleak House*, with its contemptuous portrait of the philanthropic Mrs. Jellyby, and *Uncle Tom's Cabin*: Altick, p. 283. Altick's discussion of *Uncle Tom's* reception is the most productive in terms of gender, but see also Douglas Lorimer, *Color, Class and the Victorians* (Leicester: Leicester University Press, 1978); and Howard Temperley, *British Antislavery, 1833–1870* (London: Longman, 1972).

42. Altick, *The Shows of London*, pp. 341–342.

43. The children had been previously compared in America to a "race of gnomes with which the superstition of former times once peopled the chambers of the earth"; among other American commentators, N. P. Willis emphasized their "docility" and the absence of the "monstrous" in their appearance, and Dr. J. M. Warren cited St. Hilaire in support of his argument that they were not a "race of dwarfs" because "dwarfs cannot perpetuate their kind." Altick, *The Shows of London*, pp. 284–285. Knox's 1855 *Lancet* article on the children, previously cited, comes very late in the

debate about their origins; the children merely provide a hook for him to talk about other elements of his theories.

44. Jacqueline Rose, "The Return of Peter Pan," the new introduction to the second edition of *The Case of Peter Pan or the Impossibility of Children's Fiction* (Philadelphia: University of Pennsylvania Press, 1993), p. xv. Rose's theories about childhood and about psychic life underpin my argument at many points.

45. My special thanks to John Barrell, Diana Fuss, Paul Gilroy, David Glover, Evelynn Hammonds, Mary Poovey, Catherine Hall, Judith Walkowitz, and Vron Ware for their generous help with, and productive criticisms of, the various versions of this essay.

JAMES R. KINCAID

8

PRODUCING EROTIC CHILDREN

THIS PAPER is divided into eleven parts, eleven being a prime number. The eleven parts are not equal in length or weight, and they do not carry the same importance; nonetheless, they are exactly symmetrical and harmonious.

These are the parts:

1. Ellie Nesler's son

2. Michael Jackson

3. McMartin-Menendez

4. The Coppertone Child Home Alone

5. Questions We Love to Ask

6. My Thesis

7. Resisting the Obvious

8. Recovered Memory

9. Scandal—That's What We Need

10. Me

11. You

I. ELLIE NESLER'S SON

Ellie Nesler's son is named Willy, Willy Nesler. He is now about thirteen years old, living, I think, in Jamestown, California, where, in 1993, in April, he was in a courtroom waiting to testify in the preliminary hearing of one Daniel Driver, accused of seven counts of child-molesting. The papers say Willy Nesler was one of the alleged victims; they also say that, according to his mother, he was vomiting wildly the morning he was scheduled to tell his story. Anyway, before he got the chance to speak, his mother took control, silencing her boy and the accused forever. When Daniel Driver looked at that mother with what she took to be a smirk, Ellie, goaded beyond her limits, bolted from the courtroom, filched a .22 semiautomatic from her sister's purse, charged back in, and plugged the guarded and manacled Driver in the head and neck five times at close range, proclaiming, "Maybe I'm not God, but I'll tell you what: I'm the closest damn thing to it."[1] I mention Willy Nesler because at this point he becomes invisible, silent and empty, a vacancy at the center of the story—filled up and written on by his mother, and the press, and the nation's outrage, our own included. Willy Nesler becomes our principal citizen, the empty and violated child, whose story we need so badly we take it into ourselves. No one wants Willy Nesler testifying, taking on substance: the erotic child is mute, under our control. Once the accused is out of the way, and the child is rendered speechless and helpless, we can proceed to our usual business: the righteous, guilt-free constructions of violent pornographic fantasies about child sexuality.

In this case, Willy Nesler's mother thrusts herself between us and the speaking child, blocking his words just in time, and giving us the screen we need. In the scores of accounts I read of the trial, Willy appears only as "Ellie's boy," "Nesler's son."[2] Ellie Nesler herself forms the displaced, disowned, and finally discarded projection we can use for a while to contemplate with impunity her thoroughly sexualized boy. For a moment, Ellie grabs the headlines, becomes a vigilante June Cleaver, the American Mom of the fifties, reborn snarling, protecting her chick. Defense funds spring up, fueled by spaghetti suppers; schoolchildren are forced to write thank-you notes; T-shirts and bumper stickers scream, "Nice Shootin' Ellie"; *Hard Copy* and Charles Kurault descend on Jamestown. All this so we can do as we like with our image of Willy Nesler. We can sentimentalize him erotically, as a townsperson does by saying, "His little soul died the day he was molested,"[3] or we can indulge in the full-scale fantasies scripted by Ellie's attorney, who asked the jury to "pick a child you know and look at their innocence and sweetness," and then imagine it being violated.[4]

This does not last very long. For a while, Ellie gave us a story so compelling in its gothic simplicities that it was irresistible: drive a stake through the heart of the pedophile and bourgeois America will be safe, along with our illusions about childhood, the family, sexuality, and our own rectitude. But Ellie's story never sold. The crowds of media talent that drew into Jamestown from Los Angeles and New York, like vultures to road kill, fled even more quickly. All of a sudden, Ellie was abandoned—left to fend for herself in the trial and reduced to claiming that she was insane at the time of the killing. In a last-ditch, double-barreled bid for sympathy, she claimed that she had been molested herself as a child, and also that she had a fatal disease; but the insanity defense failed, and nobody cared by then whether Ellie had cancer or not, or even whether those she named—her father's poker buddies and a state senator[5]—had sexually abused her.

What had happened was that Ellie turned out to be complicated, not the simple heroine we needed for gothic, but a woman with a history, a history we did not want. She had a minor criminal record; she had taken drugs, perhaps on the morning of the shooting; she had threatened to kill Daniel Driver months earlier. We no longer had the clean-cut simplicity that would allow us the screen of outrage between us and our object of interest, which had never been Ellie or Driver but Willy Nesler, the breached, silent child. Without the screen story, we were left to face the music ourselves, or go and find other stories. Since the stories are not hard to find, we hesitated not a second in getting out of Jamestown and leaving Ellie to her sentencing— ten years—while we hustled to locate more guilt-free eroticism.

2. MICHAEL JACKSON'S DRIVEWAY

In the joke, Michael Jackson's driveway is as erotic as our construction of Willy Nesler. The joke is this: How do you know Michael Jackson is having a party? By all the Big Wheels parked in his driveway. The other Michael Jackson joke has him visiting O. J. Simpson and offering to look after the children, should things go badly for Simpson. It's the same joke. Simpson's children, Willy Nesler, the drivers of all those Big Wheels: they take their parts in the narratives we manufacture, the narratives of innocence protected and pure, that is, lost and sullied. It does not matter much what line we take on the issues we can pretend these cases contain. Issues are there simply to give us, as they say, deni-ability, psychic deniability.

Take the fun in being outraged with Michael Jackson as boy-lover, and telling our friends how outraged we are. And not just with Jackson either, but with the failure of others to be as loving to children as we are: "Can you imagine anyone letting a son sleep with that man?" Actually, imagining is what we are all good at; otherwise such stories would not find ready listeners such as me and you. Had Michael Jackson not existed, we would have been forced to invent him, which is, of course, what we did.

Or take the way we can use the Jackson story to blow off steam about "the media," as if "the media" were an independent agent, an outsider whose desires and energies are foisted on us against our will. "The media," then, becomes a little like "the pedophile," a handy fabrication and focus for our passions that we can abuse and pretend to disown.

The hounding of Michael Jackson is a spectacular case in point. Michael Jackson, to whose music we have sent our children and our soft drink companies with record piles of dollars, is superchild and now super-child-molester. Michael Jordan would have done as well, or Barney. Jackson as a construction of our eroticism and our guilt, of our lavish, capitalist fantasies and generosities, and our frightened, repression-driven paranoia: he can hardly be said to exist outside our needs. Once he was a child himself, and it is commonly said that he still is; but we can make him play the part of the *guilty* child, absolving us from guilt. Jackson is reduced to his bed and his relationships, to the "sharing" of that bed. That's all he is, as he and dozens of boys (including our star boy, Culkin) pose for our collective scrapbooks. Even Jackson's recent marriage is openly construed as a reason for getting not Lisa Marie but her children into that bed.

Not mentioned in my eleven-point outline, and offered as an unde-served bonus: Woody Allen forms a more troubled, sophisticated version of this cultural drama. His story and his role shift before our eyes, as he bounces from child to child (younger and younger all the time), from villain to victim, from comedian to ogre. Allen becomes, like Oscar Wilde, the repository of a fair number of hatreds—of artists, Jews, New Yorkers, cosmopolitans generally, short guys, redheads, Knicks fans—

but primarily he becomes (as in Chaucer's "Prioress's Tale") the monster who threatens the child, and thus gives us exactly what we want.

3. McMARTIN-MENENDEZ

The McMartin trial, dealing with allegations of child-molesting and ritual Satanic abuse at a Southern California preschool, began with charges in the summer of 1983 and did not end until the summer of 1990, the trial itself running, with one short break, from April 1987 until July 1990. This, the longest criminal trial in American history, ended mostly with acquittals, along with some deadlocks and inconsequential declarations of mistrials, all signaling that we had other spectacles to attend to, and could finally let this one go. Along the way, though, we had provided ourselves with seven rich years of titillating narratives about animal sacrifice and demonic possession, about games of Tickle and Naked Movie Star, about Raymond Buckey's underwear and his collection of *Playboy* magazines, about children and sex.

Menendez is McMartin II, an artful variation on what has become our favorite public entertainment: staged dramas of child-molesting, masked as exercises in justice. Lyle Menendez, who has been compared to Judy Garland and Montgomery Clift as a "great neurotic actor,"[6] testifies, with a tough-guy sob we have all become attached to, "He raped me." Not only that—he testifies the very next day that he had, as an eight-year-old, molested his fellow defendant, Erik, then six, with a tooth-brush. "I'm sorry," Lyle said to his brother, right there in the courtroom, not omitting the sob.

According to most spectators, Erik is not so gifted, despite his acting ambitions, and really pours out too many details without anything like his brother's mastery of narrative pace and flow. Erik talks, all in a rush, about the taste of his father's semen, sweetened with cinnamon; he speaks of his mother squeezing blisters on his penis; he mentions categories of incestuous activities and the names each had—Knees, Nice, Rough, and Sex—respectively oral, hand, needles and tacks, and anal. He is in too much of a bustle to add flourishes from bad novels: his father lighting candles and slowly placing them about them room before saying to the boy, like an X-rated Vincent Price, "One last fuck before I kill you." Still, even Erik manages to do the job. One alternate juror on the Donahue show confesses, "Phil . . . it was sickening. . . . I could *visualize* this pedophile father—he's down the hall in the bedroom, he is sodomizing his six-year-old child."[7]

What is being visualized so clearly is a child, a figure in this drama so important that it seems to replace the actual bodies of the grown-up and athletically bulky Lyle and Erik. Both are referred to, not only by their attorneys but by many of our deputies in the press, as children, kids, boys, sometimes prefixed by "little." It is this image of the child that we are paying for in the trial, and we use the besweatered young men as transparent agencies, peering back through them to the child within, down the hall in the bedroom.

4. THE COPPERTONE CHILD HOME ALONE

But what about Macaulay Culkin? What about the adorable child? The adorable child is not our only child-species, as Lyle and Erik demonstrate, but adoration is still dear to our erotic centering of the child. The vacantly androgynous Culkin on the beach, his swimming trunks being pulled down behind cutely by a cute little dog: that's the national pinup.[8] I grant you that Culkin is fast losing his hold on this role, and his ability to present himself to us with no face and no body, as a blankness we can fill in. Still, the desire that once rushed into his emptiness lingers on, and he is still the ghost of a cultural wish-fulfillment dream to find the perfectly evacuated child, isolated and suitably domesticated, at home in bourgeois familiarity. The film *Home Alone* covers its own appeals just barely, using Three-Stooges comedy, and loading the child with sadistic potency in the make-believe layering of "fun" that allows us to enjoy the erotic formulations without beginning to acknowledge them: the child alone, defenseless, needing us. The sequel is a lot less smooth about all this, coarsening itself to the point of having Culkin make comments about seeing naked butts, and forcing him to jump into a swimming pool with a suit so many sizes too big that it peels off when he hits the water—surprise, surprise.

As Culkin reluctantly acquires a body of his own, and thus fades from our fantasies, others are found to take his place, in films like *The Client* or *The Little Rascals*, where adorable children inherit Culkin's position, one he took over in turn from a long line of culturally mandated cuties: Ricky Schroeder, Henry Thomas, Jay North, Tatum O'Neal, Jodie Foster, Brooke Shields, Mark Lester, Shirley Temple, Freddie Bartholomew, and on into the night.

Last year's Clint Eastwood film, *A Perfect World*, offers a darker, less obviously "cute" version of Culkin: a small boy played by T. J. Lowther, in a role which is actually given some substance, thus reducing his potential as a target for our usual erotic adoring. All the same, he plays out explicitly a variety of our most distressing and titillating narratives about child sexuality, in scenes that either reproduce or parody (depending on one's position) the child as object of sexual attention. He spends the first half of the movie in his briefs, and the last half in a Halloween costume that gets torn so as, again, to expose his underpants. At one point, the vicious convict, commenting on the boy's "cute underwears," inserts his hand into them to examine the penis, pronouncing it "puny." Later the good convict (Kevin Costner), sensing that the boy is reluctant to undress before him, and learning that it is all because he is ashamed of his "puny" penis, says, "Let me see it," takes a long look, and tells him it's OK, thus reassuring us that our own voyeurism here is also absolutely OK. The film works over again the erotic pedagogical territory tromped on in *The Earthling*, *Treasure Island*, *Searching for Bobbie Fisher*, *Kidnapped*, *Redneck*, *Willie Wonka*, *The Man Without a Face*, *The Champ*, *Shane*, and *The Client*.

5. QUESTIONS WE LOVE TO ASK

But first: questions we don't love to ask. Let us take the stories of Ellie Nesler, Menendez, Woody Allen, Michael Jackson, the day-care trial du jour, and ask about the source, the nature, and the size of the pleasures we take from such stories. What are these stories, where do they come from, and why do we tell them with such relish? What kind of relish is it? Why do we want to hear these feverish tales about the sexuality of children, and why do we listen to them so eagerly? What is it about the child and its eroticism that so magnetizes us? In short, Why do we tell the stories we tell? Why do we need to hear them? Those are plain sorts of questions; but we don't often attend to them. We prefer others:

1. How can we spot the pedophiles and get rid of them?

2. Meanwhile, how can we protect our children?

3. How can we induce our children to tell us the truth, and all of it, about their sexual lives?

4. How can we get the courts to believe children who say they have been sexually molested?

5. How can we get the courts to believe adults who suddenly remember they were sexually molested as children?

6. How can we get ourselves to believe others when they say they remember being sexually molested years ago?

7. How can we know if maybe some people are not making these things up, misremembering?

8. How can we know if bumbling parents, cops, and (especially) therapists are not implanting false memories?

Though some of these questions seem to take revenge on other questions, they all have one thing in common: they demand the same answer, "We can't."

I think that is why both the standard and the backlash stories are so popular: they have about them an urgency and a self-flattering righteous oomph. Asking them, I can get the feeling that I care very much, and that I am really on the right side in these vital issues of our time. Even better, these open-ended, unanswerable questions generate variations on themselves, and allow us to keep them going, circulating them among ourselves without ever experiencing fatigue, never getting enough of what they are offering.

And what they are offering is a nicely protected way of talking about the subject of child sexuality. I do not deny that we are also talking about detection and danger. Certainly we care about the poor, hurt children. But we care also about maintaining the particular erotic vision of children that is putting them in this position in the first place.

6. MY THESIS

You have already beat me to it, but here it is anyway, blunt and persuasive. My argument is that erotic children are manufactured—in the sense that we produce them in our cultural factories, the ones that make meanings for us. They tell us what "the child" is, and also what "the erotic" *is*. I argue that for the last two hundred years or so, they have confused us, have failed to distinguish the two categories, have allowed them dangerously to overlap. And the result of all that is the examples I've mentioned to this point. All these are public spectacles of child eroticism, an eroticism that can be flaunted and also screened, exploited and denied, enjoyed and cast off, made central and made criminal.

This new thing, the post-Romantic child, has been deployed as, among other things, a political and philosophical agent, a weapon used to assault substance and substitute in its place a set of negative inversions: innocence, purity, emptiness. Childhood in our culture has come to be largely a coordinate set of *have nots*: the child is that which *does not have*. Its liberty, however much prized, is a negative attribute, as is its innocence and purity. Moreover, all these, throughout the nineteenth century, became more and more firmly attached to what was characterized as sexually desirable, innocence in particular becoming a fulcrum for the nineteenth and twentieth century's ambiguous construction of sexuality and sexual behavior. Innocence was what came to you in heaven, or in marriage, as a kind of prize. Innocence was that which we have been trained to adore and covet, to preserve and despoil, to speak of in hushed tones and in bawdy songs.

The same goes for purity, of course, another empty figure that allows the admirer to read just about anything he likes into that vacancy, including a flattering image of his very self. The construction of the modern "child" is very largely an evacuation, the ruthless sending out of eviction notices. Correspondingly, the instructions we receive on what to regard as sexually arousing tell us to look for (and often create) this emptiness, to discover the erotic in that which is most susceptible to inscription, the blank page. On that page we can write what we like, write it and then long for it, love it, have it. Children are defined, and longed for, according to what *they* do not have.

Bodies are made to conform to this set of cultural demands. Heathcliff and Cathy (aged twelve) are symbols of titanic passion; Shirley Temple was enticing until puberty, when she instantly became a Republican frump; Rick Schroeder lost our interest when he stopped calling himself "Ricky"; Macaulay Culkin teeters on the brink of unerotic oblivion; Tom Sawyer's later adventures do not interest us. Baby-smooth skin is capable of making us pant with desire, while unsmooth, or contoured skin is not: Is this because flatness is innately more titillating than texture, or because flatness signifies nothing at all and thus does not interfere with our projections? In the same way, desirable faces must be blank, washed out of color, eyes big and round and expressionless, hair blond or colorless altogether, waists, hips, feet, and minds small. The physical makeup of the child has been translated into mainstream images of the sexually and materially alluring. We are told to look like children, if we can and for as long as we can, to pine for that look. (These cultural directives equating the erotic with eternal youth operate, perhaps, with special ferocity on women, but not only on women: think of Tom Cruise, Marky Mark, John Kennedy Jr., Matthew Broderick, Prince Charles, David Letterman, Jimmy Connors, Tom Brokaw, Mick Jagger, Jack Nicholson, George Burns—all cute little boys forever.)

It is worth noting that these various narratives of the child not only focus and allow desire, but also erase various social and political complications, performing essential cultural work that is not simply erotic. By formulating the image of the alluring child as inevitably bleached, bourgeois, and androgynous, these stories mystify material reality, and render nearly invisible, certainly irrelevant, questions we might raise about race, class, and even gender. Such categories are scrubbed away in this state, laved and snuggled into the grade-A homogeneity we might call Shirley Shroeder Culkin/Macaulay Ricky Temple. When poor children are allowed, as they sometimes are, to play this part, they are elevated (helped) into the class above them; boys and girls leave gender markers behind and meld together; children of color find themselves blanched to ungodly sallowness, Moby-Dicked, we might say. In all our stories, there is but one erotic child, and his name is Purity: neither rich nor poor, neither male nor female, neither black nor brown (yellow and red being out of the question). These swirling tales of desire allow nothing that would distract us from the primary fantasy.

In any case, the major point and dilemma is that we are instructed to crave that which is forbidden, a crisis we face by not facing it, by becoming hysterical, and by writing a kind of pious pornography, a self-righteous doublespeak that demands both lavish public spectacle and constant guilt-denying projections onto scapegoats.

Child-molesting becomes the virus that nourishes us, that empty point of ignorance about which we are most knowing. It is the semiotic shorthand that explains everything, that tells us to look no further: having been on either side of the child-molesting scene defines us completely. Lawyers know this, as do politicians and storytellers. In *Forrest Gump* for instance, as in a hundred other recent narratives, the fact that the heroine was abused by her father, who was also drunk and lower-class, explains to our full satisfaction why she is suicidal, drug-infested, looking for love in all the wrong places, and willing to settle for the dim-witted hero.

It is not a pretty landscape we have constructed, nor one with clearly marked exits. We think we know a great deal about this subject of child-molesting; we are told that many things connected with it are obvious. But it is possible that this obviousness is the glue that cements the double bind.

7. RESISTING THE OBVIOUS

So we might try to avoid the stupefyingly obvious: common and natural assumptions that seem to be continuous with the problem of child-molesting. We might even resist the most compelling ritual gesture of all: acknowledging that, of course, sexual child abuse does exist, and exists on a very large scale. We need not deny it; we just do not want to begin the discussion in the territory left to us once we offer that disclaimer. I suspect that this disclaimer is a vital part of the discourse that eroticizes the child, and keeps us blind to what we are doing. It forces the discussion into channels of diagnosis and cure, mandates certain assumptions about what is and is not important, allows us to see some things, and blinds us to others. It traps us into offering one more set of tips on how to determine whether or not child-molesting "happened." But what if we explored another set of happenings: what is happening to us and to our children as we tell our customary stories of the child and of sexuality?

It is not rewarding to keep acknowledging that "molestation happens." One notices that every debunker of every salacious popular myth (even brilliant debunkers like Elizabeth Loftus and Paul McHugh) begins by saying, in effect, "Now, don't misunderstand me; I know that millions of children are sexually abused." I think we need to fly past that net. That we are compelled to say that molestation happens is an insistence that it must. Where would we be without it? Its material presence is guaranteed by our usual stories, stories of displacement and denial, stories that act to keep alive the images that guarantee the molesting itself or at least our belief in it. Now, it is true that the stories themselves are based on a cultural inheritance that is very deep and complex. I do not claim that if we outlawed the stories, then the attraction to children would end. Censorship would not help us. It is just that the molesting and the stories protesting the molesting walk the same beat. When we seek to adjust the protesting stories by saying "Yeah, but let's take recovered memory out of the plot," we do nothing to disrupt the circuitry, only to further remove from investigation its generating sources. Why do we talk about sex with children as if it were an isolated physical catastrophe, divorced from our talk? Maybe the child-molesting problem is married to the way we think about "the child-molesting problem."

8. RECOVERED MEMORY

But haven't we already recognized our position, and aren't we moving even now to correct it? The pendulum is swinging, we might say, and we now are starting to see that things are more complicated than we supposed, that not absolutely everyone mentioned in connection with child-molesting may be guilty. We are now willing to grant that there are neurotics out there, and misrememberers, and clumsy therapists, and even liars. In our zeal, we may have falsely convicted some and driven others to suicide; we may have been so eager to hear children make accusations that we were not critical enough of what they were saying; we may even have implanted those accusations by being so insistent; we may have victimized ourselves, some of us, by asking ourselves to remember molesting scenes of years ago, asking in such an expectant way that we remembered in detail things that never happened.

We like to think we see all this now, with a clarity that is perhaps not unflinching, but growing in sharpness and focus. And the result of this creditable advance, we suppose, is that we have abandoned the old, melodramatic, gothic way of seeing intergenerational sex, the simple plot wherein there were grotesque villains, easy to spot, attacking a pure, uncomplicated virtue.

Or *maybe* all this complicating in reference to the dubiousness of recovered memory and of children's testimony about sexual issues is really just a matter of keeping the talk going by slightly rejiggling the terms. Maybe it's not so much a complication as a reversal, a way of maintaining the same structure of titillating talk and effective self-protection. Turning the accuser into the accused, swapping villain and victim, does not, when you look at it, seem like that much of a change. Demonizing Freud and psychoanalysis can be done without a paradigm leap. It is still a gothic melodrama, filled with self-protective name-calling. The game stays as it was; we all just switch sides: the accused now deserves sympathy and the accuser condemnation. But the primary discourse stays. In fact, these new twists are so intriguing they demand even more talk, serving the same old needs.

9. SCANDAL—THAT'S WHAT WE NEED

Scandal: the Oxford English Dictionary (OED) says it is, at root, a trap; it is believed to be from the IndoGermanic *skand*, to spring or leap. Early on, "scandal" meant to cause perplexity of conscience, to hinder the reception of faith or obedience to Divine Law, to present a stumbling block. Ignoring all the alternate meanings given by the OED, let us settle on this cluster. Scandal is a trap sprung on the main bullies of any culture: faith, law, and submission to them. Scandal is the enemy of cultural hegemony; it is the offense that frees us from piety; it is the gross material fact that thumbs its nose at all metaphysical policemen. We are drawn to scandal by a hope to trip up the cultural censors, by a dream of escaping culture or transforming it. Compliance, we sense, will get us nowhere, great as the rewards for compliance may be. Let me prove all this to everyone's satisfaction.

Take the most banal of all scandals, political scandal—and ask yourself what draws you to it. Why are the erotic doings of, say, Bill Clinton so much more interesting than his policies? Not, let me suggest, because he is himself erotic; like most politicians, where he is, eros is not. Most of us would do a great deal to avoid imagining the actual doings of Clinton's body. Let me assume, then, that what draws us to scandal is the energy and promise of scandal itself, not the particulars of any one scandal. It is the offense that matters, that holds out promise, that gives us hope.

10. ME

I caused a scandal myself, but it was a comic miniscandal, altogether insufficient for the job I have in mind. Still, how would you like it if you got a review, a prominent review, by an Oxford don in the *London Times* (albeit *The Sunday Times*) and the best thing in that review was the following: "It is astonishing that a Professor of English could be so poorly informed." The review goes on to call my book, *Child-Loving: The Erotic Child and Victorian Culture*,[9] "fatally flawed," but that amounts almost to praise compared to the allegation that, although I do not exactly "recommend the practice or admit to it myself," being annoyingly "evasive" on what I really do in my spare time, the book I have written makes it clear that I am "a passionate champion of pedophilia."[10] In a separate article in the same edition, *The Sunday Times* said: "Kincaid's theories support those of the infamous Paedophile Information Exchange, or PIE," banned in Britain several years ago for allegedly dealing in child pornography. To cement the connection between me and PIE, *The Sunday Times* contacted Lord Bernard Braine, Tory MP for Castle Point and crusader for sexual decency, who said he was sending a copy of my book to the Home Secretary so he could ban it. "I simply cannot believe," said Lord Braine, "a reputable publisher could consider printing a book with such views. For any rational human being to give currency to what the vast majority of people regard as the vilest crime possible is deeply shocking." This article was headlined, "Anger over US don's support for paedophiles."[11]

This was nothing compared to the coverage in *The Daily Mail*, which was more forthright in its headline: "Paedophile Book 'Should Be Banned'." *The Daily Mail* said my book portrays pedophiles as "kindly people who cause no ill-effects"; and they sought out Lord Braine again, who says, "We have enough social problems in this country without encouraging publications of this kind." Ann Winterton, Conservative MP for Congleton, agreed—"I am appalled that this book is being published in Britain"—and so does Dame Jill Knight, Tory MP for Edgbaston: "It is crucial for the normal development of children that their innocence be preserved." *The Daily Mail* also quoted some experts in the field as saying that "Child sexual abuse can have very damaging effects," suggesting, I guess, that I was the passionate champion of the reverse view. Michael Hames, head of Scotland Yard's Obscene Publications Squad, gave the judicious overview: "People will be rightly outraged. This book won't offend against the law, but it will give comfort to paedophiles."[12]

11. YOU

But my book only tapped, predictably, a small feeder line of outrage, and caused hardly more than a belch. For the truly scandalous, I look to you readers, the leaders of our profession. The OED tells us that being scandalous means being willing to take on big-time opprobrium, and that takes big shoulders, and many of them. The only way, though, to rewrite the script is, I think, first to jar loose the present one, to drain its power by drawing it into the trap that scandal can set and then spring.

Disgrace can do that, can revise the narrative, perhaps into one kinder to us and to children as well. For one thing is clear: our present gothic scapegoating stories, our stories of denial and projected desire, are doing few of us any good. Perhaps we can write ourselves into the plot directly, give up our immunity. We might then be anxious to find narratives other than the gothic, to cast about for other genres so we can avoid playing the monster part. Such alternate genres, I think, would be mixed, modulated, abandoning, for instance, stark essentialist notions of sexuality and sexual behavior in favor of the idea of a range of erotic feelings even within and toward children. Such scandalous narratives, finally, might see more calmly the way children and eroticism have been constructed for us, and might help us decide that the problems involved in facing these things are much smaller than those that come down on us when we evade them. We know that a child's memory is developed not simply from data but from learning a canonical narrative; we know that what we are and have been comes to us from narrative forms that take on so much authority they start looking like nature. We suspect that events themselves are complicit with the narrative authority that forms and licenses them. Why not snub the authority and change the stories? We might find that, all along, we have been afraid of the wrong things. We might even find stories that are not fueled by fear.

But none of this is going to happen without a fuss, without a most distressing and ignominious set of scandals—which is where you come in.

NOTES

1. *Los Angeles Times*, July 23, 1993, p. A26.

2. It was not until *Redbook* published Beverly Lowry's account of the imprisoned Ellie Nesler's struggle with cancer, "Should Ellie Nesler Go Free?" (August, 1994, pp. 82–85, 114–117), that Willy's name surfaced. It is possible, of course, that his name was withheld from the newspaper accounts out of consideration for his age (though this is by no means a universal practice); but such erasures still have the effect of eroticizing the emptiness. They also fold the child into the adult, as a possession or an extension: "Ellie's boy" is really a part of Ellie (Ellie's foot), a function of Ellie (Ellie's job), and an object (Ellie's afghan).

3. Frankie Tinkle, "mother of three" and lifelong resident, as quoted in the *San Francisco Chronicle*, August 13, 1993, p. A17.

4. Tony Serra, San Francisco attorney and Nesler's lawyer, quoted in the *San Francisco Chronicle*, August 12, 1993, p. A18.

5. According to the *Los Angeles Times* (September 10, 1993, p. A32), Nesler blurted out this accusation during the sanity phase of her trial, charging that psychiatrists covered up for a probation officer she says molested her when she was fourteen, the cover-up being arranged, she yelled, "because he's a state senator." She named no names, but State Sen. Patrick Johnston issued a statement acknowledging that he had been Nesler's probation officer and denying the allegation.

6. Dominick Dunne, "Menendez Justice," *Vanity Fair* (March, 1994), p. 111. Other details are drawn from this article, from television news coverage and Court TV, and from newspaper accounts running in the *Los Angeles Times*.

7. Transcript from *The Donahue Show*, February 2, 1994, p. 9; concerning the statements of Ms. Judy Zamos, identified as "Jury Alternate in Lyle's Trial."

8. Interestingly (I guess), a prominent child actor, Culkin's costar in *The Good Son* and his rival for the big bucks, Elijah Wood, serves as the model for a Coppertone kid in Rob Reiner's *North*. The child is used in a scene as the model for a tourist billboard, where his trunks are pulled down repeatedly by a dog, causing Wood to protest, repeatedly, about having his "crack," "the most private crevice on my body," shown. Nonetheless, shown it is, albeit as a representation (graphic).

9. Published by Routledge, 1992.

10. John Carey, "The Age of Innocents," *Sunday Times* (London), March 7, 1993, "Features," pp. 9–11.

11. James Dalrymple, *Sunday Times* (London), March 7, 1993, n.p.

12. Edward Verity, "Paedophile Book 'Should Be Banned'," *The Daily Mail* (London), March 8, 1994, n. p.

9

DRUCILLA CORNELL

THE RIGHT
TO ABORTION
AND THE
IMAGINARY
DOMAIN

I. INTRODUCTION

IN THIS ESSAY I will argue that the right to abortion must be guaranteed, as it is absolutely essential to the establishment of minimum conditions of individuation. The traditional conceptions of individuality offered by liberal thinkers mistakenly assume individuality as a given. Against this position, I argue that individuation is a fragile achievement, and one, as the word implies, that is necessarily dependent on constitutive relations with others. I, therefore, accept the communitarian insight that "selves" only come into "being" in a web of relations and socio-symbolic ties in which we are entangled from the beginning of our lives. However, I adamantly oppose the rejection of rights and the critique of "overindividuation" advocated by some "communitarian" feminists.[1]

Philosophical insight into how "selves" are constituted does not necessarily lead to any conclusions about the role of rights and the importance of individuation for those "selves" designated as women. It is only if one ignores the significance of patrilineage as well as the legal and social institutions that implicitly or explicitly rest on patriarchy and therefore on a specific form of stratified social differentiation, that one can wax sentimental about the value of family and community, and warn against the corrosive powers of overzealous feminists and lesbian-and-gay-rights activists. But if one rejects the idea that every individual or subject has a substantial core that, by definition, makes him—I use the word "him" deliberately because this very idea of the person has been criticized for its erasure of sexual difference—equal as a person before the law, then even the foundations upon which conceptions of rights or equality stand must be rethought. Any defense of the right to abortion that reinstates the reductionist alternatives I have described above demands nothing less than the rethinking of these basic concepts.

My argument will proceed as follows: first, I will argue that the right to abortion should be treated as an equivalent right for women to what I will term "bodily integrity,"[2] understood from within the context of mother-right and reproductive freedom. The wrong in denying a right to abortion is not a wrong to the "self," but a wrong that prevents the development of the minimum conditions of individuation necessary for any meaningful concept of selfhood. I will provide a psychoanalytic account of how individuation demands the projection and the recognition by others of bodily integrity.

Second, I will argue that because the conditions of individuation are social and symbolic the right to bodily integrity cannot be understood as a right to privacy, if that right is understood as a right to be left alone.[3] Thus, it is not enough for the state to refrain from actively blocking women's "choice" to have abortions. The right to bodily integrity, dependent as it is on social and symbolic recognition, demands the establishment of conditions in which safe abortions are available to women of every race, class, and nationality. I place the word "choice" in quotations marks because the word itself trivializes how basic the right to abortion is to women's minimum conditions of individuation. Moreover, it should be obvious that no woman *chooses* to have an unwanted pregnancy. If we could control our bodies, "ourselves," then we would not need state intervention to ensure conditions for safe abortions. The rhetoric of "choice" and "control" assumes the much-criticized dualistic conception of the subject as the king who reins over the body. Distancing ourselves from the liberal analytic conception of individuality as a pregiven core or substance demands both a different political rhetoric and a redefinition of the content of the right to abortion itself.

The demand for new rhetoric also inheres in the effort to symbolize the feminine within sexual difference, a difference that is necessarily erased by a conception of the subject that defines itself as "above sex." This erasure underlies the difficulty in liberal analytic jurisprudence of conceptualizing abortion as a right: this right cannot be separated from some notion of ourselves as embodied and sexuate beings.[4] This being said, we need to be very careful in how we conceive of the embodied self. The courts have too often relied on the "reality" of the womb as a pregiven natural difference in order to defeat equality claims under the equal protection doctrine.[5] We must find a way to resymbolize feminine sexual difference within the law so that such a resymbolization is not incompatible with claims of equality.

This analysis of the devaluation of the feminine within sexual difference is crucial if we defend the right to abortion as based on equality. To rethink equality so as to deconstruct the difference/equality debate that is often mistakenly presented as an either/or,[6] we need to understand the symbolic and normative dimensions of how bodies come to matter.[7] We need a theory of equality and of right based on the protection of minimum conditions of individuation. We can use this theory of equality to justify the measurement of feminine sexual difference as of equivalent value in relation to other expressions of sexuate "being." Equivalency, then, does not necessarily demand formal likeness or simple identity between men and women as the basis of equality. In conclusion, I will argue that we can only truly come to terms with the significance of abortion—both in terms of the psychic life of individual women and for a program of feminist legal reform—if we situate abortion only within a context of mother-right and reproductive freedom.

II. THE SOCIAL AND SYMBOLIC CONDITIONS FOR BODILY INTEGRATION AND INDIVIDUATION

My account of how and why individuation is an extremely fragile achievement, one made possible only by spinning out a meaning for and image of a coherent self from a pre-given web of social ties, symbolic relations, and primordial identifications, is based on the writings of Jacques Lacan. Lacan relied on an interpretation of Sigmund Freud's notion of the bodily ego. I believe my presentation of Lacan's theory of how an infant comes to perceive him or herself as a coherent whole or self is compatible with divergent psychoanalytic perspectives. It is not, however, compatible with philosophical positions advanced in political and legal philosophy that fail to give full weight to the social and symbolic constitution of the self. This is why my own account has a certain affinity with communitarianism and its critique of a version of radical individualism.

Insight into the relational and symbolic constitution of the self, however, does not lead to any necessary political and legal conclusions. But such insight does demand that we rethink the importance of protecting the symbolic, social, and legal conditions in which individuation can be achieved and maintained. The Lacanian account allows us to understand just how fragile the achievement of individuation is, and how easily it can be undermined, if not altogether destroyed, by either a physical or a symbolic assault on the projection of bodily integrity. The denial of the right to abortion should be understood as a serious symbolic assault on a woman's sense of self precisely because it thwarts the projection of bodily integration, and places the woman's body in the hands and imaginings of others who would deny her coherence by separating her womb from her self.[8] But before we can fully understand why the denial of the right to abortion can and should be understood as a symbolic dismemberment of a woman's body, we need to explore Lacan's explanation of the constitution of selfhood.

For Lacan, there is an impressive singularity that distinguishes human beings from other primates: their reaction on seeing their mirror image as infants. Between the ages of six and eighteen months, human infants display jubilation at the recognition of their mirror image. Lacan refers to this period as the mirror stage. In comparison, chimpanzees, for example, lose interest in an image of themselves as soon as they realize it is just an image, and not another chimpanzee. The jubilation, according to Lacan, lies in the human infant's first experience of perceiving itself as a whole. This perception of wholeness occurs when the infant is, in reality, in a state of complete helplessness. Thus, the image functions both as a projection, and as an anticipation of what the infant might become but is not now.

This disjuncture between the reality of helplessness and the projection of a unified self is an effect of our premature birth, such that our perceptual apparatus is much more advanced than our motor functions. In other words, during the mirror stage—which, I would argue,

is not a stage in the traditional sense, because one never completes it—
the infant can perceive what it cannot produce. The infant obviously
cannot provide him or herself with a mirror image so that the experience can be evoked repeatedly. Thus, the infant is completely dependent on others in order to have the experience repeated and its projected
identity and bodily integrity confirmed. In this way, the sight of another human being, including the infant's actual image in a mirror, or in
the eyes of the mother or primary caretaker, is crucial for shaping identity. This other, who in turn both appears as whole and confirms the
infant in its projected and anticipated coherence by mirroring him or
her as a self, becomes the matrix of a sense of continuity and coherence that the child's present state of bodily disorganization would belie.

It is only through this mirroring process that the infant comes to
have an identity. The body's coherence depends on the future anteri-
ority of the projection, in that what has yet to be, is imagined as already
given. The infant, then, does not recognize a self that is already "there"
in the mirror. Instead, the self is constituted in and through the mirroring process as other to its reality of bodily disorganization, and by
having itself mirrored by others as a whole.

The power that mirroring has over the infant is not, then, the recognition of similarity in the mirror, a "wow, that looks like me" reaction
to the image; rather it is the *anticipated* motor unity associated with bodily integration. Thus, it is not the exact image, but the reflection of
bodily integrity that does not match the infant's own body that *matters*.
In this sense, there is always a moment of fictionality, of imagined anticipation, in and through which the ego is constituted.

The sense of self-identity is internalized in the adult, and continues to involve the projection of bodily integrity and its recognition by
others. Our "bodies," then, are never really our own. The idea that we
own our bodies is a fantasy that imagines as completed that which always
remains in the future anterior. Therefore, to protect "ourselves" from
threats to our bodily integrity, we have to protect the future into which
we project our unity and have our bodily integrity respected by others.
To reduce the self to just "some body" is to rob it of this future anterior. This is the meaning of my earlier statement that the mirror stage
is not really a stage at all because the self never completes it. As I understand it, the mirror stage is never simply overcome in a "higher" stage

of development; it is a turning point through which the self must always come around, again and again, to guard continuously against social and symbolic forces that lead to dismemberment, disintegration, and total destruction of the self.

I want to turn briefly to Lacan's critique of ego psychology. Lacan's notion is that the self as an ego and not a subject is caught in a vicious circle of ego confirmation. This Lacanian circle of egoism is destructive, not only because it forever turns in on itself and is fated to be repeated, but because in its repetitions, which seek to realize the illusion of autoreflection as the truth of the ego, the Other upon whom this illusion is dependent is then erased. This moment of erasure is itself erased by a defensive posturing that reduces the Other to a mirror—an object that plays no active role in the constitution of the ego—and which, therefore, cannot threaten the ego's imagined self-sufficiency by distorting or denying the truth of the ego's projected image of itself as self-constituted. Lacan explicitly connects what he calls "the era of the ego" with the objectification of women as mirrors who, as mirror objects of confirmation for men, must not be allowed to ascend to the position of subjects.[9] I will explore the full significance of this insight in explaining why a feminist program of legal reform is so difficult to maintain and why it must include the rearticulation of the subject or, more specifically, of the subject of right.

It would be impossible here to answer fully the question of who comes after the ego, or even of what "after" could mean were it thought of as outside linear temporality. But I can at least articulate "the beginning" of that other subject. I believe this must be done within a context that assumes the recognition of the alterity of the future from which the self has been constituted and on which, through a projection, it depends for its survival as a self and not just "some body." The feminist legal reform program I advocate depends on no less than the symbolic recognition of this specifically egoistic form of misrecognition, particularly as it erases the mother and reduces women to objects that confirm the masculine ego as existing only "for itself." The egoism that finds its value only in its narcissistic investment, in its illusion of being for itself, is not only vicious, it is false. I am using the language of the Kantian moral critique of egoism deliberately.[10] The Kantian critique emphasizes that if people have value only for themselves, they are necessarily of a lesser order of worth because their worth is only narcissistic and thus only instrumentally valuable, rather than valuable in itself.[11] Within the Kantian tradition, the "in itself" implies impersonal valuation of the person as a person. The legal system, if it is to be just, recognizes the inviolability that inheres in this impersonal evaluation that has already been given.[12]

I believe my psychoanalytic account is consistent with the rejection of the evaluation of persons based on narcissistic ego investment. As I have already argued, pure narcissistic ego confirmation is both impossible and based on an unethical erasure of the Other.[13] A more interesting point is to be made, however, by asking the question: Can the value of a person just be "there" in itself? In psychoanalytic terms, such value, in the most primordial sense of even achieving a sense of oneself as a self, is always bestowed by the Other. The mystery of impersonal evaluation of the person "in itself" can be solved only if we remember the time frame of the heteroreflection that gave personhood to the infant in order to be valued as a self, "in itself." This time frame is that of the future anterior, in which the self is always coming to be through the projection and the confirmation of the projection of what he or she has been given to be by others.

If we take this time frame together with the role of the Other in constituting the person, we can begin to think of a legal system as a symbolic Other, a system that does not merely recognize but constitutes and confirms who is to be valued, who is to *matter*. Moreover, if the legal system as a symbolic Other is also understood to operate through the future anterior, then its operations are transitive, in that they constitute what is recognized. Such an understanding of the legal system as "active," as a symbolic Other, validates a feminist claim for legal reform. It allows for a fuller appreciation of how the denial of legal and social symbolization can be so significant to whoever is confirmed as a self and, in that sense, guarantees what I have called the minimum conditions of individuation.

This conception also allows us to remove rights from their so-called basis in what has come to be called negative freedom, which has traditionally been defined as freedom from state intervention for already free persons. But because the self depends upon the other for the achievement of selfhood, if the state recognizes and confirms whoever is recognized as a constituted person, then there can never be any simple negative freedom for persons. This move away from a pure conception of negative freedom is important in redefining the right to abortion to include conditions for safe abortions. Thus, the removal of state intervention from a woman's choice or right to privacy is not the only definition of abortion as a right, and defending a right to abortion need not be so restricted.

Let me now summarize, before moving to a discussion of the precise wrong to women in the denial of the right to abortion and to my argument for reconceiving the content of such a right. This analysis begins with a rejection of the current viability analysis that has been used to curtail significantly the right to abortion.[14] First, the projection and confirmation of one's bodily integrity remains fundamental to the most basic sense of self. The body is socially conceptualized at the very moment we imagine "it" is ours. This "body" is thus distinguished from the undifferentiated thereness, or what Charles Peirce called "Secondness" of the undifferentiated "matter" that subtends the imagined body.[15] Second, I believe the state and the legal system should themselves be understood as symbolic Others that confirm and constitute who is established as a person. It is only from within such a psychoanalytic framework that we can see how other-dependent the sense of self is, and why the time frame of its constitution through the future anterior demands the protection of the future self's anticipated continuity and bodily integrity. Without the protection of the future of anticipation, the self cannot project its own continuity. The denial of the right to abortion makes such an anticipation of future wholeness impossible for women.

III. THE SIGNIFICANCE OF PROJECTION AND ANTICIPATION IN THE CONTEXT OF ABORTION

My intent is to rearticulate the wrong of the denial of the right to abortion by redefining it as an equivalent right and justifying its protection under the rubric of equality. I will do so by showing how both the fragility of a coherent selfhood and the time frame of anticipation necessary for the projection of bodily integrity demand that we rethink this wrong. The ability to internalize the projection of bodily integrity so that one experiences oneself as whole is central to the conception of selfhood. Our embodiment makes this very projected sense of unity all too easy to lose. Throughout our lives, the disjuncture between what we have come to think of as mind and body is always latent, and we depend on its remaining so. In a case of physical assault, one's sense of projected unity is completely shattered. Physical violence imposes a horrifying dualism of self. In a violent assault we are reduced to "some body"—as other to our body. The representation of the body as apart, as "made up" out of parts, is described by Elaine Scarry in her discussion of torture:

> But the relation between body and voice that for the prisoner begins in opposition (the pain is so real that "the question" is unreal, insignificant) and that goes on to become an identification (the question, like the pain, is a way of wounding; the pain, like the question, is a vehicle of self-betrayal) ultimately ends in opposition once more. For what the process of torture does is to split the human being into two, to make emphatic the ever present but, except in the extremity of sickness or death, only latent distinction between a self and a body, between a "me" and "my body." The "self" or "me," which is experienced on the one hand is more private, more essentially at the center, and on the other hand as participating across the bridge of the body in the world, is "embodied" in the voice, in language. The goal of the torturer is to make the one, the body, emphatically and crushingly present by destroying it, and to make the other, the voice, absent by destroying it.[16]

The self-betrayal of which Scarry speaks here is the betrayal of answering the torturer's questions "against one's will." I want to take Scarry's insight into just how shattering it is to have the fictitiousness of the integrated body and the self's coherence so brutally exposed, and to place this into the context of abortion. At this point, I must also add a description of the full horror of this self-betrayal, of the ripping apart of the self and of undergoing both the apartness of the body and its dismemberment into parts in a self-inflicted abortion in which the hand operates against the womb.

In Torborg Nedreaas's novel *Nothing Grows By Moonlight*,[17] the anonymous voice of the woman narrator describes the anguish of a self-inflicted abortion in precise terms of the loss of self, as I have used the word, and of world, as Scarry uses it:

Then I grabbed the knitting needle. I had to dry my hands. Drops of sweat were
running down my temples. Then it growled again, the sound rose, the growling sprang
loose from the horizon and flashed across the sky. Two sharp flashes of lightning,
then a waterfall of rain. It clattered behind the mountain, reluctantly, subdued. It
came like cannon fire, letting loose and being flung like flashing sheets of iron across
the sky. There was a blinding light from a lightning flash, two flashes; then all hell
broke loose. The sky exploded with a boom right above my head. The mountains on
the other side of the fjord burst and collapsed. A thousand cannonballs fell and
rolled around for a while across the earth made of iron. Lightning followed in their
footsteps.[18]

The voice's raging despair blends with the narrator's remembrance of
the storm's violence as it creates a surreal world around her, and as her
own world collapses. Her remembrance is embodied in the metaphor
of her own anguish as "the hell that broke loose in the storm." The
voice continues:

I'd gotten one hand inside. The rest of my body was numb with fear. My tongue
was without sensation and swollen in my throat. Nausea as sitting frozen in the
back of my brain. The room was illuminated in blinding flashes, wiped away, and lit
again. The white world was collapsing above me in a madness of noise.

My fingers had gotten hold of something. It was without sensation. But pains of
fear were flowing through my fingers, which had found the uterus opening. I snarled
through my teeth, "God, God, let the earth perish. Now I'll do it, now I'll do it.[19]

The self-betrayal here is the self-dismemberment undertaken to
prevent the body from overtaking one's self. The body's potential over-
bearance is the pregnancy, which the narrator believes she cannot allow
to come to fruition in light of her class impoverishment and the ostra-
cization she and the child would endure because she is unmarried. The
cruel contradiction is that dismemberment is the only way she can preserve the illusion that her body is her own, an illusion that is brutally
shattered by the infliction of the unbearable pain by her own hand:

Then I set to. Drops of sweat ran down the bridge of my nose, and I noticed that
I was sitting there with my tongue hanging out of my mouth. Because something
burst. I could hear it inside my head from the soft crunch of tissues that burst. The

pain ran along my spine and radiated across my loins and stomach. I screamed. I
thought I screamed, but there wasn't a sound. More, more, push more, find another
place. It had to be wrong. And I held the very tip of the weapon between my thumb
and forefinger to find the opening to my uterus once more. It was difficult but I
thought I'd succeeded. The steel needle slid a little heavily against something. It went
far up. Then a piercing lightning of pain through my stomach, back and brain told
me it had hit something. More, more, don't give up. Tissues burst. The sweat blind-
ed my eyes. I heard a long rattling groan coming out of me while my hand let the
weapon do its work with deranged courage.[20]

I recognize, of course, that not all illegal abortions are self-inflicted,
and thus do not necessarily represent the kind of self-betrayal the narrator describes. Yet there is no doubt that prior to *Roe v. Wade*,[21] class, racial,
and national oppression left many women with no option other than to
endure a self-inflicted abortion.[22] This is why I deliberately rely on a working-class voice to tell the story of the anguish of a self-inflicted abortion.
I also use the passive voice implied by the word "endure," because it mocks
the attempt to label this kind of terrible physical suffering a "choice."

Testimonials to the horror of illegal abortions have not changed
the picture of the reduction of women to "some body" within the
conditions of safety that legal abortions provide. The experience of
splitting through the exposure of the fictitiousness of bodily integrity still remains. One could argue that this kind of splitting, which so
effectively dismembers the "self" as it reduces the imagined unified
body to its parts is present in all experiences related to illness and medical treatment. But there are many studies that show that, as the right
of bodily integrity is accorded more respect, and the patient is treated more like a "self" and not just a diseased body, the primordial sense
of self is assaulted less. As the self is attacked in its projected coherence by the splitting of illness, the sense of entitlement to a self
protected by the legal recognition of the right to bodily integrity is
even more necessary.

Of course, bodily integrity always remains imaginary. But there is
no self without this imaginary projection. Scarry makes this point when
she insists that violent assaults on the body always imply an attack on
the conditions under which the self has been constituted, and thus
through which it could be reconstituted. Rendering abortion illegal

undermines the entitlement to a self at a time when it is most needed to protect the necessary projection that there is a self that is still
"there," and more specifically, that the womb is part of that self, not
apart from it. Wombs do not wander, except in the wild imagination
of some men who have come up with very colorful stories of what a
womb "is."[23] To separate the woman from her womb or to reduce her
to it is to deny her the conditions of selfhood that depend on the ability to project bodily integrity.

The denial of the right to abortion enforces the kind of splitting
that inevitably and continuously undermines a woman's sense of self.
Her womb and body are no longer hers to imagine. They have been
turned over to the imagination of others, and those imaginings are
then allowed to reign over her body as law. The wrong in denial of the
right to abortion is often thought to be that the woman is forced to
turn over her body to the fetus as an invader. The wrong as I recon-
ceive it involves a woman, at a crucial moment, having her body turned
over to the minds of men.

Judith Jarvis Thompson's essay on abortion provides an example
of the first argument.[24] She argues that we do not, under our law or
moral institutions, believe that any person should be forced to rescue
another person. To draw out the implications of this position,
Thompson uses the analogy of a person being hooked up to a very
talented violinist whose life is in danger, and whose accomplishments
and value to society are clearly established, in order to save the artist's
life. She argues that even in this situation, we would not impose a duty
to rescue. If we would not impose such a duty in that case, why would
we contradict our law and moral institutions by insisting that women
should be required to rescue fetuses whose lives have yet to begin?[25]
But Thompson's argument itself involves an imagined projection of
the relationship between the fetus and the mother, and one I believe
should not be allowed to hold sway over our own imaginings, because
the portrayal does not adequately envision the uniqueness of the condition of pregnancy. This failure is inseparable from the subsumption
of feminine sexual difference within the so-called human in which
pregnancy is analogized with a relationship between two already independent persons. This formulation, in other words, assumes that the
womb and the fetus are other to the woman, rather than a part of her

body. Such an assumption implies a "view" of the woman's body and her "sex," and a conception of the meaning of pregnancy, that cannot be separated from imagined projections that erase the specificity of feminine sexual difference. If we reimagine the pregnant woman as her unique self, and also as pregnant, we get another picture. To quote Barbara Katz Rothman:

> Consider in contrast the woman-centered model of pregnancy I have presented: the baby not planted within the mother, but flesh of her flesh, part of her. Maybe, as very early in an unwanted pregnancy, a part of her like the ovum itself was part of her, an expendable or even threatening part, or maybe, as is most often the case by the end of a wanted pregnancy, an essential part of her, a treasured aspect of her being. If one thinks of pregnancy this way, then the rights argument is an absurdity. It is not the rights of one autonomous being set against the rights of another, but the profound alienation of the woman set against part of herself.[26]

How one "sees" a woman and her "sex" is central to understanding the status of the fetus. Although Rothman speaks explicitly of suits against the woman by her fetus, I am concerned here with her challenge to the prevalent image of pregnancy. Any analogy of a fetus to an already autonomous being rests on the erasure of the woman; it reduces her to a mere environment for the fetus. This vision of the woman is connected necessarily to one's view of the fetus, because the fetus can only be seen as a person if the woman is erased or reduced to an environment. Once the woman is put back into the picture, the pregnancy is no longer like any of the conditions to which it is analogized because, as I have already argued, it is unique. Thus, I agree with George Fletcher when he argues:

> The point is, rather, that any attempt to draw an analogy to abortion will be imperfect and deceptive. . . . The relationship between the fetus and its carrying mother is not like that between the dialysis-needy musician and a stranger with good kidneys. Nor is it like any other ingenious hypothetical cases that Kis poses in an attempt to elicit our moral intuitions about killing and letting die. The fetus is not like a pedestrian whom a driver hits (when her bakes fail) in order to avoid hitting two others. Nor is it like the drowning boy whom a swimmer may save or not. Nor is it like a man overboard in a shipwreck whom we keep out of the overfilled

lifeboat. These other standard characters make up the pantheon of moral philosophy as it has been plied at least since Carneades imagined the problem of two
shipwrecked sailors fighting for the same plank to avoid drowning.[17]

All of these examples involve cases of individuals who are clearly
human beings. Fletcher's insight is to argue that whatever the fetus is,
it is not a fully developed human being, and therefore analogies such
as the one Judith Jarvis Thompson uses to other justified or excused
killings cannot hold. Abortion, then, is not killing in any traditional
sense, and cannot be adequately discussed under that rubric. As a result,
Fletcher concludes that we need another framework in order to adequately analyze abortion. I agree with him, and it is obviously my
intention to provide such an alternative framework.

My addition here, however is that the erasure of the uniqueness of
the fetus, which Fletcher empathizes, cannot be separated from the erasure of the uniqueness of the condition of pregnancy, which in turn
cannot be separated from the failure of our legal system to symbolize
and reimagine the specificity of the feminine within sexual difference.
More sharply put, the status of the fetus comes into question once the
uniqueness of pregnancy as a condition different from all others is recognized, and thus turns on the idea of how the woman and her "sex"
are viewed. The construction of the womb as a container, as an environment for the fetus, is just that—a construction, an imaginary projection
that gives meaning to what cannot actually be seen. Here we have an
extraordinarily clear example how a woman's "sex" is constructed. To
imagine a womb as a container is to imagine "it," not to know "it" in its
truth. But for purposes of trying to provide an adequate framework to
defend abortion as a right, we also need to "see" just how divergent constructions of the woman's sex, and particularly of her womb, will
necessarily affect how the fetus is conceived of and how abortion will
be viewed. If we think of the womb as a part of the woman, if her body
is respected as opaque, as bound, if the woman's "insides" cannot be
forcibly "exposed" as an outside, then the idea that the woman and her
body can be rendered transparent is denied. This view of the woman as
a container for the fetus reduces her "sex" to a maternal function.
Rothman, for example, re-envisions women as "whole selves" with reproductive power and creativity. As she notes, this redefinition changes the

way abortion is conceptualized. If we reduce women (consciously or unconsciously) to the maternal function, then we "see" them as mothers, ironically, even as they seek, through abortion, to avoid becoming mothers. To quote Rothman:

> By creating the fetus, this unborn child as a social being, we turn this woman into "its mother"—defining her in terms of the fetus even as she seeks to avoid making a baby, avoid becoming a mother.
>
> If women controlled abortion, controlled not only the clinics, but the values and the thinking behind abortion, would we make such a distinction between contraception, not letting this month's egg grow, and abortion, not letting this month's fertilized egg grow? Or could we put early abortion back together with contraception, into the larger idea of birth control, and say that until we feel we've made a baby, an abortion is stopping a baby from happening, not killing one? Seeing women as creators, not containers, means seeing abortion as refusing to create, not destroying that which we contain.[28]

Reducing a woman to the maternal function in the crude form of designating her "sex" as a container explicitly denies her the right of bodily integrity, and thus the conditions of selfhood in which a woman can project the meaning of her own "insides" as "hers." What is a woman under this fantasy of her "sex"? She is a *what*, a thing, a container, an environment, not a *who*, a self. We do not need to be essentialists to argue that the feminine "sex" is both more than and other to this reduction of her "sex" to a container.

To summarize, the way in which a fetus and the woman is "seen"—and I put "seen" in quotation marks to remind us again of my argument that one does not see a woman directly but imagines her through projections of the significance or lack of same of her sex—is right at the heart of the abortion debate. This is a classic example of precisely why a feminist program of legal reform and the rearticulation of rights cannot proceed without the reimagining and the resymbolization of the feminine within sexual difference which take back "ourselves" from the masculine imaginary.

Men and women create themselves by projecting the body as integrated, as being one's "own." The body matters as a psychic object, and its reality always has a phantasmatical dimension. Bodily integrity is actualized through the externalized fantasy one has of one's body, although this externalized idea of one's body as one's "own" can be effectively undermined. Any experience of illness graphically teaches us that lesson. But it is precisely the very fragility of bodily integrity that makes its protection so crucial. To deny women the conditions in which they can project bodily integrity by turning their bodies over to the projections of others is to deny them a basic condition of selfhood. There is also an important temporal dimension to the projection and anticipation of bodily integrity which can help us to grasp how devastating the denial to the right to abortion can be to women. The temporal dimension can also help us in understanding more deeply what is wrong with the image of maternal relationship that Judith Jarvis Thompson gives us in her discussion of abortion.

For Thompson, the individual wakes up to find oneself—and I am using the word "oneself" to reflect the way in which Thompson's rhetoric removes the issue of abortion from "sex"—connected against one's will to a dialysis-needy musician. I have already argued that, in order to develop an adequate analytic framework, we have no choice but to confront "sex" and, more specifically, the way in which feminine sexual difference is both imagined and then symbolized in the law so as to reflect and reinforce such imaginary projections. The classic example is the image of the womb as a container. But there is a temporal dimension inherent in Thompson's analysis that it is also important both to note and to criticize. If one took the time frame implied in the suddenness of waking and finding oneself connected to the musician into the context of abortion, then it would seem that the wrong of the denial of abortion begins to take effect only at the moment that the woman finds herself connected and thus with the imposed duty to rescue. But under my analysis of how bodily integrity must be continuously confirmed, the wrong in the denial of the right to abortion begins long before that.

There are innumerable pre-*Roe* accounts of how the fear of unwanted pregnancies and illegal abortions haunted women's sense of themselves long before they actually became pregnant. As part of that generation, I remember the horrific stories of knitting needles, backalley washrooms, lives lost, and long-lasting damage to women's reproductive capacities. Sex was haunted by the specter and the fear of what an unwanted pregnancy would mean for the woman when abortion was illegal. I am ware that many right-to-lifers would defend the reaction to such a specter as one of the advantages of rendering abortion illegal, since it might help prevent young people from engaging in the "sin" of unmarried sex. Freedom of sexual expression is crucial to any sexuate being's well-being and given that my notion of the imaginary domain demands the freedom to continuously reimagine one's sexuality, I clearly disagree with this position. But for now, I want to reemphasize that what is at stake in the imposition of this specter is the serious undermining of women's ability to project their own bodily integrity over time. This undermining has serious implications, because it becomes internalized as the inability to imagine oneself as whole. The very constitution of selfhood can not be separated from the protection of the future projection of the woman's self as a whole body. The threat takes effect before any woman actually has to face an unwanted pregnancy. Here we have an important example of how the symbolization of women's "sex" has a constitutive effect on what we have to come to think of as selfhood. Not only is a woman's individuality not just given, it is limited in its very definition by certain symbolizations of her "sex" in the law. This reduces her to those definitions. To deny a woman the right to abortion is to make her body not "hers" at the same time that it reduces her to her "sex," limitedly defined as maternal function. Such restrictive symbolizations deny a woman her imaginary domain.

I have suggested that there is a truth implicit in Thompson's otherwise misguided comparison of pregnancy with an enforced relationship with a dialysis-needy violinist. In her presentation of the condition of the one who is forcibly tied to the musician we have an image of how imposed restrictions on bodily integrity affect a sense of self. Thompson's thesis is that one must be able to keep one's body for oneself as an essential aspect of one's very personhood. But because she desexualizes her own discourse, she undermines the power of her own argument in defense of that thesis. We can fully understand the wrong in the denial of abortion if we understand just how dependent a sense of self is on projections of bodily integrity. Put simply, there is no adequate way to think about abortion without having also to think about "sex." That point should be obvious. The reality that it has not been is reflected in the tortured and failed attempts to find an analogy for abortion in so-called human experience. My additional suggestion here is that this failure is not a coincidence but is itself an expression of how the feminine within sexual difference has been subsumed in the human, and thus erased or symbolized as the maternal function, a symbolization that makes it difficult if not impossible to defend the right to abortion. Once we understand that the conditions for women "being for themselves" have been systematically denied them by the dearth of symbolizations of their "sex," then we can see how perceptions of what a woman is have been shaped by the law, and must be actively challenged in the validity of their meaning in a feminist program of legal reform. This challenge in the context of abortion demands that we rearticulate the right beyond its current encasement in an analytical structure that is inseparable, as I have already argued, from the reduction of feminine sexual difference to the maternal function, a reduction necessary for the construction of the fetus as a social being different from other persons only because of its environment. Now that I have redefined the wrong of the denial of the right to abortion, let me turn to the rearticulation of the right that I believe flows from it.

IV. THE REARTICULATION OF THE RIGHT TO ABORTION

Abortion should be protected as an equivalent right necessary for the establishment of the minimum conditions of individuation for women, which must include the protection of the individual's projection of bodily integrity.[29] The move from the objectification of the feminine within sexual difference as a "what" (in the case of abortion, for example, as a container for a fetus) to a "who," a sexuate being with her own imaginary, is precisely what my own rearticulation of the right to abortion recognizes.

The right to abortion should not be understood as the right to choose an abortion, but as the right to realize the legitimacy of the individual woman's projections of her own bodily integrity, consistent with her imagination of herself at the time that she chooses to terminate her pregnancy. Once the right is rearticulated in this manner, we can provide an alternative analysis that completely rejects the conclusion of *Webster v. Reproductive Health Services*,[30] in which the Supreme

Court stated that it is consistent with the right to abortion to allow states to enjoin public facilities and employees from providing abortions, because such an injunction purportedly does not place a governmental obstacle in the way of the right defined abstractly as "the right to choose." This alternative analysis rejects also the denial of Medicaid coverage for abortions, which was similarly defended as no impediment to "the right to choose."

We can further reject the "undue burden" analysis set forth in *Planned Parenthood of Eastern Pennsylvania v. Casey*,[31] in which the Court upheld a series of state restrictions on both the exercise of the right to abortion and states' rights to determine who should shape the way a woman's decision to terminate her pregnancy should be viewed. My rearticulation of the right is consistent with the imaginary dimension of the projection of bodily integrity. Once we understand that the right to abortion is essential to bodily integrity and individuation, we can see that what is at stake in the states' efforts to regulate abortion is the woman's right to be insulated from state imposition of the views of others on her own imaginary. States have argued that their programs regulating abortion are intended to inform women of the seriousness of the act of terminating a pregnancy. Such efforts deny the woman's status as a fully individuated human being, capable of acting and of giving meaning to that action without help from the State. It is not only an issue of "who" can make the ultimate decision, as Justices Souter, Kennedy, and O'Connor argue in their opinion in *Casey*, that attempts to justify the legitimacy of certain of the provisions of the Abortion Control Act passed in Pennsylvania in 1982 in order to regulate abortion.[32] It is also "how" that decision may be exercised. The protection of "how" is essential for the establishment of respect for women as fully individuated sexuate beings with their own imaginaries and therefore with their own understandings of what it means to end a pregnancy.

This rearticulation is transitive, in that it hopes to promote the bringing into "being" of what has been both explicitly and implicitly denied as "True": the equivalent value of the feminine within sexual difference. This denial is particularly evident in court cases that have denied the validity of women's equality claims in the supposed name of recognizing a difference that is just "there" in its meaning prior to any evaluation. The debate over whether or not women should have the right to abortion as well as how that right is to be articulated forces us to face the fact that how a woman's body matters is inseparable from how "it" is symbolized and whether "it" is evaluated as of equivalent value to the masculine body.[33] The reevaluation of the feminine within sexual difference as of equivalent value inevitably changes how a woman's body is thought to matter in the sense of both material reality and significance.

NOTES

1. It is not surprising to find some prominent communitarian feminists at the forefront of the battle against the right to abortion. See Mary Ann Glendon, *Rights Talk: The Impoverishment of Political Discourse* (New York: The Free Press, 1991), and Elizabeth Fox-Genovese, *Feminism Without Illusions: A Critique of Individualism* (Chapel Hill and London: University of North Carolina Press, 1991).

   For me, the description "communitarian feminist" is itself an oxymoron if one takes seriously the feminist proposition that a legal system, which implicitly incorporates patriarchal assumptions, erases the specificity of the feminine within sexual difference, symbolizing the feminine as the maternal function or reducing it to a "natural difference" used to justify unequal treatment. Both alternatives are reductionist, and thus deny women the full play of the imaginary domain, involving the endless process of rebirth and recreation that is only possible if the minimum conditions of individuation are protected by law.

2. My explanation of integrity seeks to encompass the concept of the process of integration.

3. The original analysis of the common law right to privacy was presented by Samuel Warren and Louis D. Brandeis, "The Right to Privacy," *Harvard Law Review*, Vol. 4 (1980), p. 193. Warren and Brandeis advocated the protection of the "inviolate personality" of each person. Justice Brandeis set forth the basis for the modern right when he recognized a right to protection of one's private life from government intrusion. He called it "the right to be left alone—the most comprehensive of rights and the most valued by civilized man." *Olmstead v. U.S.*, 277 U.S. 438 (1928) (Brandeis, J. dissenting).

4. Luce Irigaray writes that as living, sexuate beings, our identity cannot be constructed without conditions of respect for difference and the equality of rights to bring out such differences. Forced sexual choice denies us the most fundamental recognition of our differences and therefore, any potential for the attainment of equality of rights. See Luce Irigaray, "How to Define Sexuate Rights?" in *The Irigaray Reader*, ed. Margaret Whitford, trans. David Macey (Oxford: Basil Blackwell, 1991), and Luce Irigaray, *je, tu, nous, Toward a Culture of Difference*, trans. Alison Martin (New York and London: Routledge, Chapman and Hall, 1993).

5. The Supreme Court has repeatedly upheld the regulation of a reproductive freedom against equal protection challenges. In *Geduldig v. Ajello*, 417 U.S. 484 (1974), the Court held that state regulation of pregnancy is not sex-based because such regulation does not categorically distinguish the class of women from the class of men. However, in *Michael M. v. Superior Court*, 450 U.S. 464 (1981), the Court suggested that state regulation of pregnancy, by its nature, cannot discriminate on the basis of sex, for such regulation pertains to a real and categorical difference between genders.

6. Drucilla Cornell, "Gender, Sex, and Equivalent Rights," in *Feminists Theorize the Political*, eds. Judith Butler and Joan Scott (New York: Routledge, 1992), and Joan Scott, "Deconstructing Equality Versus Difference: Or, the Uses of Poststructuralist Theory for Feminism," in *Conflicts in Feminism*, eds. Marianne Hirsh and Evelyn Fox Keller (New York: Routledge, 1990).

7. This formulation derives from Judith Butler. See her *Bodies That Matter* (New York: Routledge, 1993).

8. I am using the word "self" here to indicate what Lacan means by ego identity in the mirror stage. Jacques Lacan, *Écrits: A Selection*, trans. Alan Sheridan (New York and London: W. W. Norton and Company, 1977).

9. See Teresa Brennan, *History after Lacan* (New York and London: Routledge, 1994).

10. See Thomas Nagel, *The Value of Inviolability* (1992, unpublished manuscript on file with author, New York University Law School), for an excellent and succinct discussion of the significance of this distinction in Kantian morality and, more specifically, how it relates to the value of inviolability.

11. *Ibid.*

12. *Ibid.*

13. See Drucilla Cornell, *The Philosophy of the Limit* (New York: Routledge, 1992).

14. *Planned Parenthood of Eastern Pennsylvania v. Casey*, 112 S. Ct. 2791 (1992).

15. See Charles Peirce, *The Collected Papers of Charles Sanders Peirce*, Vols. I and II, eds. Charles Hartshorne and Paul Weiss (Cambridge: The Belknap Press of Harvard University Press, 1960).

16. See Elaine Scarry, *The Body in Pain* (New York: Oxford University Press, 1985), pp. 48–49.

17. Torborg Nedreaas, *Nothing Grows by Moonlight* (Lincoln: University of Nebraska Press, 1987).

18. *Ibid.*, p. 189.

19. *Ibid.*

20. *Ibid.*, p. 189–190.

21. *Roe v. Wade* 410 U.S. at 113 (1973).

22. *Roe v. Wade* 410 U.S. at 149–150.

23. See, generally, Scarry, *The Body in Pain*.

24. Judith Jarvis Thompson, "A Defense of Abortion," *Philosophy and Public Affairs*, Vol. 1, No. 1 (Fall, 1971).

25. *Ibid.*

26. Barbara Katz Rothman, *Recreating Motherhood: Ideology and Technology in a Patriarchal Society* (New York: W.W. Norton and Company, 1989), pp. 160–161.

27. George Fletcher, "Reflections on Abortion" (Unpublished manuscript on file with the author, Columbia University School of Law).

28. Rothman, p. 123.

29. For an explanation of the notion of "equivalent rights," see Cornell, "Gender, Sex, and Equivalent Rights."

30. *Webster v. Reproductive Health Services*, 492 U.S. 490 (1989).

31. *Planned Parenthood of Eastern Pennsylvania v. Casey*, 2791.

32. *Ibid.*

33. Judith Butler, *Bodies That Matter*, p. 32.

CONTRIBUTORS

NANCY ARMSTRONG is Nancy Duke Lewis Professor at Brown University. She teaches in the departments of Comparative Literature, English, and Modern Culture and Media. She is the author of *Desire and Domestic Fiction: A Political History of the Novel*, and coauthor with Leonard Tennenhouse of *The Imaginary Puritan: Literature, Intellectual Labor, and the Origins of Personal Life*. She has also coedited with Leonard Tennenhouse two essay collections: *The Violence of Representation: Essays in Literature and the History of Violence* and *The Ideology of Conduct: Essays in Literature and the History of Sexuality*.

REY CHOW teaches in the Department of English and Comparative Literature at the University of California, Irvine. She is the author of *Woman and Chinese Modernity* and *Writing Diaspora*, and most recently, *Primitive Passions: Visuality, Sexuality, Ethnography, and Contemporary Chinese Cinema*.

DRUCILLA CORNELL is Professor at the Benjamin N. Cardozo School of Law. She is the author of several books, including *Beyond Accomodation: Ethical Feminism, Deconstruction, and the Law; The Philosophy of the Limit;* and *Transformations: Recollective Imagination and Sexual Difference*. She is also the coeditor of two volumes in legal studies: *Hegel and Legal Theory* and *Deconstruction and the Possibility of Justice*. Her essay is drawn from her recently published book *The Imaginary Domain: Discourse on Pornography, Sexual Harassment, and Abortion*.

DIANA FUSS is Associate Professor of English at Princeton University. She is the author of two books, *Essentially Speaking: Feminism, Nature and Difference* and *Identification Papers*, and the editor of *Inside/Out*.

MARJORIE GARBER is Professor of English at Harvard University and Director of the Center for Literary and Cultural Studies at Harvard.

The author of *Vice Versa: Bisexuality and the Eroticism of Everyday Life* and *Vested Interests: Cross-Dressing and Cultural Anxiety*, she has also written three books on Shakespeare (*Shakespeare's Ghost Writers: Literature as Uncanny Causality*, *Coming of Age in Shakespeare*, and *Dream in Shakespeare: From Metaphor to Metamorphosis*), and has edited collections of essays on cultural topics from media spectacles to the Rosenberg case and the McCarthy era. She has two dogs, Wagner and Yofi.

BARBARA JOHNSON is Professor of English and Comparative Literatures at Harvard University. Her numerous publications include *The Critical Difference: Essays in the Contemporary Rhetoric of Reading*, *A World of Difference*, and *The Wake of Deconstruction*. She is also the editor of *Freedom and Interpretation: Oxford Amnesty Lectures* and coeditor of *Consequences of Theory*.

CORA KAPLAN is Professor of English at Rutgers University, where she is also director of the Institute for Research on Women. She is the author of *Sea-Changes: Culture and Feminism*, the author of the critical anthology of women's poetry, *Salt and Bitter and Good: Three Centuries of English and American Poets*, and the coeditor of *Formations of Fantasy*. She is currently working on a book entitled *Giant Propensities: Nationality, Gender, and the Rise of Racial Thinking in Victorian Britain, 1840–1865*.

JAMES R. KINCAID is Aerol Arnold Professor at the University of Southern California. His most recent books are *Child-Loving: The Erotic Child and Victorian Culture* and *Annoying the Victorians*. The present essay forms part of a larger work, tentatively entitled *Manufacturing Virtue: The Culture of Child-Molesting*.

HARRIET RITVO is Arthur J. Conner Professor of History at MIT. She is the author of *The Animal Estate: The English and Other Creatures in the Victorian Age* and the coeditor of *The Macropolitics of Nineteenth-Century Literature: Nationalism, Imperialism, Exoticism*. Her essay in this volume is drawn from a book in progress, tentatively entitled *The Platypus and the Mermaid: Animal Classification as British Culture, 1700–1900*.

DAVID WILLS is Professor of French at Louisiana State University. He is the author of *Self De(con)struct: Writing and the Surrealist Text*, coauthor with Peter Brunette of *Screen Play: Derrida and Film Theory*, coauthor with Alec McHoul of *Writing Pynchon: Strategies in Fictional Analysis*, and coeditor with Peter Brunette of *Deconstruction and the Visual Arts: Art, Media, Architecture*. His essay in this volume is drawn from his recently published book, *Prosthesis*.

PHOTO CREDITS

Frontispiece   page ii
Mark Tansey, *Innocent Eye Test*, 1981, oil on canvas, 78 x120". The Metropolitan Museum of Art New York, promised gift of Charles Cowles, in honor of William S. Lieberman, 1988; Courtesy Curt Marcus Gallery, New York. © Mark Tansey.

CHAPTER I

Figure 1.1   page 15
Untitled (Cinderella in Evening Gown). 1992, 92.C.06.x2. Photo: William Wegman.

Figure 1.2   page 23
J. R. Ackerley with his dog Queenie (Tulip in *My Dog Tulip*). Photo: Francis King.

Figure 1.3   page 26
Sigmund and Anna Freud with Wolf. Photo: Freud Museum, London; Sigmund Freud Copyrights; A. W. Freud *et al*.

Figure 1.4   page 27
Freud with Jo-Fi's pups Fo and Tattoun, Hohe Warte, 1933. Photo: Freud Museum, London; Sigmund Freud Copyrights; A. W. Freud *et al*.

Figure 1.5   page 27
Freud and his chow Lun Yi at the home of Princess Marie Bonaparte, en route from Vienna to London, June 1938. Photo: Freud Museum, London; Sigmund Freud Copyrights; A. W. Freud *et al*.

Figure 1.6   page 31
Marie Bonaparte, Princess George of Greece (1882–1962), with the chow, Topsy. Late 1930s. Photo: A. W. Freud *et al*.

CHAPTER 4

Figure 4.1   page 105
London Bridge 1895–1896. From G. H. Martin and David Francis, "The Camera's Eye," *The Victorian City: Image and Realities*, eds. H.J. Dyos and Michael Wolff (London: Routledge & Kegan Paul, 1978).

Figure 4.2   page 107
Thomas Annan, *Close No. 193, High Street, The Old Closes and Streets of Glasgow* (1868). From *The Golden Age of British Photography 1839–1900* (New York: Aperture, 1984), p. 145.

Figure 4.3   page 108
Gustave Doré, *Bluegate Fields*. From *A Pilgrimage* (London, 1872).

Figure 4.4   page 109
A Butcher's Shop (c. 1900). From G. H. Martin and David Francis, "The Camera's Eye," *The Victorian City: Image and Realities*, eds. H. J. Dyos and Michael Wolff (London: Routledge & Kegan Paul, 1978).

Figure 4.5   page 110
"Slum Life in Our Great Cities" (1890). From G. H. Martin and David Francis, "The Camera's Eye," *The Victorian City: Image and Realities*, eds. H. J. Dyos and Michael Wolff (London: Routledge & Kegan Paul, 1978).

Figure 4.6 page 111
John Thompson, *The Temperance Sweep* (c. 1876–1877). From Stephen White, *John Thompson, Life and Photographs: The Orient, Street Life in London, Through Cyprus with the Camera* (London: Thames and Hudson, 1985), plate 152.

Figure 4.7 page 112
Paul Martin, *Loading up at Billingsgate Market: Cutout Figure* (c. 1894). From Roy Flukinger, Larry Schaaf, and Standish Meacham, *Paul Martin, Victorian Photographer* (Austin: University of Texas Press, 1877), p. 45.

Figure 4.8 page 113
Paul Martin, *Loading up at Billingsgate Market* (c. 1894). From Roy Flukinger, Larry Schaaf, and Standish Meacham, *Paul Martin, Victorian Photographer* (Austin: University of Texas Press, 1977), p. 44.

Figure 4.9 page 114
Oscar Gustav Rejlander, *The Two Ways of Life* (1857). From Helmut Gernsheim, *The History of Photography: From the Camera Obscura to the Beginning of the Modern Era* (New York: McGraw Hill, 1969), plate 104.

Figure 4.10 page 115
A. J. Munby, *Hannah Cullwick*. From Leonore Davidoff, "Class and Gender in Victorian England," *Sex and Class in Women's History*, eds. Judith L. Newton, Mary P. Ryan, and Judith R. Walkowitz (London: Routledge & Kegan Paul, 1983), p. 16.

Figure 4.11 page 116
A. J. Munby, *Hannah Cullwick*. From Leonore Davidoff, "Class and Gender in Victorian England," *Sex and Class in Women's History*, eds. Judith L. Newton, Mary P. Ryan, and Judith R. Walkowitz (London: Routledge & Kegan Paul, 1983), p. 49.

Figure 4.12 page 117
Clementina, Lady Hawarden, Photographic Study (c. 1860). From *The Golden Age of British Photography 1839–1900* (New York: Aperture, 1984), p. 125.

Figure 4.13 page 118
The Music Lesson (1857). From Helmut Gernsheim, *The History of Photography 1850–1880, The Age of Collodion* (London: Thames and Hudson, 1988), p. 76.

Figure 4.14 page 119
Mourning Group, Windsor Castle (1862). From Francis Dimond and Roger Taylor, *Crown and Camera: The Royal Family and Photography 1842–1910* (New York: Penguin, 1987), p. 24.

Figure 4.15 page 120
Poster (1908). From Gavin Weightman and Steve Humphries, *The Making of Modern London 1815–1914* (London: Sidgwick & Jackson, 1983), p. 124.